Gipsy Smith

HIS LIFE AND WORK

by Himself

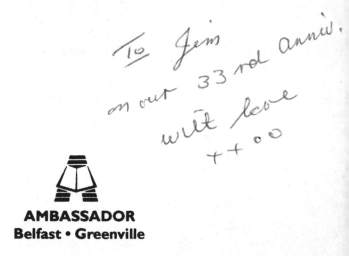

To Jim
on our 33 rd anniv.
with love
+ + o o

AMBASSADOR
Belfast • Greenville

First Published 1901
This Edition 1996

Copyright © 1996 Ambassador Productions Ltd.

ISBN   1   898787   57   3

Published by

AMBASSADOR PRODUCTIONS, LTD.
Providence House
16 Hillview Avenue,
Belfast, BT5 6JR

Emerald House
1 Chick Springs Road, Suite 102
Greenville, South Carolina, 29609

Gipsy Smith

HIS LIFE AND WORK

by Himself

Introductions by

G. CAMPBELL MORGAN

and

ALEXANDER MCLAREN, D.D.

NOTE TO MY READERS

THIS story of my life is sent forth to the world with a diffidence amounting almost to reluctance on my part, but I have often been urged to tell the tale of my not unromantic career in full, and these persistent requests are my justification for the present volume.

I gladly acknowledge the invaluable literary help which I have received from my friend Mr. W. Grinton Berry, M.A., in its preparation.

I do not pose as a practical or skilled author, and Mr. Berry's help has been simply indispensable.

G. S.

INTRODUCTION
TO AMERICAN EDITION
By G. CAMPBELL MORGAN

MY first acquaintance with Gipsy Smith was made in 1886 when I entered upon work in Hull, which he had originated. Going at the invitation of the committee then in oversight of the work at Wilberforce Hall to conduct services for fourteen days, I remained thirteen months, and thus had opportunity to observe the results of his labors. I found very many whole-hearted followers of Jesus Christ in dead earnest about the conversion of others. These, most of them, had been brought to God under the preaching of this man. Many of them remain in the churches of the town unto this day, and retain their first love to Christ and devotion for His cause. During this time I often met Gipsy, and from the first my heart was joined to his as a brother beloved, and I count him still as my close personal friend and a highly valued fellow-laborer in the kingdom and patience of Jesus Christ.

During these years I have noted with great joy his remarkable development, until to-day he stands at the very front of those who are doing the work of the Evangelist. His early life, as this book clearly shows, consisted of certain facts which were against the chances of his success, and yet, taking a higher viewpoint of consideration, they were in his favor.

His lack of educational advantages would have seemed likely to bar his progress. He recognized this, and set himself from the first with a devotion and earnestness which were magnificent to remedy the defect. He has been a hard worker and hard reader, and this has found its reward in the fact that to-day he has acquired a style and delivery that is full of force and beauty. One of our great London dailies said of him recently that he is one of the finest exponents of the possibilities of Anglo-Saxon speech since the days of John Bright.

It is possible to hear him again and again, as I have done, without detecting a flaw in his grammar or pronunciation; and one is filled with wonder at his wonderful triumph in this direction.

In his case the very early lack has been the stimulus of constant effort, and there has been no arrest of development consequent upon the mistaken notion—alas, too common among more favored men —that he had his education long ago.

Greatly in his favor is the fact that he was a child of nature, nurtured near to her heart. When that Spirit who breatheth where He listeth brought him into living contact with Christ, the gain of this early environment was manifest.

To know him to-day is to catch the sweet, healthy freshness of woods and flowers and dear old mother earth, and to breathe the fragrance of the life lived far from the stifling atmosphere of great cities. I never talk with him without taking in a wholesome quantity of ozone. His most remarkable growth has been spiritual. In tone and temper, and those fine qualities of spirit which are the fairest productions of Christian life, he has steadily advanced, and to-day more than ever is a child of God in outward conduct and inward character.

Though thus a child of the country, his mission has been pre-eminently that of a messenger of the Gospel to great cities. It is one of the most heart-stirring and spirit-reviving sights I know to watch a dense mass of city folk, toilers in the factories, clerks from the offices, professional men, and those of culture and leisure, listen to him as he pleads with tender eloquence the cause of the Master.

Gipsy Smith is an evangelist by right of a "gift," bestowed by the Spirit of God, as certainly as there ever was such in the history of the Church. In his case, moreover, we have a conspicuous example of the fact that the Spirit bestows such gifts on those by natural endowment fitted to receive and use them. There is no conflict between a man as God made him and the work of grace in him when he is utterly abandoned to the will of God.

This story of his life is full of deep interest, as it breathes the very spirit of the man—artless, intense, transparent. For it I bespeak a reading on the part of all those who love the Lord Jesus and are interested in the story of His methods with the messengers of His grace.   I welcome the book as a fresh living message of that grace, and as adding another to the long list of lives that show forth the excellencies of Him who calls men out of darkness into His marvellous light.

This brief prefatory work is a work of love, for out of the fulness of the heart the mouth speaketh, and of my friend who is at once Gipsy and Gentleman, because wholly Christian, I can truly say, thank my God upon every remembrance of him.

INTRODUCTION

By Rev. Dr. Alexander McLaren

THERE is little need for any introduction to this book; but my friend Gipsy Smith having done me the honor of asking me to prefix a few words to it, I gladly comply with his request. I have at least one qualification for my present position—namely, my long and close knowledge of the man who here tells his life-story, and I can say with absolute confidence and sincerity that that knowledge has discovered to me a character of rare sweetness, goodness, simplicity, and godliness, and possessed of something of that strange attractiveness with which popular beliefs have endowed his race. But the fascination is explicable on better grounds than magic spells; it is the charm of a nature which draws others to itself, because it goes out to meet them, and is loved because it loves.

The life told in this book has its picturesque and its pathetic sides, but is worthy of study for deeper reasons than these. It witnesses to the transforming power of Jesus Christ, entering a soul through that soul's faith. A gipsy encampment is the last place whence an evangelist might be expected to emerge. Almost alien to our civilization, with

little education, with vices and limitations inherited
from generations who were despised and suspected,
and with the virtues of a foreign clan encamped on
hostile ground, the gipsies have been all but overlooked by the churches, with one or two exceptions,
such as the work of Crabbe half a century since
among those of Hampshire and the New Forest.
But the story in this book brings one more striking
and welcome evidence that there are no hopeless
classes in the view of the gospel. We are accustomed to say that often enough, but we do not always act as if we believed it, and it may do some
of us good to have another living example of Christ's
power to elevate and enrich a life, whatever its an-
tecedents, disadvantages, and limitations. Gipsy
or gentleman, "we have all of us one human heart,"
and the deepest need in that heart is an anodyne for
the sense of sin, and a power which will implant in
it righteousness. Here is a case in which Christ's
gospel has met both wants. Is there anything else
that would or could do that?

For another reason this book deserves study, for
it raises serious questions as to the Church's office
of "evangelizing every creature." Gipsy Smith has
remarkable qualifications for that work, and has
done it all over the country with a sobriety, transparent sincerity, and loyalty to the ordinary ministra-
tions of the churches which deserve and have received general recognition. But what he has not
is as instructive as what he has. He is not an orator,
nor a scholar, nor a theologian. He is not a genius.

But, notwithstanding these deficiencies in his equipment, he can reach men's hearts, and turn them from darkness to light in a degree which many of us ministers cannot do. It will be a good day for all the churches when their members ask themselves whether they are doing the work for which they are established by their Lord, if they fail in winning men to be His, and whether Christ will be satisfied if, when He asks them why they have not carried out His commands to take His gospel to those around them who are without it, they answer, " Lord, we were so busy studying deep theological questions, arguing about the validity of critical inquiries as to the dates of the books of the Bible, preaching and hearing eloquent discourses, comforting and edifying one another, that we had to leave the Christless masses alone." This book tells the experience of one man who has been an evangelist and nothing more. May it help to rouse the conscience of the church to feel that it is to be the messenger of the glad tidings first of all, whatever else it may be in addition! May it set many others to bethink themselves whether they, too, are not sufficiently furnished "for the work of an evangelist" to some hearts at least, though they have neither learning nor eloquence, since they have the knowledge of One who has saved them, and desires through them to save others.'

ALEXANDER McLAREN.

CONTENTS.

Contents

Yours heartily
Gipsy Smith

GIPSY SMITH

CHAPTER 1

BIRTH AND ANCESTRY—WITH SOME NOTES OF GIPSY CUSTOMS

I WAS born on the 31st of March, 1860, in a gipsy tent, the son of gipsies, Cornelius Smith and his wife, Mary Welch. The place was the parish of Wanstead, near Epping Forest, a mile and a half from the "Green Man," Leytonstone. When I got old enough to ask questions about my birth my mother was dead, but my father told me the place, though not the date. It was only quite recently that I knew the date for certain. A good aunt of mine took the trouble to get some one to examine the register of Wanstead Church, and there found an entry giving the date of the birth and christening of Rodney Smith. I discovered that I was a year younger than I took myself to be. The gipsies care little for religion and know nothing really of God and the Bible, yet they always take care to get their babies christened, because it is a matter of business. The clergyman of the nearest parish church is invited to come to the encampment and perform the ceremony.   To the "gorgios" (people who are not gipsies) the event is one of rare and curious interest.   Some of the ladies of the congregation are sure to accompany the parson to see the gipsy baby, and they cannot very well do this without bringing presents for the gipsy mother and more often for the baby.   The gipsies believe in christenings for the profit they can make out of them.   They have, besides, some sort of notion that it is the right thing to do.

I was the fourth child of my parents.   Two girls and a boy came before me and two girls came after me.   All my brothers and sisters, except the last born, are alive.   My eldest sister is Mrs. Ball, wife of Councillor Ball, of Hanley, the first gipsy in the history of the country to occupy a seat in a town council.   And he is always returned at the head of the poll.   Councillor Ball, who is an auctioneer, has given up his tent and lives in a house.   My brother Ezekiel works on the railway at Cambridge, and is a leading spirit of the Railway Mission there. He was the last of the family to leave the gipsy tent, and he did it after a deal of persuasion and with great reluctance.   My father and I, on visiting Cambridge, got him to take up his quarters in a nice little cottage there.   When I returned to the town some months later and sought him in his cottage, I found that he was not there and that he had gone back to his tent.   "Whatever made you leave the cottage, Ezekiel?" I asked.   "It was so cold," he replied.   Gipsy wagons and tents are very comfort-

able—"gorgios" should make no mistake about that.
My second sister, Lovinia, is Mrs. Oakley, and lives
at Luton, a widow. I had a mission at Luton last
year, and she was one of those who came to Christ.
My father, myself, and others of us had offered thousands of prayers for her, and at that mission, she,
a backslider for over twenty-five years, was restored.
God gave me this honor—the joy of bringing my
beloved sister back to the fold. I need not say that
I think of that mission with a special warmth of
gratitude to God. Mrs. Evens—Matilda, the baby
of the family—helped me a great deal in my early
evangelistic labors, and together with her husband
has done and is doing good work for the Liverpool
Wesleyan Mission.

Eighty out of every hundred gipsies have Bible
names. My father was called Cornelius, my brother
Ezekiel. My uncle Bartholomew was the father of
twelve children, to every one of whom he gave a
scriptural name — Naomi, Samson, Delilah, Elijah,
Simeon, and the like. Fancy having a Samson and
a Delilah in the same family! Yet the gipsies have
no Bibles, and if they had they could not read them.
Whence, then, these scriptural names? Do they
not come down to us from tradition? May it not
be that we are one of the lost tribes? We ourselves
believe that we are akin to the Jews, and when one
regards the gipsies from the point of view of an outsider one is able to discover some striking resem-
blances between the gipsies and the Jews. In the
first place, many gipsies bear a striking facial re-

semblance to the Jews. Our noses are not usually
quite so prominent, but we often have the eyes and
hair of Jews. Nature asserts herself. And although, as far as the knowledge of religion is concerned, gipsies dwell in the deepest heathen darkness, in the days when I was a boy they scrupulously observed the law of the Sabbath, except when the
"gorgios" visited them and tempted them with
money to tell their fortunes. It was a great trouble to
my father—I am speaking of him in his unregenerate
days—to have to pull up his tent on the Sabbath
day. And I have known him go a mile on Saturday to get a bucket of water, so that he should not
have to travel for it on the Sunday. And the bundles
of sticks for the fire on Sunday were all gathered the
day before. Even whistling a song tune was not allowed on the Sunday. When I was a boy I have
been knocked over more than once for so far forget-
ting myself as to engage in this simple diversion on
the Sunday. Sunday to the gipsies is a real rest-day.
And at the same time it is the only day on which
they get a properly cooked mid-day meal! Then,
again, the ancient Jewish law and custom of marriage is the same as that which is in vogue, or was in
vogue, until quite recently among the gipsies. Sixty
years ago a marriage according to the law of the
land was unknown among the gipsies. The sweethearting of a gipsy young man and maiden usually
extends over a long period, or, as "gorgios" would
say, the rule is long engagements. Very often they
have grown up sweethearts from boy and girl. It

was so with my brother Ezekiel and his wife. There is never such a thing as a gipsy breach of promise case, and if there were the evidence would probably be scanty, for gipsy sweethearts do not write to each other—because they cannot. Ninety-nine out of every hundred of them have never held a pen in their hands. When the young people are able to set up for themselves they make a covenant with each other. Beyond this there is no marriage ceremony. There is nothing of jumping over tongs or broomsticks, or any other of the tomfooleries that outsiders attribute to gipsies. The ceremonial is the same as that which was observed at the nuptials of Rebekah and Isaac. Isaac brought Rebekah into his tent, and she became his wife, and he lived with her. The gipsies are the most faithful and devoted of husbands. I ought to add that the making of the marriage covenant is usually followed by a spree.

When a gipsy becomes converted, one of the first things about which he gets anxious is this defective marriage ceremonial. At one of my missions an old gipsy man of seventy-four sought and found his Saviour. He went away happy. Some days after he came back to see me. I perceived that something was oppressing his mind. "Well, uncle, what's the matter?" I asked. By the way, I should say that gipsies have great reverence for old age. We should never think of addressing an old man or woman by his or her name—not Mr. Smith or Mrs. Smith, John or Sally, but always uncle or aunt, terms of

affection and respect among us.   Uncle looked at me
gloomily and said: "The truth is, my dear, my wife
and I have never been legally married." They had
been married according to the only fashion known
among the gipsies, and I told him that in the eyes of
God they were true husband and wife. But he
would not be persuaded. "No," he said, "I am
converted now; I want everything to be straight.
We must get legally married." And they did, and
were satisfied.

Like the Jews, the gipsies have in a wonderful
way preserved their identity as a race.   Their separate existence can be traced back for centuries.
Throughout these long years they have kept their
language, habits, customs, and eccentricities untouched.   The history of gipsies and of their tongue
has baffled the most laborious and erudite scholars.
We can be traced back until we are lost on the plains
of India, but even in these far-off days we were a
distinct race.   Like the Jews, the gipsies are very
clean.   A man who does not keep his person or be-
longings 'clean is called "chickly" (dirty), and is
despised.   They have hand-towels for washing themselves, and these are used for nothing else.   They are
scrupulously careful about their food.   They would
not think of washing their table-cloth with the other
linen.   Cups and saucers are never washed in soapy
water.   I saw my uncle trample on and destroy a
copper kettle-lid because one of his children by mistake had dropped it in the wash-tub.   It had become
"unclean."   A sick person has a spoon, plate, and

basin all to himself. When he has recovered or if he dies they are all destroyed. It is customary at death to destroy the possessions of the dead person or to bury them with him. When an uncle of mine died, my aunt bought a coffin large enough for all his possessions—including his fiddle, cup and saucer, plate, knife, etc.—except, of course, his wagon. My wife and my sister pleaded hard for the cup and saucer as a keepsake, but she was resolute. Nobody should ever use them again.

To return to my father. He earned his living by making baskets, clothes-pegs, all sorts of tinware, and recaning cane-chairs. Of course in his unconverted days he "found" the willows for the baskets and the wood for the clothes-pegs. Gipsies only buy what they cannot "find." My father had inherited his occupation from many generations of ancestors. He also pursued the trade of horse-dealer, a business in which gipsies are thoroughly expert. What a gipsy does not know about horses is not worth knowing. The trade is one in which tricks and dodges are frequently practised. A Dr. Chinnery, whom I met on one of my visits to America, told me of a gipsy horse-dealer for whose conversion he had been particularly anxious and with whom he had frequently talked. Said this gipsy, "Can I be a Christian and sell horses?" Dr. Chinnery urged him to try, and he did. The poor gipsy found the conjunction of callings very difficult, but he managed to make it work. After two or three years, Dr. Chinnery asked him how he was getting

on. He answered that when he had a good horse
to sell he told those with whom he was dealing that
it was a good horse. Since he had become a Christian they believed him. If it was a horse about
which he knew little, or a horse of which he had
doubts, he said: "My friends this (naming the sum)
is my price. I do not know anything about the
horse; you must examine him yourselves, and assure yourselves of his fitness. Use your judgment;
you buy him at your own risk." It will be seen
from this anecdote that the gipsies are not wanting in *finesse*. This gipsy had also not a little of
the Yankee cuteness which is breathed in with the
American air. His Christianity did not in the least
hinder, but rather helped, his horse-dealing.

The gipsy women sell what their husbands make,
and of course when we were all little my mother did
the selling for us. The women are the travellers for
the concern; the men are the manufacturers. This
old trade of making baskets is passing out of the
hands of the gipsies; they can buy these goods for
less than it costs to make them, and consequently
they confine themselves to selling them. Recaning
chairs and mending baskets is still done by some.
Most of the men deal in horses and in anything else
which is possible to their manner of life, and out of
which they can make money. I estimate that there
are from 20,000 to 25,000 gipsies in the British Isles.
The women-folk among them still do most of the
selling, but I am afraid that too frequently they
carry their wares about with them merely as a blind.

The occupation of most of them is fortune-telling. It is the fashion and the folly of the " gorgios " that have to a large extent forced this disgraceful profession upon gipsy women. Soothsaying is an Eastern custom, a gift that Westerners have attributed to Orientals. The gipsies are an Eastern race, and the idea has in course of generations grown up among outsiders that they, too, can reveal the secrets of the hidden future. The gipsies do not themselves believe this; they know that fortune-telling is a mere cheat, but they are not averse to making profit out of the folly and superstition of the " gorgios." I know some of my people may be very angry with me for this statement, but the truth must be told.

We travelled in the counties of Essex, Suffolk, Norfolk, Cambridge, Bedford, and Hertford. In my young days I knew these parts of England well, but since I left my gipsy tent, nearly a quarter of a century ago, I have not seen much of them. I had no education and no knowledge of "gorgio" civilization, and I grew up as wild as the birds, frolicsome as the lambs, and as difficult to catch as the rabbits. All the grasses and flowers and trees of the field and all living things were my friends and companions. Some of them, indeed, got almost too familiar with me. The rabbits, for instance, were so fond of me that they sometimes followed me home. I think I learned then to have a sympathetic nature, even if I learned nothing else. My earliest clear impression of these days, which have now retreated so far into the past, is that of falling from the front of my father's wagon. I had given the horse a stroke, as boys will do. He made a sudden leap and jerked me off onto the road. What followed has passed from my mind, but my father tells me I was run over by his wagon, and if my loud screams had not attracted his attention I should have been run over also by his brother's wagon, which followed his.

It was my mother's death, however, which woke me to full consciousness, if I may so put it. This event made a wound in my heart which has never to this day been really healed, and even at this moment, though I am now in middle life, I often feel my hungry soul pining and yearning for my mother. " Rodney, you have no mother!"—that was really the first and the ineffaceable impression of my boy's life.

CHAPTER II

MY MOTHER

WE were travelling in Hertfordshire. The eldest of the family, a girl, was taken ill. The nearest town was Baldock, and my father at once made for it, so that he might get a doctor for his child. I remember as if it were yesterday that the gipsy wagon stood outside the door of the doctor's house. My father told him he had a sick daughter. The doctor mounted the steps of the wagon and, leaning over the door, called my sick sister to him and examined her. He did not enter our poor wagon. We were only gipsies. "Your daughter has the small-pox," he said to my father; "you must get out of the town at once." He sent us to a by-lane about one and a half miles away—it is called Norton Lane. In a little bend of this lane, on the left-hand side, between a huge overhanging hawthorn and a wood on the right-hand side, making a natural arch, father erected our tent. There he left mother and four children. He took the wagon two hundred yards farther down the lane, and stood it on the right-hand side near an old chalk-pit. From the door he could see the tent clearly and be within call. The wagon was the sick-room and my father was the nurse. In a few days the doctor, coming to the

tent, discovered that my brother Ezekiel also had
the small-pox, and he, too, was sent to the wagon,
so that my father had now two invalids to nurse.
Poor mother used to wander up and down the lane
in an almost distracted condition, and my father
heard her cry again and again: "My poor children
will die, and I am not allowed to go to them!" Mother
had to go into Baldock to buy food, and, after preparing it in the tent, carried it half-way from there
to the wagon. Then she put it on the ground and
waited till my father came for it. She shouted or
waved her silk handkerchief to attract his attention.
Sometimes he came at once, but at other times he
would be busy with the invalids and unable to leave
them just at the moment. And then mother went
back, leaving the food on the ground, and sometimes before father had reached it, it was covered with
snow, for it was the month of March and the weather
was severe. And mother, in the anxiety of her loving
heart, got every day, I think, a little nearer and
nearer to the wagon, until one day she went too near,
and then she also fell sick. When the doctor came
he said it was the small-pox.

My father was in the uttermost distress. His
worst fears were realized. He had hoped to save
mother, for he loved her as only a gipsy can love.
She was the wife of his youth and the mother of his
children. They were both very young when they
married, not much over twenty, and they were still
very young. He would have died to save her. He
had struggled with his calamities bravely for a whole

month, nursing his two first-born with whole-hearted love and devotion, and had never had his clothes off, day or night.   And this he had done in order to save her from the terrible disease.   And now she, too, was smitten.   He felt that all hope was gone, and knowing he could not keep us separate any longer, he brought the wagon back to the tent.   And there lay mother and sister and brother, all three sick with small-pox.   In two or three days a little baby was born.

Mother knew she was dying.   Our hands were stretched out to hold her, but they were not strong enough.   Other hands, omnipotent and eternal, were taking her from us.   Father seemed to realize, too, that she was going.   He sat beside her one day and asked her if she thought of God.   For the poor gipsies believe in God, and believe that he is good and merciful.   And she said, "Yes."

"Do you try to pray, my dear?"

"Yes, I am trying, and while I am trying to pray it seems as though a black hand comes before me and shows me all that I have done, and something whispers, 'There is no mercy for you!'"

But my father had great assurance that God would forgive her, and told her about Christ and asked her to look to Him.   He died for sinners.   He was her Saviour.   My father had some time before been in prison for three months on a false charge, and it was there that he had been told what now he tried to teach my mother.   After my father had told her all he knew of the gospel she threw her arms around his neck and kissed him. Then he went outside, stood behind the wagon, and wept bitterly. When he went back again to see her she looked calmly into his face, and said, with a smile: "I want you to promise me one thing. Will you be a good father to my children?" He promised her that he would; at that moment he would have promised her anything. Again he went outside and wept, and while he was weeping he heard her sing:

> "I have a Father in the promised land.
> My God calls me, I must go
> To meet Him in the promised land."

My father went back to her and said: "Polly, my dear, where did you learn that song?"

She said: "Cornelius, I heard it when I was a little girl. One Sunday my father's tents were pitched on a village green, and seeing the young people and others going into a little school or church or chapel —I do not know which it was—I followed them in and they sang those words."

It must have been twenty years or so since my mother had heard the lines. Although she had forgotten them all these years, they came back to her in her moments of intense seeking after God and His salvation. She could not read the Bible; she had never been taught about God and His Son; but these words came back to her in her dying moments and she sang them again and again. Turning to my father, she said: "I am not afraid to die now. I feel that it will be all right. I feel assured that God will take care of my children."

Father watched her all that Sunday night, and knew she was sinking fast. When Monday morning dawned it found her deep in prayer. I shall never forget that morning. I was only a little fellow, but even now I can close my eyes and see the gipsy tent and wagon in the lane. The fire is burning outside on the ground, and the kettle is hanging over it in true gipsy fashion and a bucket of water is standing near by. Some clothes that my father has been washing are hanging on the hedge. I can see the old horse grazing along the lane. I can see the boughs bending in the breeze, and I can almost hear the singing of the birds, and yet when I try to call back the appearance of my dear mother I am baffled. That dear face that bent over my gipsy cradle and sang lullabies to me, that mother who if she had lived would have been more to me than any other in God's world—her face has faded clean from my memory. I wandered up the lane that morning with the hand of my sister Tilly in mine. We two little things were inseparable. We could not go to father, for he was too full of his grief. The others were sick. We two had gone off together, when suddenly I heard my name called: "Rodney!" and running to see what I was wanted for, I encountered my sister Emily. She had got out of bed, for bed could not hold her that morning, and she said to me, "Rodney, mother's dead!" I remember falling on my face in the lane as though I had been shot, and weeping my heart out and saying to myself, "I shall never be like other boys, for I have no mother!" And somehow that feeling has never quite left me, and even now, in my man's life, there are moments when mother is longed for.

My mother's death caused a gloom indescribable to settle down upon the tent life. The day of the funeral came. My mother was to be buried at the dead of night. We were only gipsies, and the authorities would not permit the funeral to take place in the day-time. In the afternoon the coffin was placed on two chairs outside the wagon, waiting for the darkness. Sister and brother were so much better that the wagon had been emptied. My father had been trying to cleanse it, and the clothes, such as we had for wearing and sleeping in, had been put into the tent. While we were watching and weeping round the coffin—father and his five children—the tent caught fire, and all our little stock of worldly possessions were burned to ashes. The sparks flew around us on all sides of the coffin, and we expected every moment that that, too, would be set on fire. We poor little things were terrified nearly to death. "Mother will be burned up!" we wept. "Mother will be burned up!" Father fell upon his face on the grass crying like a child. The flames were so strong that he could do nothing to stop their progress; and, indeed, he had to take great care to avoid harm to himself. Our agonies while we were witnessing this, to us, terrible conflagration, helpless to battle against it, may easily be imagined, but, strange to relate, while the sparks

fell all around the coffin, the coffin itself was untouched.

And now darkness fell and with it came to us an
old farmer's cart. Mother's coffin was placed in the
vehicle, and between ten and eleven o'clock my father,
the only mourner, followed her to the grave by a
lantern light. She lies resting in Norton church-
yard, near Baldock. When my father came back
to us it was midnight, and his grief was very great.
He went into a plantation behind his van, and throwing himself upon his face, promised God to be good,
to take care of his children, and to keep the promise
that he had made to his wife. A fortnight after the
little baby died and was placed at her mother's side.
If you go to Norton church-yard now and inquire for
the gipsies' graves they will be pointed out to you.
My mother and her last born lie side by side in that
portion of the grave-yard where are interred the remains of the poor, the unknown, and the forsaken.

We remained in that fatal lane a few weeks longer:
then the doctor gave us leave to move on, all danger
being over. So we took farewell of the place where
we had seen so much sorrow.

I venture to think that there are some points of
deep spiritual significance in this narrative. First
of all, there is the sweet and touching beauty of my
father's endeavor to show my mother, in the midst
of his and her ignorance, the way of salvation as far
as he was able. My dear father tried to teach her
of God. Looking back on that hour he can see
clearly in it the hand of God. When he was in prison

as a lad, many years before, he heard the gospel
faithfully preached by the chaplain. The sermon
had been on the text, "I am the good Shepherd, and
know My sheep, and am known of Mine." My
father was deeply distressed and cried to God to save
him, and had there been any one to show him the
way of salvation he would assuredly have found
peace then.

At the time of my mother's death, too, my father
was under deep conviction, but there was no light.
He could not read, none of his friends could read,
and there was no one to whom he could go for instruction and guidance. The actual date of his conversion was some time after this, but my father is
convinced that if he had been shown the way of salvation he would have there and then surrendered his
life to God.

Another significant point was this: what was it
that brought back to my mother's mind in her last
hour the lines:

> "I have a Father in the promised land.
> My God calls me, I must go
> To meet Him in the promised land"?

Was it not the Holy Ghost, of whom Christ said,
"But the Comforter, which is the Holy Ghost, whom
the Father will send in My name, He shall teach you
all things, and bring all things to your remembrance,
whatsoever I have said unto you"? (John xiv. 26).
My mother had lived in a religious darkness that
was all but unbroken during her whole life, but a ray of

light had crept into her soul when she was a little girl, by the singing of this hymn. That was a part of the true light which lighteth every man that cometh into the world. No minister ever looked near our gipsy tent, no missioner, no Christian worker. To me it is plain that it was the Holy Ghost who brought these things to her remembrance—as plain as the sun that shines, or the flowers that bloom, or the birds that sing. That little child's song, heard by my mother as she wandered into that little chapel that Sunday afternoon, was brought back to her by the Spirit of God and became a ladder by which she climbed from her ignorance and superstition to the light of God and the many mansions. And my mother is there, and although I cannot recall her face, I shall know it some day.

I became conscious after my mother's death that I was a real boy, and that I had lost something which I should never find. Many a day when I have seen my aunts making a great deal of their children, giving them advice and even thrashing them, I have cried for my mother—if it were only to thrash me! It tore my hungry little heart with anguish to stand by and see my cousins made a fuss of. At such times I have had hard work to hide my bitter tears. I have gone up the lane round the corner, or into the field or wood to weep my heart out. In these days, my dreams, longings, and passions frightened me. I would lie awake all night exploring depths in my own being that I but faintly understood, and thinking of my mother. I knew that she had gone beyond the clouds, because my father told me so, and I believed everything that my father told me. I knew he spoke the truth. I used to try to pierce the clouds, and often-times I fancied I succeeded, and used to have long talks with my mother, and I often told her that some day I was coming up to her.

One day I went to visit her grave in Norton church-yard. As may be imagined, that quiet spot in the lonely church-yard was sacred to my father and to us, and we came more often to that place than we should have done had it not been that there in the cold earth lay hidden from us a treasure that gold could not buy back. I shall never forget my first visit to that hallowed spot. Our tent was pitched three miles off. My sister Tilly and I—very little things we were—wandered off one day in search of mother's grave. It was early in the morning when we started. We wandered through fields, jumped two or three ditches, and those we could not jump we waded through. The spire of Norton church was our guiding star. We set our course by it. When we reached the church-yard we went to some little cottages that stood beside it, knocked at the doors and asked the people if they could tell us which was mother's grave. We did not think it necessary to say who mother was or who we were. There was but one mother in the world for us. The good people were very kind to us. They wept quiet, gentle tears for the poor gipsy children, because they knew at once from our faces and our clothes that we were gipsies, and they knew what manner of death our mother

had died. The grave was pointed out to us. When
we found it, Tilly and I stood over it weeping for a long
time, and then we gathered primrose and violet roots
and planted them on the top. And we stood there
long into the afternoon. The women from the cottages gave us food, and then it started to our memory
that it was late, and that father would be wondering
where we were. So I said, "Tilly, we must go home,"
and we both got on our knees beside the grave and
kissed it. Then we turned our backs upon it and
walked away. When we reached the gates that led
out of the church-yard we looked back again, and I
said to Tilly, "I wonder whether we can do anything
for mother?" I suddenly remembered that I had
with me a gold-headed scarf-pin which some one had
given me. It was the only thing of any value that
I ever had as a child. Rushing back to the grave,
upon the impulse and inspiration of the moment,
I stuck the scarf-pin into the ground as far as I could,
and hurrying back to Tilly, I said, "There, I have
given my gold pin to my mother!" It was all I had
to give. Then we went home to the tents and wagons.
Father had missed us and had become very anxious.
When he saw us he was glad and also very angry,
intending, no doubt, to punish us for going away
without telling him, and for staying away too long.
He asked us where we had been. We said we had gone
to mother's grave. Without a word he turned away
and wept bitterly.

CHAPTER III

A MISCHIEVOUS LITTLE BOY—WITH SOMETHING
ABOUT PLUMS, TROUSERS, RABBITS, EGGS,
AND A CIRCUS

THE wild man in my father was broken forever.
My mother's death had wrought a moral revolution
in him. As he had promised to her, he drank much
less, he swore much less, and he was a good father
to us. When my mother died he had made up his
mind to be a different man, and as far as was possible
in his own strength he had succeeded. But his soul
was hungry for he knew not what, and a gnawing
dissatisfaction that nothing could appease or gratify
was eating out his life.

The worldly position of our household, in the
mean time, was comfortable. My father made clothes-
pegs and all manner of tinware, and we children
sold them. If I may say so, I was the best seller
in the family. Sometimes I would get rid of five or
six gross of clothes-pegs in a day. I was not at all
bashful or backward, and I think I may say I was
a good business man in those days. I used so to
keep on at the good women till they bought my pegs
just to get rid of me. "Bother the boy," they would
say, "there is no getting rid of him!" And I would

say, "Come, now, madame, here you have the best
pegs in the market. They will not eat and will not
wear clothes out; they will not cry, and they will
not wake you up in the middle of the night!" Then
they would laugh, and I used to tell them who I was,
and that I had no mother. This softened their hearts.
Sometimes I sold my pegs wholesale to the retail
sellers. I was a wholesale and a retail merchant.

I got into trouble, however, at Cambridge. I was
trying to sell my goods at a house there. It chanced
to be a policeman's house. I was ten or eleven years
of age, too young to have a selling license, and the
policeman marched me off to the police-court. I
was tried for selling goods without a license. I was
called upon to address the court in my defence.
And I said something like this: "Gentlemen, it is
true I have no license. You will not let me have a
license; I am too young. I am engaged in an honest
trade. I do not steal. I sell my clothes-pegs to help
my father to make an honest living for himself and
us children. If you will give me a license my father
is quite willing to pay for it, but if you will not, I do
not see why I should be prevented from doing honest
work for my living." This argument carried weight.
My ingenuousness impressed the court, and I was
let off with a small fine.

I think I can tell some amusing things about these
days. My dress consisted of an overall (and an
underall too), a smock-frock of the sort that is still
worn in the Eastern counties. When I took this off,
I was ready for bed. The frock had some advan-

tages. It had pockets which it took a great deal to fill. They were out of sight, and no one could very well know what was in them. One day I was up a tree, a tree that bore delicious Victoria plums. I had filled my pockets with them, and I had one in my mouth: I was in a very happy frame of mind, when, lo! at the foot of the tree appears the owner of the land. He gave me a very pressing invitation to come down. At once I swallowed the plum in my mouth, in case he should think that I was after his plums. He repeated his pressing invitation to come down.

"What do you want, sir?" I asked, in the most bland and innocent tones, as if I had never known the taste of plums.

"If you come down," he said, "I will tell you."

I am not used to climbing up or climbing down, but I had to come down because I could not stay even up a plum-tree for ever, and my friend showed no disposition to go. He said, "I will wait until you are ready," and I did not thank him for his courtesy. I did not make haste to come down, neither did I do it very joyfully. When I got to the foot of the tree my friend got me by the right ear. There was a great deal of congratulation in his grip. He pulled me over rapidly and unceremoniously to another tree.

"Do you see that tree?" he said.

"Yes, sir."

"Do you see that board?"

"Yes, sir."

"Can you read it?"

"No, sir."

"Well, I will read it for you: 'Whosoever is found trespassing on this ground will be prosecuted according to law.'"

Since that day I have never wanted anybody to explain to me what "whosoever" means. This memorable occasion fixed the meaning of the word on my mind for ever. The irate owner shook me hard. And I tried to cry, but I could not. Then I told him that I had no mother, and I thought that touched him, although he knew it, for he knew my father. Indeed, that saved me. He looked at me again and shook me hard. "If it were not for your father," he said, "I would send you to prison." For wherever my father was known in his unconverted days, by farmer, policeman, or gamekeeper, he was held in universal respect. At last he let me off with a caution. He threw an old boot at me, but he forgot to take his foot out of it. But I was quite happy, for my pockets were full of plums. I dared not say anything about it to my father. My father would have been very angry with me, because, even in his wild days, he would not allow this sort of thing in his children if he knew. Then there were farmers who were kind to us—very; and we had to be specially careful what we did and where we went. If our tent was pitched near their places, my father would say to us, "I do not want you to go far from the wagons to-day," and we knew at once what that meant.

My father was a very fatherly man. He did not believe in sparing the rod or spoiling the child. He was fond of taking me on his knees with my face downward. When he made an engagement with me he kept it. He never broke one. He sometimes almost broke me. If a thrashing was due, one might keep out of father's reach all day, but this merely deferred the punishment; there was no escaping him at bed-time, because we all slept on one floor, the first. Sometimes he would send me for a stick to be thrashed with. In that case I always brought either the smallest or the biggest—the smallest because I knew that it could not do much harm, or the largest because I knew my father would lay it on very lightly. Once or twice I managed to get out of a thrashing in this way: One was due to me in the evening. In the afternoon I would say to him, "Daddy, shall I go and gather a bundle of sticks for your fire?" and he would say, "Yes, Rodney." Then when I brought them to him I would hand him one, and he would say, "What is this for?" "Why, that is for my thrashing," I would answer. And sometimes he would let me off, and sometimes he would not. Occasionally, too, I used to plead, "I know mother is not far behind the clouds, and she is looking down on you, and she will see you if you hit me very hard." Sometimes that helped me to escape, sometimes it did not. But this I will say for my father: he never thrashed me in a temper, and I am quite sure now that I deserved my thrashings, and that they all did me good.

As I grew older I became ambitious of some thing better and greater than a smock-frock, namely—a pair of trousers. My father did not give an enthusiastic encouragement to that ambition, but he told me that if I was a good boy I should have a pair of his. And I was a good boy. My father in those days stood nearly six feet high, was broad in proportion, and weighed fifteen stones. I was very small and very thin as a child, but I was bent on having a pair of trousers. My father took an old pair of his and cut them off at the knees; but even then, of course, they had to be tucked up. I was a proud boy that day. I took my trousers behind the hedge, so that I might put them on in strict privacy. My father and brother, enjoying the fun, although I did not see it, waited for me on the other side of the hedge. When I emerged they both began to chaff me. "Rodney," said my brother, "are you going or coming?" He brought me a piece of string and said, "What time does the balloon go up?" And, in truth, when the wind blew, I wanted to be pegged down. I did not like the fun, but I kept my trousers. I saw my father's dodge. He wanted me to get disgusted with them and to go back to the smock-frock; but I knew that if I went on wearing them he would soon get tired of seeing me in these extraordinary garments and would buy me a proper pair.

A day came when we were the guests of the Prince of Wales at Sandringham—that is, we pitched our tents on his estate. One day I helped to catch some rabbits, and these trousers turned out to be very useful. In fact, immediately the rabbits were caught, the trousers became a pair of fur-lined garments; for I carried them home inside the trousers.

At length my father bought me a pair of brand-new corduroys that just fitted me, but I was soon doomed to trouble with these trousers. One day I found a hen camping out in the ditch, and there was quite a nestful of eggs there. I was very indignant with that hen for straying so far from the farm-yard. I considered that her proceedings were irregular and unauthorized. As to the eggs, the position to me was quite clear. I had found them. I had not gone into the farm-yard and pilfered them. On the other hand, they had put themselves in my way, and I naturally thought they were mine, and so I filled my pockets with them. I was sorry that I had to leave some of these eggs, but I could not help it. The capacity of my pockets in my new trousers was less generous than in the old ones.. My next difficulty was how to get out of the ditch without breaking any of the eggs. But I was a youngster of resource and managed it. And now I had to take my way across a ploughed field. This meant some very delicate pedestrian work. Then I heard a man shout, and I thought that he wanted me, but I did not desire to give him an interview. So I ran, and as I ran I fell; and when I fell the eggs all cracked. I got up, and, looking round, saw nobody. The man who I thought was pursuing me was only shouting to a man in another field. It is truly written, "The wicked flee when no man pursueth." I thought I had found these eggs, but my conscience found me. I have never found eggs again from that day to this.

One other episode of my childish days will I inflict upon my readers. It was the time of the Cambridge Fair, and our wagons were standing on the fair-ground. The fun of the fair included a huge circus—Sanger's, I think it was. In front of the door stood the clown, whom it was the custom among us to call "Pinafore Billy." This is the man who comes out and dilates on the wonders and merits of the performance, tells the people that the show is just about to begin, and invites them to step in. My highest ambition as a boy was to become a Pinafore Billy. I thought that that position was the very height of human glory, and I would have done anything and taken any trouble to get it. Now I wanted to get into the circus, and I had no money. A man was walking round the show with a long whip in his hand driving boys off, in case they should attempt to slip in under the canvas. I went up to this whip-man and offered to help him. He was very scornful, and said, "What can you do?" I said, "I will do what I can; I will help to keep the boys off." So he said, "Very well; what will you do?" I answered, "You go round one way and I will go the other." It was agreed, but as soon as he started to do his half of the round and turned his back on me, and had got round the tent, I slipped under the canvas. I thought by doing so I should at once be in the right part of the circus for seeing the show, but instead of that I found myself in a sort of dark, dismal part underneath

the raised seats of the circus. This was where the
horses were kept. I saw at once I was in a fix, and
to my horror I perceived a policeman walking round
inside and coming towards me. I was at my wits'
end; but luckily I perceived some harness lying
about, and seizing a loose cloth close at hand, I began to polish the harness vigorously. When the
policeman did come up to me he said, "My boy,
that is a curious job they have given you to do in
such a place as this." "It is very hard work," I
said, and went on polishing as vigorously as ever,
never looking up at the policeman's face. I was
afraid to, for I knew that my looks would betray my
guilt. Then the policeman went on. I really do
not know how I made my way into the circus. However, I found myself sitting among the best seats
of the house, and I am sure that I attracted great
attention, for here was I, a poor little gipsy boy,
dressed in corduroys and velvets, sitting among
all the swells. I was not long in peace. My conscience at once began to say to me, "How will you
get out? You dare not go out by the door in case
you meet the whip-man that you offered to help."
I felt myself to be a thief and a robber. I had not
come in at the door, but I had climbed up some other
way. I do not remember quite how I got out of this
terrible dilemma, but I know that I escaped without
suffering, and was very glad, indeed, to find myself
outside again with a whole skin.

These are the worst of the sins that I have to confess. My boyhood's days were, on the whole, very

innocent. I did not drink or swear. I am afraid, however, that I told lies many a time. I had no opportunity for cultivating bad habits, for all the companions I had were my sisters and my brother, and so I was kept from serious sin by the narrowness and the limitations of my circumstances.

CHAPTER IV

THE MORALS OF THE GIPSIES

PERHAPS this is a fit place to say a few words about the morals of the gipsies. I want to say at once that the character of my people stands very high. I never knew of a gipsy girl who went astray. I do not say that that never happened, but that I never knew a fallen woman in a gipsy-tent. The gipsy boy is told from his earliest days that he must honor and protect women. He drinks in this teaching, so to say, with his mother's milk, and he grows up to be very courteous and very chivalrous. The gipsy sweethearts do their courting in the day-time, and where they can be seen by their parents. The " gorgio " sweethearts would probably find these conditions rather trying. Gipsy sweethearts do not go out for walks by the light of the moon, neither do they betake themselves to nooks and corners out of sight and out of reach of everybody. All the sweet things the gipsy man says to the gipsy maid must be uttered, if not in the hearing of their parents, at least in their sight.

My brother Ezekiel and his wife were sweethearts from childhood. One day, when they were approaching the estate of manhood and womanhood, Ezekiel was sitting talking to his girl in the presence of her mother. "I know," said Ezekiel's prospective mother-in-law, "that you young people want a walk. You shall have one. I will go with you." And this is the kind of thing which occurs invariably during gipsy courtships. Sweethearts would never think of going off alone for a little walk, yet the gipsies find this no bar to pleasant and successful courting. The result of these customs is that gipsy courtships are not marred by untoward and unpleasant incidents. The hearts of the young men and young women are pure, and this purity is guarded by their parents like gold. The gipsy men, indeed, pride themselves on the purity of their women, and that says a great deal for the men. Practically all gipsies get married. There are very few old maids and old bachelors. The gipsy husband and wife live on the most intimate terms. The wife knows all that her husband knows. I would not say that a gipsy husband knows all that his wife knows, any more than a "gorgio" husband knows all that his wife knows. They usually have large families. There is no more groundless slander than the statement that gipsies steal children. They have every reason for not so doing. They have plenty of their own. My great-uncle was the father of thirty-one children, and a brother of my father's was the father of twenty-four, I think. I have never heard that they sought to add to their number by theft.

The young gipsy couple start their married life by purchasing a wagon. This costs anywhere from

£40 to £150, and is obtained from a " gorgio " wagon-builder. Oddly enough, the gipsies never learn the trade of making their own wagons. The wagons are very warm and very strong, and last a great many years. The young husband is, of course, the manufacturer of the goods, and his wife the seller. When she leaves the wagon in the morning to go her rounds she arranges with her husband where the wagon shall be placed at night, and thither she betakes herself when her day's toil is over. In the course of the day she may have walked from fifteen to twenty miles. Gipsies have plenty of exercise and a sufficiency of food. This explains their very good health. If the husband has been refused permission to stand his wagon on the arranged spot and has had to move on, he lets his wife know where he is going by leaving behind him a track of grass.

Gipsies are very lovable and very loyal to one another. They are respectful, and even reverential, to old age. I never knew of a gipsy who ended his or her days in the workhouse. The gipsy young man would rather work the flesh off his fingers than tolerate any such thing. They would feel ashamed to abandon those who had done so much for them.

The gipsies do not hate the " gorgios," but they feel that they are suspected and mistrusted, and that everybody is afraid of them. They feel that all " gorgios " are against them, and therefore they are against the "gorgios." If a kindness is done them by a " gorgio " they never cease to talk about it. They remember it all their days and their children are

told of it too. Quite recently a curious illustration
of this trait came to my knowledge. I was travelling from Cambridge to Thetford, and had as my
companion a clergyman of the Church of England.
"Some years ago," he said to me, "a gipsy family
came to my parish. The father was ill, and I went
to see him. I read to him, I prayed with him, and
my wife brought him some nourishing soup. This
poor man became a sincere seeker after Christ, and
I have every reason to believe he was converted. I
followed up my friendship with him. When he left
the parish and went a few miles farther away I kept
in touch with him, and wrote to a brother clergyman
and arranged with him to follow up what I had tried
to do for this dying man. This he gladly did, and
the man passed away happy in the knowledge of
sins forgiven. Two or three years after I was driving out of Norwich when I met two young gipsy
fellows with a donkey which they were going into
Norwich to sell. I was in need of a donkey, so I got
down and began to talk to them. I questioned them
about the donkey. They said it was a very good
one, and from its appearance I thought so too. Then
we went on to discuss the price. I finally decided to
purchase the donkey. I had some further conversation with them, telling them where to take the donkey, and when I would be home to pay for the same.
In the mean time I observed with somewhat of alarm
that these two young fellows were exchaging curious glances. We were about to fix up the bargain
when one of them said to me, 'Are you Mr. So-and-so?'

'Yes, I am.' 'Oh, well, sir, we have heard of your great kindness to poor So-and-so when he was dying, and we cannot sell you this donkey: it is a bad one; we could not take you in; but if you will let us we will give you a good donkey, a genuine, good article.' And they got me a fine animal, which has done a good deal of work, which I still have, and have been delighted with.''

The gipsies are naturally musical. In fact, I believe that the only naturally musical people in the world are the Jews and gipsies, and this is another point of affinity between the two races. The gipsies love to dance in the lanes to the music of the harp, the dulcimer, and violin. They do not object to the " gorgios " looking on, but they would rather they did not join in the merriment. They like to live their own life with absolute freedom and without interference.

But, alas! there is a debit side to this moral balance account. The gipsies drink a good deal. Beer is their beverage. Spirits as a rule they take sparingly. They do not drink for the mere sake of drinking, but only when they meet friends. Their drinking is an unfortunate outcome of their highly social dispositions. They may be abstemious for days, weeks, and even months, but when they begin to drink they go in for it thoroughly. Cans and bottles do not satisfy them. Buckets are what they need; and the spree sometimes lasts for nearly a week. Gipsy women, however, are abstemious. I have only known one who was really a drunkard. And then gipsies swear, some of them, indeed, fearfully. They do not lie to each other, but to the "gorgios." They are paid to lie, to tell fortunes. This vile business, which has really been forced upon them by the " gorgios," utterly debauches the consciences of the gipsies. And I should like all our educated women to know that every time they pay a gipsy woman to tell their fortune they make it the more difficult for that woman to become a Christian. The gipsies, too, are pilferers. They do not commit big robberies. They do not steal horses or break into banks, nor do they commit highway robberies, or find a few thousands, or fail for a few. But they take potatoes from a field or fruit from an orchard—only what is sufficient for their immediate needs. The potatoes they take from a field are only those they need until they get to the next potato field. Sometimes, too, late at night, they will put five or six horses into a field to feed, and take them out early in the morning. They are also in the habit of finding young undergrowth stuff that they use for their clothes-pegs and baskets. Most of them never dream that there is any sin or wrong in such actions. They regard them merely as natural, ordinary, commonplace events in their daily lives.

CHAPTER V

MY FATHER, AND HOW HE FOUND THE LORD

To return to the story of my own life. I have said that the gipsies are very musical, and my father was a good illustration of this statement. He was a very good fiddler—by ear, of course. He tells a story of the days when he was learning to play in his mother's tent. Dear old lady, she got tired of the noise the boy was making, and she told him to stop. As he did not stop, she said, "If you don't I will blow out the candle." This she did. That, of course, made no difference to the young musician; he went on playing, and grannie said, "I never saw such a boy; he can play in the dark!" For years my father had greatly added to his ordinary earnings by fiddling to the dancers in the public-houses at Baldock, Cambridge, Ashwell, Royston, Bury St. Edmunds, and elsewhere. Even after my mother's death, though his fiddling led him into great temptations, my father continued this practice, and he sometimes took me with him. When he fiddled I danced. I was a very good dancer, and at a certain point in the evening's proceedings my father would say, "Now, Rodney, make the collection," and I went round with the hat. That is where

I graduated for the ministry. If ever my father took more drink than was good for him, with the result that he did not know whether he was drawing the bow across the first string or the second, I went round again with my cap. What I collected that time I regarded as my share of the profits, for I was a member of the firm of Smith & Son, and not a sleeping partner either. How delighted I was if I got a few coppers to show to my sisters! These visits with my father to the beer-shop were very frequent, and as I think of those days, when I was forced to listen to the vile jokes and vulgar expressions of the common laborers, I marvel at the grace which shielded me and prevented me from understanding what was being said.

All this time, while my father was living this life of fiddling and drinking and sinning, he was under the deepest conviction. He always said his prayers night and morning and asked God to give him power over drink, but every time temptation came in his way he fell before it. He was like the chaff driven before the wind. He hated himself afterwards because he had been so easily overcome. He was so concerned about his soul that he could rest nowhere. If he had been able to read the word of God, I feel sure, and he, looking back on those days, feels sure, that he would have found the way of life. His sister and her husband, who had no children, came to travel with us. She could struggle her way through a little of the New Testament, and used to read to my father about the sufferings of Christ and His death upon the tree for sinful men. She told my father it was the sins of the people which nailed Him there, and he often felt in his heart that he was one of them. She was deeply moved when he wept and said, "Oh, how cruel to serve Him so!" I have seen father when we children were in bed at night, and supposed to be asleep, sitting over the fire, the flame from which was the only light. As it leaped up into the darkness it showed us a sad picture. There was father, with tears falling like bubbles on mountain streams as he talked to himself about mother and his promise to her to be good. He would say to himself aloud, "I do not know how to be good," and laying his hand upon his heart he would say, "I wonder when I shall get this want satisfied, this burden removed." When father was in this condition there was no sleep for us children. We lay awake listening, not daring to speak, and shedding bitter tears. Many a time I have said the next mornin to my sisters and my brother, "We have no mother, and we shall soon have no father." We thought he was going out of his mind. We did not understand the want or the burden. It was all quite foreign to us. My father remained in this sleepless, convicted condition for a long time, but the hour of his deliverance was at hand.

> " Long in darkness we had waited
>   For the shining of the light:
> Long have felt the things we hated
>   Sink us into deeper night."

One morning we had left Luton behind us. My eldest sister was in the town selling her goods, and my father had arranged to wait for her on the roadside with our wagon. When our wagon stopped my father sat on the steps, wistfully looking towards the town against the time of his daughter's return, and thinking, no doubt, as he always was, of my mother and his unrest. Presently he saw two gipsy wagons coming towards him, and when they got near he discovered to his great delight that they belonged to his brothers Woodlock and Bartholomew. Well do I remember that meeting. My father was the eldest of the three, and although he was such a big man, he was the least in stature. The brothers were as surprised and delighted to meet my father as he was to meet them. They fell on each other's necks and wept. My father told them of his great loss, and they tried to sympathize with him, and the wives of the two brothers did their best to comfort us motherless children. The two wagons of my uncles faced my father's, but on the opposite side of the road. The three men sat on the bank holding sweet fellowship together, and the two wives and the children of the three families gathered around them. Soon my father was talking about the condition of his soul. Said he to Woodlock and Bartholomew: "Brothers, I have a great burden that I must get removed. A hunger is gnawing at my heart. I can neither eat, drink, nor sleep. If I do not get this want satisfied I shall die!" And then the brothers said: "Cornelius, we feel just the same. We have talked about this to each other for weeks."

Though these three men had been far apart, God had been dealing with them at the same time and in the same way. Among the marvellous dispensations of Providence which have come within my own knowledge, this is one of the most wonderful. These men were all hungry for the truth. They could not read, and so knew nothing of the Bible. They had never been taught, and they knew very little of Jesus Christ. The light that had crept into their souls was "the true light that lighteth every man that cometh into the world." "He, the Spirit, will reprove the world of sin, righteousness, and judgment."

As the brothers talked they felt how sweet it would be to go to God's house and learn of Him, for they had all got tired of their roaming life. My father was on the way to London, and fully resolved to go to a church and find out what it was his soul needed. The three brothers agreed to go together, and arranged to take in Cambridge by the way. They drove their wagon to the Barnwell end of the town, where there was a beer-shop. The three great big simple men went in and told the landlady how they felt. It is not often, I feel sure, that part of a work of grace is carried on in a beer-shop, and with the landlady thereof as an instrument in this divine work. But God had been dealing with the landlady of this beer-house. When the brothers spoke to her she began to weep, and said, "I am somewhat in your case, and I have a book upstairs that will just suit you, for it makes me cry every time I read it." She brought the book down and lent it to the brothers to read. They went into the road to look after their horses. A young man who came out of the public-house offered to read from the book to them. It was *The Pilgrim's Progress.* When he got to the point where Pilgrim's burden drops off as he looks at the cross, Bartholomew rose from his seat by the way-side and excitedly walking up and down, cried: "That is what I want, my burden removed. If God does not save me I shall die!" All the brothers at that moment felt the smart of sin, and wept like little children.

On the Sunday the three brothers went to the Primitive Methodist Chapel, Fitzroy Street, Cambridge, three times. In the evening a certain Mr. Gunns preached. Speaking of that service, my father says: "His points were very cutting to my soul. He seemed to aim directly at me. I tried to hide myself behind a pillar in the chapel, but he, looking and pointing in that direction, said, 'He died for thee!' The anxious ones were asked to come forward, and in the prayer-meeting the preacher came to where I was sitting and asked me if I was saved. I cried out, 'No; that is what I want.' He tried to show me that Christ had paid my debt, but the enemy of souls had blinded my eyes and made me believe that I must feel it and then believe it, instead of receiving Christ by faith first. I went from that house of prayer still a convicted sinner, but not a converted one."

We now resumed our way to London, and had reached Epping Forest when darkness came on. My father put his horse in somebody's field, intending, of course, to avoid detection of this wrong-doing by coming for it early in the morning. That night he dreamed a dream. In the dream he was travelling through a rugged country over rocks and bowlders, thorns and briers. His hands were bleeding and his feet torn. Utterly exhausted and worn out, he fell to the ground. A person in white raiment appeared to him, and as this person lifted up his hands my father saw the mark of the nails, and then he knew it was the Lord. The figure in white said to my father, showing him His hands, "I suffered this for you, and when you give up all and trust Me I will save you." Then my father awoke. This dream shows how much the reading of *The Pilgrim's Progress* had impressed him. He narrated the dream at the breakfast-table on the following morning. When he went to fetch his horses his tender conscience told him very clearly and very pointedly that he had done wrong. As he removed the horses from the field and closed the gate he placed his hand on it and, summoning up all his resolution, said, "That shall be the last known sin I will ever wilfully commit."

My father was now terribly in earnest. There were a great many gipsies encamped in the forest at the time, including his father and mother, brothers and sisters. My father told them that he had done with the roaming and wrong-doing, and that he meant

to turn to God.   They looked at him and wept.   Then
my father and his brothers moved their vans to Shepherd's Bush, and placed them on a piece of building
land close to Mr. Henry Varley's chapel.   My father
sold his horse, being determined not to move from
that place until he had found the way to God.   Says
my father: "I meant to find Christ if He was to be
found.   I could think of nothing else but Him.   I
believed His blood was shed for me."   Then my
father prayed that God would direct him to some
place where he might learn the way to heaven, and
his prayer was answered.   One morning he went
out searching as usual for the way to God.   He met a
man mending the road, and began to talk with him—
about the weather, the neighborhood, and such-
like things.   The man was kindly and sympathetic,
and my father became more communicative.   The
man, as the good providence of God would have it,
was a Christian, and said to my father, "I know what
you want; you want to be converted."   "I do not
know anything about that," said my father, "but
I want Christ, and I am resolved to find Him."
"Well," said the working-man, "there is a meeting
to-night in a mission-hall in Latimer Road, and I
shall come for you and take you there."   In the
evening the road-mender came and carried off my
father and his brother Bartholomew to the mission-
hall.   Before leaving, my father said to us, "Children,
I shall not come home again until I am converted,"
and I shouted to him, "Daddy, who is he?"   I did
not know who this Converted was.   I thought my

father was going off his head, and resolved to follow
him. The mission-hall was crowded. My father
marched right up to the front. I never knew him
look so determined. The people were singing the
well-known hymn:

> " There is a fountain filled with blood
>   Drawn from Emmanuel's veins,
> And sinners, plunged beneath that flood,
>   Lose all their guilty stains."

The refrain was, "I do believe, I will believe, that
Jesus died for me." As they were singing, my
father's mind seemed to be taken away from everybody and everything. "It seemed," he said, "as if
I was bound in a chain and they were drawing me
up to the ceiling." In the agony of his soul he fell
on the floor unconscious, and lay there wallowing
and foaming for half an hour. I was in great distress, and thought my father was dead, and shouted
out, "Oh dear, our father is dead!" But presently
he came to himself, stood up and, leaping joyfully,
exclaimed, "I am converted!" He has often spoken
of that great change since. He walked about the
hall looking at his flesh. It did not seem to be all
quite the same color to him. His burden was gone,
and he told the people that he felt so light that if
the room had been full of eggs he could have walked through and not have broken one of them.

I did not stay to witness the rest of the proceedings. As soon as I heard my father say, "I am con-

verted," I muttered to myself, "Father is converted;
I am off home." I was still in utter ignorance of
what the great transaction might mean.

When my father got home to the wagon that night
he gathered us all around him. I saw at once that
the old haggard look that his face had worn for years
was now gone, and, indeed, it was gone for ever.
His noble countenance was lit up with something
of that light that breaks over the cliff-tops of eternity. I said to myself in wonderment, "What marvellous words these are—'I do believe, I will believe,
that Jesus died for me.'" My father's brother Bartholomew was also converted that evening, and the
two stopped long enough to learn the chorus, and
they sang it all the way home through the streets.
Father sat down in the wagon, as tender and gentle
as a little child. He called his motherless children
to him one by one, beginning with the youngest,
my sister Tilly. "Do not be afraid of me, my dears.
God has sent home your father a new creature and
a new man." He put his arms as far round the five
of us as they would go, kissing us all, and before we
could undersand what had happened he fell on his
knees and began to pray. Never will my brother,
sisters, and I forget that first prayer. I still feel its
sacred influence on my heart and soul; in storm and
sunshine, life and death, I expect to feel the benediction of that first prayer. There was no sleep for
any of us that night. Father was singing, "I do
believe, I will believe, that Jesus died for me," and
we soon learned it too. Morning, when it dawned,

found my father full of this new life and this new joy.
He again prayed with his children, asking God to
save them, and while he was praying God told him
he must go to the other gipsies that were encamped
on the same piece of land, in all about twenty families.
Forthwith he began to sing in the midst of them, and
told them what God had done for him. Many of
them wept. Turning towards his brother Bartholomew's van, he saw him and his wife on their knees.
The wife was praying to God for mercy, and God
saved her then and there. The two brothers, Bartholomew and my father, then commenced a prayer-
meeting in one of the tents, and my brother and
eldest sister were brought to God. In all, thirteen
gipsies professed to find Christ that morning.

CHAPTER VI

OLD CORNELIUS WAS DEAD

AND now commenced a new life for my father. He felt so new inside that he was sure he must look new outside. And so he did. There was a hand-glass in the wagon. My father was continually examining himself in it. He looked at himself all over, at least as much of him as could be perceived in the glass, and when he had done this minute inspection he would say to himself, "Is this old Cornelius?" It was not. The old Cornelius was dead. The new Cornelius was a great surprise and delight to my father, and also to his children. As it is written, "If any man be in Christ, he is a new creature: old things are passed away; behold, all things are become new." Christ makes new men and a new creation.

No sooner had my father begun this new life than he had to withstand the assaults of Satan. His attention was first drawn to his old fiddle. He took it down, and I felt sure he was going to play "I do believe," and I asked him to do so. He said, "No, my dear, I am going to sell this fiddle." I said, "No, daddy, do not sell it; let Ezekiel and me play it. You can teach us how to." My father said,

" No, that fiddle has been the cause of my ruin. It has led me into drink, and sin, and vice, and bad company. It shall not be the ruin of my boys. It shall not be where I am. I will get rid of it, and I shall not have one again until I feel strong enough to be able to manage it." So my father sold the fiddle and began to preach to the men that bought it from him.

Very soon the third brother, Woodlock, was brought to God. The critical event in his life took place in Mr. Varley's vestry. As soon as Mr. Varley heard of the conversion of my father and his brothers, he invited them to his Tabernacle. He put up a mission tent on the ground where the gipsies were encamped and called it the Gipsy Tabernacle. A lady came to teach the gipsy children in the day-time and some young men in the evening read to them. The three brothers made a solemn league and covenant with each other that they would never fall out, and that for Christian work they would never be parted. This pledge they kept until death dissolved the bond. If you wanted one of them for a meeting, you had to invite the three. These three men were as simple as children. One of the first hymns they learnt and the one that they were most fond of singing was

> " Gentle Jesus, meek and mild,
> Look upon a little child."

And, after all, they were only children, felt themselves children always, and possessed all their days a truly childlike spirit. Each of them was as sweet as a sister, as tender as a mother, and as playful as a kitten. They were very fond of singing, and we children loved to sing, too. As for anything deeper, we did not yet understand the need of it. We had no books, and if we had had books we could not have read them. Our first idea of God came from father's beautiful life in the gipsy tent—a life which was like the blooming of a flower whose beauty won us all. If father had lived one life in a meeting and another in the gipsy tent, he would not have been able to rejoice to-day over his five children converted. But the beauty of father's character was most seen in his home life. We dearly loved to have him all to ourselves. Nobody knew what a fine, magnificent character he was as well as we children. Whenever we were tempted to do things that were at all doubtful, we at once thought of father, and if we had any suspicion that the course of conduct we contemplated would not be pleasing to him, we at once abandoned all idea of following it. Father's life was the leaven which leavened the whole lump.

One Sunday morning, seven or eight weeks after their conversion, the three brothers set out to visit their father and mother. The old couple were camped in Loughton Forest, near High Beech. They walked all the way from Shepherd's Bush to Loughton, and when they got within hearing distance they began to sing, "Gentle Jesus, meek and mild." Granny heard the voices of her boys and knew them,

as every mother would have known them. She got
up, and peering with her old, weary eyes over the
bushes, said to herself, "Why, bless me, if them's
not my boys coming!" It does not matter how old
you are, as long as your mother is living you will
still be a boy. Then granny, turning to grandfather, said, "I say, Jim, come out of the tent and
see if these ain't my boys!" And the three stalwart
men still marched triumphantly on with proud, smil-
ing, beaming faces, singing, "Gentle Jesus, meek
and mild." Then says old granny, "What in the
world is the matter with you?" "Oh," says my
father, "mother, we have found Christ; we have
found Jesus; we are converted!" My poor grandfather walked round the tent, saying, "My boys
have come home to teach me what I ought to have
taught them!" Granny soon had a meal ready for
her boys. "Before we eat," said my father, "we
always pray now"; and they all knelt down. As
soon as they got off their knees, grandfather began
to cry for mercy, and soon found peace. Grandfather's brother was camping with him, and he, too,
sought and found the Saviour. He was ninety-
nine years of age, and lived two years after this, dying
a triumphant Christian death. Grandfather and
grandmother were both seventy, and lived five years
after their conversion.

Presently the brothers returned to London, and
soon were deeply engaged in Christian work. The
gipsies were all turned off the ground where they
had been staying, and the Gipsy Tabernacle went

with them. My father hired a field at the rent of
£25 a year, and all the gipsies followed him there.
The tents were pitched around the field with the
mission tent in the centre, and meetings were continually held. Once again, however, they got into
trouble. Several of the antagonists of the gipsy
Christians got drunk, fought and made a great dis-
turbance, with the result that the gipsies were sent
away from the land. We still travelled about a
little, chiefly between Cambridge and London. The
winter months we spent usually in Cambridge and
the summer months on the east side of London. My
father was anxious that his children should learn
to read, and he sent us occasionally to school. By
this he reckons that I must have had about six
or eight weeks' schooling at the most, one winter.
These weeks comprise all my collegiate career. I
had just enough schooling to learn my letters and
a little more. The school was at Cambridge, the
seat of learning; so I am a Cambridge man. While
working day by day to support their children my
father and his two brothers never lost an opportunity of preaching the Gospel in chapel, in mission-
room, and in the open air.

I remember their work in the summers of '73, '74,
and '75. Their method of proceeding was in this
wise: father would get out his fiddle, for by this time
he had another one which he used in his meetings,
and which proved a great attraction. He was accompanied by his two brothers and all the children
of the three families. They would start singing and

keep on singing until three or four hundred people gathered. And then they would commence an
evangelistic service. The work that stands out
most clearly in my mind is that which took place
at Forest Gate. There was a great revival there,
and as a result a large mission hall was erected,
which is standing now, I believe.

About this time my father and his brothers got
into touch with the Rev. William Booth, the founder
of the Christian Mission. Mr. Booth gave them
much encouragement in their work, and told them
that the way to keep bright and happy was to work
for God. He persuaded the three brothers to undertake a week's mission at Portsmouth. The town
was placarded with the announcement that the three
converted gipsies with their "hallelujah fiddle"
were coming. So successful was the work that that
week extended into six, and to us children in our
tent, father being absent, it seemed almost like six
years. When he was away, both father and mother
were away. For he was mother as well as father to
us. The six weeks seemed much longer to us than
to the children of my uncles, for they had their mothers. At last we were told of the day of his return.
We thought he would come back early, and we were
ready for him at six o'clock in the morning. Alas!
he did not come until six at night. It was his custom when he came home to embrace us one by one,
and speak words of tenderness to us. On this occasion, as on others, we all made way for the baby,
namely, my sister Tilly. It was my turn next. I

came after her. But Tilly stayed such a long time in my father's arms that I became very impatient. "Look here," I said, "it is my turn now; you come out!" "All right," said Tilly, quite cheerfully, "you get me out of my father's arms if you can." I knew that I could not do that; so I said, "Never mind, there is room for me, too, and I am coming in," and I went. There is room, too, in our Heavenly Father's arms for all. He pours out His love over His children with more fulness and tenderness than ever earthly father did; and remember no one can take us from our father's arms.

My father now became possessed with a strong desire to go to Baldock, the scene of his troubles, awakening, and conviction. He had played his fiddle in the public-houses there for years. He felt he had done great mischief, and that now it was his duty to do what he could to repair that harm. He and his two brothers started for Cambridge. It was their custom to do evangelistic work as they proceeded on their way, and consequently their progress was not rapid. They stopped for the night just outside Melbourne and placed their wagons at the side of the road. The horses were tied to the wheels of the wagons and were given plenty of food. Then the brothers went to bed. At four o'clock there was a knock at the front door, and a voice shouted, "Hallo there!"

"Who are you?" my father asked.

"I am a policeman, and I have come to take you into custody."

"Why?"

"There is a law made that if any gipsies are found stopping on the road for twelve miles round they are to be taken up without a summons or a warrant."

"You must take care," said my father, "what you do with me, because I am a King's son!"

When my father got up and dressed himself he found that there were four policemen awaiting the brothers. They were handcuffed like felons and marched off to the lock-up, a mile and a half distant. All the way the three converted gipsies preached to the policemen and told them that God would bring them to judgment if they neglected Him, that they would be witnesses against them at the great day, and would then declare in the presence of the Lord Jesus Christ that they had faithfully warned them to flee from the wrath to come. The officers made no reply and marched on. It is very certain that they had never had such prisoners before, and had never heard such a lengthy discourse as they did that night. For my father preached to them a sermon a mile and a half long. In the cells the gipsies fell on their knees in prayer and asked God to touch the hearts of the policemen. Then they sang—

"He breaks the power of cancelled sin,
    He sets the prisoner free."

The keeper said that they must not make such a noise. The gipsies asked him if he had read of

Paul and Silas having been put into prison, and he said, "Yes." Then they inquired of the policemen whether they knew what Paul and Silas did. They answered, "They sang praises to God." "And so will we," said the gipsies; and they began to sing again—

> " His blood can make the vilest clean;
> His blood avails for me."

The keeper gave them rugs to keep them warm, and his wife brought them hot coffee and bread and butter. My father gave her a little tract, entitled "The blood of Jesus Christ cleanses from all sin," and told her the story of our Lord's death for sinners. She drank in every word, and there and then trusted Christ as her Saviour. In the morning the brothers were brought before the magistrates and fined 25s. each, or in default they must go to prison for fourteen days. They had no money, but their fines were paid—by whom they never knew.

When the three gipsy brothers got to Baldock they told the people that they had been locked up at Melbourne, and the news spread on every hand, with the result that the interest in the meetings was very greatly increased. The first service was outside a public-house, and the landlady and her daughter were converted. The meetings were held in a meadow, and so great were the crowds that policemen were sent to keep order.

CHAPTER VII

CHRISTMAS IN THE TENT—A STORY OF THREE PLUM-PUDDINGS

WHEN my father and his brothers travelled about the country, all their families accompanied them. By this time my father had prayed my sisters Emily and Lovinia and my brother Ezekiel into the kingdom. They came in the order of their ages. I was the next, and in my heart I, too, was longing for God. My father used to pray continually in my hearing, "Lord, save my Rodney!"

All this time my father was very poor, and one winter at Cambridge we were in the hardest straits. My father was sitting in his van, looking solemn and sad. That day one of my aunts, I knew, had been buying provisions for the Christmas feast on the morrow. This had excited my interest, and, boy-like, I wanted to know what we were going to have for Christmas, and I asked my father. "I do not know, my dear," he said, quietly. There was nothing in the house, and he had no money. Then the devil came and tempted him. His fiddle was hanging on the wall, and he looked at it desperately and thought to himself, "If I just take down my fiddle and go to a public-house and play to the people there, my

children, too, will have a good Christmas dinner."
But the temptation was very soon overcome. My
father fell on his knees and began to pray. He
thanked God for all His goodness to him, and when
he arose from his knees he said to his children, "I
don't know quite what we shall have for Christmas,
but we will sing." He began to sing with a merry
heart:

> " In some way or other
> The Lord will provide:
> It may not be *my* way,
> It may not be *thy* way;
> But yet in His *own* way
> The Lord will provide."

Just then, while we were singing, there was a knock
at the door of the van.

"Who is there?" cried my father.

It was the old Cambridge town missionary, Mr.
Sykes.

"It is I, Brother Smith. God is good, is He not?
I have come to tell you how the Lord will provide.
In a shop in this town there are three legs of mutton
and groceries waiting for you and your brothers."

A wheelbarrow was needed to bring home the
store. The brothers never knew who gave them
these goods. But the word of God was verified:
"No good thing will He withold from them that
walk uprightly."

I remember one of my pranks in these days very
vividly. My sister Tilly and I were out selling our

goods. By this time the gipsies were very well known in the town. Going from door to door, we came to the house of Mrs. Robinson, a Baptist minister's wife. She knew my father and his brothers well, and she bought some things of us. Then, after the business transactions were over, she began to speak to us in a kindly way, and it ended by her giving us three parcels, one for each of the three brothers. We carried them off in triumphant glee. But we could not resist the temptation to open the paper parcels and see what they contained. To our delight we discovered three plum-puddings. Each of us started on one. But we found out to our disgust that they were only partly cooked, and then it occurred to us—if we had been older and wiser it would have occurred to us earlier—that we really must not take home to our uncles these puddings that we had begun to eat. The one we had left untouched we carried home like dutiful children to our father, and there we thought the matter ended. A few days afterwards Mrs. Robinson met Uncle Bartholomew and asked him how he liked his plum-pudding? He stared at her vacantly. What plum-pudding? He did not know of any plum-pudding. Would she kindly explain herself? Mrs. Robinson told him that she had given Cornelius Smith's children three puddings, one for each of the brothers. Uncle Bartholomew was forced to declare that his had never come to him. He spoke about the matter to my father, and I will sum up the situation by saying that my father explained it very clearly to us.

Never since that day have I had the least appetite for plum-pudding, and I believe that my sister Tilly shares this unnatural peculiarity with me.

Quite recently Miss Robinson, the daughter of Mrs. Robinson, and a prominent worker in connection with the Y.W.C.A., met me at a mission and asked, "Are you the gipsy boy who knows something about plum-puddings?" At once the incident came back to my memory and we laughed together heartily. But let me say to all my young friends, "Be sure your sins will find you out. You cannot even eat your uncle's plum-puddings without being discovered and punished for it."

And this recalls to my recollection how, before my dealings with Mrs. Robinson, I had palmed off a nest of sparrows as a nest of young linnets, and got paid for it as if they were the latter.

CHAPTER VIII

THE DAWNING OF THE LIGHT

BUT, although I was a mischievous boy, I was not a really bad boy. I knew in my heart what religion meant. I had seen it in the new lives of my father, sisters, and brother. I had seen the wonderful change in the gipsy home—the transformation that had taken place there. I had seen the transformation-scene if I had not felt it, and in my heart there was a deep longing for the strange experiences which I knew to be my father's. I remember well a visit that my father paid to Bedford about this time. I shall never forget my thoughts and feelings while I listened to the people as they spoke of John Bunyan. They took us to see the church where he used to preach, and showed us his monument. During our stay in the town, I spent some portion of every day near the monument. I had heard the people say he had been a tinker and a great sinner, but had been converted, and that through his goodness he became great. And, oh! how I looked up as he stood on that pedestal, and longed to be good like him. And I wondered if I should always live in the "wagon" and spend a life of uselessness. I walked to the village where

John Bunyan was born, and went into the house he had lived in. I stood and wept and longed to find the same Jesus Christ that had made Bunyan what he was. I never lost sight in my mind's eye of the bright visions that visited me while I was in Bedford.

I had got it into my mind that religion was a thing which first took hold of the head of the house, and then stepped down in the order of ages. My heart was heavy because I felt that I was standing in the way of my sister Tilly, who was younger than I. I remember one evening sitting on the trunk of an old tree not far from my father's tent and wagon. Around the fallen trunk grass had grown about as tall as myself. I had gone there to think, because I was under the deepest conviction and had an earnest longing to love the Saviour and to be a good lad. I thought of my mother in heaven, and I thought of the beautiful life my father, brother, and sisters were living, and I said to myself, "Rodney, are you going to wander about as a gipsy boy and a gipsy man without hope, or will you be a Christian and have some definite object to live for?" Everything was still, and I could almost hear the beating of my heart. For answer to my question, I found myself startling myself by my own voice: "By the grace of God, I will be a Christian and I will meet my mother in heaven!" My decision was made. I believe I was as much accepted by the Lord Jesus that day as I am now, for with all my heart I had decided to live for Him. My choice was made forever, and had I at once confessed Christ, I believe that the witness of the Spirit would have been mine, the witness which gives one the assurance of acceptance. I knew I had said "I will" to God. I made the mistake of not declaring my decision publicly, and I believe that thousands do likewise. The devil tells them to keep it quiet. This is a cunning device by which he shuts hundreds out of the light and joy of God's salvation.

Still I was not satisfied. A few days afterwards I wandered one evening into a little Primitive Methodist Chapel in Fitzroy Street, Cambridge, where I heard a sermon by the Rev. George Warner. Oddly enough, I cannot remember a word of what Mr. Warner said, but I made up my mind in that service that if there was a chance I would publicly give myself to Christ. After the sermon a prayer-meeting was held, and Mr. Warner invited all those who desired to give themselves to the Lord to come forward and kneel at the communion-rail. I was the first to go forward. I do not know whether anybody else was there or not. I think not. While I prayed the congregation sang:

> "I can but perish if I go,
>   I am resolved to try,
>   For if I stay away I know
>   I must for ever die."

And:

> "I do believe, I will believe,
>   That Jesus died for me,
>   That on the cross He shed His blood
>   From sin to set me free."

Soon there was a dear old man beside me, an old
man with great flowing locks, who put his arm round
me and began to pray with me and for me. I did
not know his name. I do not know it even now. I
told him that I had given myself to Jesus for time
and eternity—to be His boy forever. He said:

"You must believe that He has saved you. 'To
as many as received Him, to them gave· He power
to be the sons of God; even to them that believed
on His name.'"

"Well," I said to my dear old friend, "I cannot
trust myself, for I am nothing; and I cannot trust in
what I have, for I have nothing; and I cannot trust
in what I know, for I know nothing; and so far as I
can see my friends are as badly off as I am."

So there and then I placed myself by simple trust
and committal to Jesus Christ. I knew He died for
me; I knew He was able to save me, and I just believed Him to be as good as His word. And thus
the light broke and assurance came. I knew that
if I was not what I ought to be, I never should be
again what I had been. I went home and told
my father that his prayers were answered, and he
wept tears of joy with me. Turning to me, he said,
'Tell me how you know you are converted?" That
was a poser for a young convert. I hardly knew
what to say, but placing my hand on my heart,
I said, "Daddy, I feel so warm here." I had got a
little of the feeling that the disciples had when they
had been talking with Jesus on the way to Em-
maus: "Did not our heart burn within us?" The

date of my conversion was the 17th of November, 1876.

How my father rejoiced at my turning to the Lord. He said to me: " I knew you were such a whole-souled boy that, before the devil spoiled you, I coveted you for Jesus Christ. I knew that you would be out-and-out one way or the other. I seemed to see that there were in you great possibilities for Jesus Christ."

Next morning I had, of course, as usual to go out and sell my goods. My first desire was to see again the little place where I had kneeled the night before ere I commenced my work for the day. There I stood for some minutes gazing at the little chapel, almost worshipping the place. As I stood, I heard a shuffling of feet, and turning round I saw the dear old man who had knelt by my side. I said to myself, " Now that I have my goods—clothes-pegs and tin-ware—with me, he will see that I am a gipsy, and will not take any notice of me. He will not speak to the gipsy boy. Nobody cares for me but my father." But I was quite wrong. Seeing me, he remembered me at once, and came over to speak to me, though he walked with great difficulty and with the aid of two sticks. Taking my hands in his, he seemed to look right down into my innermost soul. Then he said to me: " The Lord bless you, my boy. The Lord keep you, my boy." I wanted to thank him, but the words would not come. There was a lump in my throat, and my thoughts were deep beyond the power of utterance. My tears contained in their silver cells the words my tongue could not utter.

The dear old man passed on, and I watched him turning the corner out of sight for ever. I never saw him again. But when I reach the glory-land, I will find out that dear old man, and while angels shout and applaud, and the multitudes who have been brought to Christ through the gipsy boy sing for joy, I will thank that grand old saint for his shake of the hand and for his "God bless you!" For he made me feel that somebody outside the tent really cared for a gipsy boy's soul. His kindness did me more good than a thousand sermons would have done just then. It was an inspiration that has never left me, and has done more for me than I can describe. Many a young convert has been lost to the Church of God, who would have been preserved and kept for it, and made useful in it, all for the want of some such kindness as that which fell to my lot that day.

CHAPTER IX

LEARNING TO READ AND WRITE—PREACHING
TO THE TURNIP-FIELD—SINGING THE GOS-
PEL IN THE COTTAGES

I BELIEVE that with my conversion came the awakening of my intellect, for I saw things and understood them as I had not done before. Everything had a new meaning to me. I had already begun to spell out a little, but now my desire for reading was tremendously intensified. I now had something to learn for, and I seemed to have, I did not know how, a settled assurance that I should one day preach the gospel. At the time of my conversion I could only spell and understand words of one syllable. I used to get my Bible down and begin to read it, alas! sometimes the wrong way up, in my father's tent or in the corner of a field, away from everybody. Many a time have I wept and prayed over that Bible. I wanted my heart filled with the spirit of it.

One day I was passing a huge sign-board with a red ground and gilt letters. As a matter of fact I believe now, if my memory serves me right, that it was a brewer's sign-board. I stared at it in wonder and distress. I was so anxious to know what it said. A lady passed, going to market, and I asked her if she would read the sign-board for me. "Why do you want to read that?" she said. "Oh," I answered, "I really am anxious to know what it says." Then she read the words, and I thanked her. She asked me if I knew my letters, and I said, "Yes, I can go over them both backwards and forwards." She patted my black head and said, "You will get on some day." Her kind words were deeply stamped on my memory.

My first books were the Bible, an English Dictionary, and Professor Eadie's Biblical Dictionary. That last volume was given to me by a lady. I expect my father had told her that I desired to preach. These three mighty volumes—for they were mighty to me—I used to carry about under my arm. My sisters and brothers laughed at me, but I did not mind. "I am going to read them some day," I said, "and to preach, too." I lost no opportunity of self-improvement and was always asking questions. I still believe in continually asking questions. If I came across anything I did not understand, I asked what it meant—I did not mind. If I heard a new word I used to flee to my dictionary. I always kept it beside me when I read or tried to read. Then I began to practice preaching. One Sunday I entered a turnip-field and preached most eloquently to the turnips. I had a very large and most attentive congregation. Not one of them made an attempt to move away. While walking along the road with my basket under my arm I used to go on preaching. I knew a great many passages of Scripture and hymns, and my discourses consisted of these all woven together. My father, too, began to see that this was no mere boyish ambition, and encouraged it. A Mr. Goodman, in Brandon, Norfolk, advised my father to send me to Mr. Spurgeon's Pastors' College, and I was greatly excited over the idea. But events so shaped themselves that this project was never carried out.

At this time, too, I did my first bit of real Christian work. One day I was hawking my wares, and, as usual, ever anxious to get a chance of telling people about Jesus. I went to a large house, and two maids came to the door to see me. I began to preach to them about the Saviour, and I discovered that they were both of them Christian girls. They took me into the kitchen, and we had a nice little conversation together. On the table was a collecting-box, which they told me was one of the British and Foreign Bible Society's boxes. I asked them for a box. Their master was the secretary of the Bible society for Cambridge, and when they told him, he gave me a box. I carried this in my basket for many weeks, collecting halfpennies and pennies for the Society. When I took the box back to the man who gave it me I had collected from 15s. to £1. I never felt so proud in my life.

I was on very good terms with the women in the villages. After I had done my best to get them to buy my goods I would say to them, "Would you like me to sing for you?" And they usually said,

"Yes." Sometimes quite a number of them would gather in a neighbor's kitchen to hear me, and I would sing to them hymn after hymn, and then perhaps tell them about myself, how I had no mother, how I loved Jesus, and how I meant to be His boy all my life. Sometimes the poor souls would weep at my simple story. I came to be known as "the singing gipsy boy." One day one of these women was speaking to my eldest sister about her brother, and my sister said, "Which brother?" "Oh," she answered, "the one who sings and stretches out his neck like a young gosling." I could sing then with great force, though I was very small in those days and very thin. My favorite hymn was:

> " There is a fountain filled with blood
>   Drawn from Emmanuel's veins,
>   And sinners, plunged beneath that flood,
>   Lose all their guilty stains."

There is an old lady still living in West Ratton who bought a reel of cotton from me when I was a boy, and allowed me to conduct a service in her kitchen. She will not part with that reel of cotton for love or money. I believe that these little singing sermons were made a great blessing. I was sought after particularly by the young folks in the houses. As my ability to read grew, I learned off by heart the fifty-third and fifty-fifth chapters of Isaiah, and the fifteenth of St. Luke. I occasionally went through one of these chapters for the lesson in father's meetings. My father and his two brothers were, of course, always engaged in evangelistic work, and I used to sing with them. My father says he still frequently meets old people who talk about those days.

In the spring of 1877 we removed from Cambridge to London, travelling in our wagons. We did the journey in easy stages, which took us five or six days. The gipsy brothers held open-air services in the villages as they passed through them. Their coming was hailed with delight and enthusiasm. It was a fine spectacle—these three big, full-blooded, consecrated men, standing in the open air, with their children around them, singing and preaching the gospel. One poor man came to hear us. The hymn they sang and that my father played on his violin was called, " Will you go?" This man came and tapped the fiddle on the back and said, " Didn't that old fiddle say, ' Will you go?' " The fiddle won great fame as the " hallelujah fiddle," and the people used to come long distances to the meetings sometimes merely to see it.

During the summer we stood our tents on a piece of building land at Forest Gate. One day I was out selling my goods, or trying to. My luck varied considerably. A good day would mean that I made a clear profit of perhaps 2s. 6d. That implied about 7s. 6d. worth of sales. On a bad day, I might make only a shilling profit or even a good deal less. But on the whole, a father with his wife and children, if they were all helping, would do pretty well. Our expenses, of course, were small, but my father's conversion increased them, because now he invariably

paid for the land on which he stood his wagon and
tents.   If I remember rightly, the rent was about
1s. 6d. or 2s. 6d. a week.   There were no taxes to pay
and no appearances to keep up.   There was no money
spent on luxuries or on drink, and we lived in a very
plain style.   Gipsies have just two good meals a day
—breakfast at 7.30 or 8 A.M. and supper about 5 P.M.
Breakfast consisted of bacon or ham, or boiled meat
with bread and potatoes, and supper was the same.
The gipsies are great tea-drinkers.   Throughout
the day we had to beg or buy something to keep us
going.   Most of the gipsy food is either boiled or
fried, for they have no ovens.   They go to bed early
and they rise early, about five or six o'clock.   They
live on plain food and not too much of it, and consequently they are very healthy.

I remember one incident of this time vividly.   It
was a very wet day, and I had taken shelter in an
unfinished building.   The rain was coming down
in torrents, and there seemed no immediate prospect
of its stopping.   I felt I could not do better than
spend the time in prayer.   I knelt down in the
kitchen among the shavings, sawdust, and sand,
with my cap on one side of me and my basket on
the other, and began to speak to my Lord.   I do
not know how long I continued in supplication.   It
was a sweet and gracious time passing very quickly.
I was startled by hearing something like a sob or a
sniff, and, looking through the unfinished kitchen
window, I saw on the wall which separated the two
gardens three men with their caps off.   They had

been listening to my petitions, and had been deeply affected thereby. Their tears fell with the rain-dops. If I had been a little older, or had possessed a little more courage, I should there and then have begun to preach the gospel to them; but I was shy, nervous, and frightened, and, taking up my basket and cap, bolted out like a wild deer into the rain.

CHAPTER X

I BECOME AN EVANGELIST—THE CHRISTIAN
MISSION AND REV. WILLIAM BOOTH—MY FIRST
FROCK-COAT AND MY FIRST APARTMENTS

I NOW approached my seventeenth birthday.
My desire to become a preacher grew stronger as
the days passed by. One Sunday morning I rose
with the determination to undertake something in
that line. I arrayed myself in my Sunday best,
consisting of a small brown beaver hat, a velvet
jacket with white pearl buttons, a vest with the same
adornments, a pair of corduroys, and a yellow handkerchief with a dash of red in it round my neck.
If gipsies have a weakness in the love of clothing,
it is for silk handkerchiefs. I sallied forth in this
attire. The people were just starting off for church
and chapel. I stood in a little corner some way
from the wagons. I knew the people must pass
that way. I took off my hat and I began to sing,
and after singing I prayed, and after prayer there
was another hymn. By this time a few people had
stopped to see what was going to happen. I dare
say a good many persons about knew me by sight,
for I took care that I was never long in a place before the people knew me. I had a way of introduc-

ing myself. I was a child of nature, and I introduced myself as naturally as the flowers do. I told the people how I had found the Saviour, what my life and desires were, and that I loved Jesus and wanted everybody else to love Him, too. They listened and wept. When I had said this I began to get very anxious as to how I should end. I desired to finish off beautifully, but I did not know how. Happily, when I had finished what I had to say, I told the people that I hoped to do better next time, and then I crept back to the wagons, certainly not feeling over exultant about my first meeting. I found that my father and some of my friends had been listening to me. They applauded my zeal, but I do not remember what they said about my sermon.

In the spring of this year I got into touch with the Christian Mission, of which the Rev. William Booth, now General Booth, was superintendent. The headquarters of the mission were at 272 White- chapel Road. It had twenty-seven mission stations and thirty-five missionaries. They were under the control of Mr. Booth, who was popularly referred to by the Christian workers as the Bishop. They had an annual conference at which speeches were made and resolutions were put and voted upon, but what amount of directing or legislative power this conference possessed I do not know. It is certain that Mr. Booth was as absolute in his control of the Christian Mission as he now is—nominally at least—of the Salvation Army. While attending some meetings at the mission station in Plaistow, we heard of an all-day gathering that was to be held at the mission's headquarters in Whitechapel Road on Whit-Monday. Uncle Bartholomew and sister Emily arranged to go and take me with them. At the evening meeting there must have been about a thousand people present.

The Rev. William Booth presided. He "spotted" my uncle, my sister, and myself, for he knew the gipsy brothers well, and availed himself of their services. Further, he knew a little about me particularly. Some time previously my father had been conducting a mission at Leicester with the late Mr. William Corbridge, and he had told Mr. Corbridge that he had a boy who wanted to be a preacher, and whom he thought of sending to the Pastors' College. Mr. Corbridge, as I got to know years later, thereupon wrote to Mr. Booth, saying "Cornelius Smith, the gipsy, has a boy, Rodney, whom he thinks of sending to the pastors' College. He has a great desire to preach. Get hold of him. He might be very useful in the mission." My appearance at this Whit-Monday service no doubt brought this letter back to Mr. Booth's mind. After several persons had addressed the meeting, he said, "The next speaker will be the gipsy boy." There was only one gipsy boy in the meeting, and I was he. My first inclination was to run away, but immediately the thought came to me that that would never do. Said I to myself, "Have I not promised the Lord to do whatever He commands me? and, as I did not seek this, I feel it is from Him." Trembling,

I took my way to the platform, which, luckily, was only five or six steps off. When I reached it I shook in every limb. Mr. Booth, with that quick eye of his, saw that I was in something of a predicament, and at once he said, "Will you sing us a solo?" I said, "I will try, sir"; and that night I sang my first solo at a big public meeting. It was as follows:

"HAPPY, EVER HAPPY

" Jesus died upon the tree,
     That from sin we might be free,
     And for ever happy be,
          Happy in His love.
     He has paid the debt we owe;
     If with trusting hearts we go,
     He will wash us white as snow
          In His blood.

" Then with joy and gladness sing;
     Happy, ever happy be;
     Praises to our heavenly King—
     Happy in the Lord.

" Lord, we bring our hearts to Thee;
     Dying love is all our plea;
     Thine for ever we would be—
          Jesus, ever Thine.
     Jesus smiles and bids us come,
     In His loving arms there's room,
     He will bear us safely home—
          Home above.

"When we reach that shining shore
All our sufferings will be o'er,
And we'll sigh and weep no more
    In that land of love;
But in robes of spotless white,
And with crowns of glory bright,
We will range the fields of light
    Evermore."

The people listened with interest and attention.
I felt I had done pretty well, that I had made a good
introduction, and that now I should have a chance.
I was clearing my throat with a preliminary nervous
cough—every preacher knows quite well what I
mean—when a great tall man (afterwards Commissioner Dowdle, of the Salvation Army) shouted,
"Keep your heart up, youngster!" I said, "My
heart is in my mouth; where do you want it?" I
did not mean the people to hear this, but they did,
and they laughed, and I was not sorry that they
laughed, for while they laughed I had a bit of time
to pull myself together. As far as I can remember, this is how my address proceeded: "I am only
a gipsy boy. I do not know what you know about
many thngs, but I know Jesus. I know that He has
saved me. I cannot read as you can. I do not live
in a house as you do; I live in a tent. But I have
got a great house up yonder, and some day I am
going to live in it. My great desire is to live for
Christ and the whole of my life to be useful in His
service." My discourse was very brief, and I was
very glad when it was done. I had sense enough

to sit down immediately I had finished what I had to say. I do not know that I have been equally wise on every occasion since then. As I resumed my seat there came from many quarters of the meeting the exclamation, "God bless the boy!"

Mr. Booth kept me beside him until the meeting was over. Then he took my arm in his and led me aside from the people and said, "Will you leave your gipsy home, your father, sisters and brother, and come to me to be an evangelist in the Christian Mission?" I asked him what an evangelist was, and he told me. Then I said, "Sir, do you think I shall make a good evangelist?" He said, "Yes, I do." I replied, "Well, you know more about this than I do, and if you think I am of any use, it is an answer to my prayer and I will come." The date was fixed, 25th of June, 1877.

When I got home to our wagon, I woke them all up and told them I was going to be a preacher. They had laughed a good deal at my youthful ambition, but now it was my turn to laugh. When the morning came, I secured my three books and, putting them under my arm, walked swaggeringly up and down in front of the wagon, full of innocent joy and pride. "Rodney is going to be a preacher!" They could not quite realize it, and they talked of nothing else for days. After breakfast that morning, I looked at my gipsy clothes and said to myself, "If I am going to be a preacher, I shall have to dress like a preacher." I had saved a little money. I went to a clothier and outfitter's shop and bought a frock-coat, a vest, and a pair of striped trousers, all ready made. I paid for them and the assistant parcelled them up and pushed them over the counter to me. I drew myself up to my full height, and putting on all the dignity I could command, said, "Send them. Do you know I am going to be a preacher?" So these clothes were sent to the gipsy tent. Next I went off to purchase some linen. A young lady came to serve me and asked me what my size was. I said, "I do not know, miss, but if you give me a bit of string I will measure myself." These articles, too, I had sent home to the tents. I further reflected that when folks went travelling it was proper that they should have a box. So I bought a box for half a crown, and a piece of clothes-line to cord it up with.

At last the morning of the fateful 25th dawned. I was up early and dressed myself with much care. I know that I burst several buttons in the operation. I will not say that I felt comfortable in these clothes, because the very reverse was the truth. I felt as if I had been dipped in starch and hung up by the hair of my head to dry. My sisters were whispering to each other in the most eager and excited tones. "What a swell he looks! Look at his collar! And, I say—I declare—look at his cuffs!" They called me a Romany Rye (gipsy gentleman), and Boro Rashie, that is to say, a great preacher. I did not leave the dear tent without many tears. I was only seventeen years and three months old, and my father's tent was as dear to me as Windsor Castle is to a prince of the blood royal. I was leaving people who loved

me and understood me, and I was going to people
who certainly would not understand me. It was
like tearing my heart out to leave them. I kissed
them all and started off, then ran back again many
times; and they ran after me. Finally I tore myself away. I had two cousins to carry my box to
Forest Gate Station, on the Great Eastern Railway.
I could have carried all that I had in a brown paper
parcel, but the dignity of the occasion demanded a
box, and forbade me to carry it myself. I booked
to Aldgate Station, and I told the guard to put my
box in the van. He knew me, or at least he knew my
father, and I found it difficult to impress him sufficiently with the dignity of my new position. He
lifted the box and said with a laugh, "What is in
it?" I said: "Never you mind, sir. You are paid to
be civil and to look after passengers." Yet even
that did not greatly awe him. "All right, old man,"
he answered, laughing; "good luck to you!"

At my destination I was met by one of the missionaries, a Mr. Bennett, who took me to a good
Christian family with whom Mr. Booth had arranged
that I should stay. I think their name was Lang-
ston, and the house was in a side street not far from
the mission's headquarters, at 272 Whitechapel
Road. I remember the situation exactly. I arrived
just in time for a meal in the evening, and for the
first time in my life I had to sit up to table, and also
to use a knife and fork. I began to entertain some
feelings of gratitude towards the starch in which I
was encased, because, at least, it helped me to sit up

straight. I had resolved to watch what my neighbors did, but they served me first and told me not to
wait. At the side of my plate was a piece of linen,
beautifully glazed and neatly folded. I did not
know what it was, nor what I had to do with it. I
thought, perhaps, it was a pocket-handkerchief, and
I said so to my hosts. Immediately, I felt that I had
introduced a discord into the harmony of the dinner
party. I was sensitive enough to feel and know I
had blundered, but my hosts were kind enough not
to laugh. I said to them: "Please forgive me. I
do not know any better. I am only a gipsy boy. I
have never been taught what these things are. I
know I shall make lots of blunders, but if you correct
me whenever I make a mistake, I will be very grateful. I will never be angry, and never cross." I
felt this was the right course for me to take. I knew
that airs would not have fitted me at all.

After supper and prayers, they told me they would
show me to my apartment. My apartment! I made
a mental note of the word and resolved to look it up
in my dictionary at the first opportunity, for I still
carried about my library of three books with me.
When they shut the door of my room upon me, I felt
I was in jail—a prisoner within four walls and a ceiling! I fancied there was not room enough to breathe.
It was the 25th of June, and the East End of London!
I felt homesick and longed for my tent. Had I not
often woke up in the morning with my head, or my
arms, or my legs, outside the tent, on the grass, under
the ample dome of heaven? Here in this small room

I felt suffocated. I looked at the bedstead and wondered if it would hold me, and when, by experiment, I found that it was strong enough, I turned down the bedclothes and examined them, for I had heard of the London "company," and I strongly objected to the way they made their living. I got into bed with a run, as long as I could have it, and a leap. It was a feather bed. I had been accustomed to sleep in feathers as long as myself, that kind which grows in a wheat-field, and very often I had to make a hole with my fist for my ear to lie in. I could not sleep. For hours I lay awake thinking of my home, for I realized acutely that I was in a land of strangers. Such sleep as I had was only in snatches, and I was dreaming all the time of my father's tent and wagon.

I rose very early in the morning, and at once knelt in prayer. I told God that He knew that I was among strangers — people who could not understand my wildness and my romantic nature; that He had brought me there; and if He would only give me grace I would try to do my best. Then I had to attend to my toilet. There was, of course, a wash-hand basin and a towel. I was almost afraid to use them, in case I should soil them. I had never seen such things in use before. It had been my custom to run to a brook of a morning and to wash in that or a pool near by. I took my bath with the birds. At other times I dipped my hand in the grass laden with dew and washed myself with it. I was up and dressed long before there was any stir or movement in the house, but of course I kept to my bedroom until I made sure that somebody else was up. I spent the time over my Bible.

I felt easier at the breakfast table, because I had had some experience and at any rate I knew what a napkin was. However, I made many blunders and broke the laws of grammar, etiquette, and propriety again and again. But my hosts were kind. They did not expect too much from me. They told me when I was wrong, and I was grateful; encouraged me when I was right, and I was equally grateful: it was an inspiration to try again. You see, I was born at the bottom of the ladder, and there is no disgrace in being born at the bottom. There are thousands of people who owe everything to their father and mother, and yet walk about the earth and swagger as if they had made creation. I knew I had tremendous odds to strive against, and I strove to face them as they came one by one. I did not face them all at once, I could not: they would have swamped me. Each day brought its own difficulties, its own work, and there was strength for the day also. I received no educational training whatever from the Christian Mission. My schooling and discipline was work—visiting the people and taking part in meetings. I was the thirty-sixth missionary. I was stationed at Whitechapel Road, the headquarters of the mission, along with a Mr. Thomas, a very able preacher, who is now dead, Mr. Bennett (before mentioned), and Mrs. Reynolds. I owe a great deal to Mrs. Reynolds. She was as a mother to me. The other workers took most of the in-door services. I helped in visiting, in open-air work, and occasionally I spoke at an in-door service, but not often. Much was made of the fact that I was a real live gipsy, and I was always announced as "Rodney Smith, the converted gipsy boy." Mr. Booth found a home for me, and my father kept me supplied with clothes. What little money I had was soon spent. I worked in the Christian Mission six months without receiving any salary at all.

When I was called upon to conduct a service alone I had to face a very serious difficulty—how to deal with the lessons. I had spent as much time as I could find in learning to read, but my leisure and my opportunities were very severely limited, and I was still far from perfection in this art. I certainly could not read a chapter from Scripture right through. What was I to do with the big words? First of all, I thought I would ask a good brother to read the lessons for me. "No," I said, "that would never do. I think that the people would prefer me to read them myself." Then I thought I should get over the difficulty by spelling out to them any word that was too difficult for me. But I felt this would be like an open surrender. The plan I adopted was this— I went on reading slowly and carefully until I saw a long word coming into sight. Then I stopped and made some comments, after the comments I began to read again, but took care to begin on the other side of the long word. I used to struggle night after night in my lodgings over the hard words and names in the Bible.

But in the meetings I did, I think, pretty well.
God gave me utterance, and I found myself saying
things I had never thought about or read about.
They were simply borne in upon me and I had to
say them. In spite of mistakes—and I made many
of these—I was most happy in my work, and always
had a good congregation. At the headquarters in
Whitechapel Road I sometimes spoke to well over
a thousand people, and when I went to the mission
centres at Plaistow, Canning Town, Poplar, and
Barking, I always had crowded congregations, and
I never had a meeting without conversions. These
four happy months passed away very quickly, as
in a dream. The most memorable incident of my
work in Whitechapel was the conversion of my sister
Tilly at one of my own meetings. Some members of
the family had come with my father one Sunday to
see me and hear me preach. I have already said that
I came to Christ myself partly because I felt I was
keeping Tilly from Him. I was immediately above
her in age, and the members of our family had been
converted in order of age. It was while I was singing one of my simple gospel songs that my dear
sister was won for the Lord. Speaking from the
human side, I may say that my love for her led me
to decision for Christ, and God repaid me more than
abundantly by making me a blessing to her.

CHAPTER XI

GROWING SUCCESS—WORK AT WHITBY, SHEF-
FIELD, AND BOLTON—MEETING MY FUTURE
WIFE--ROMAN CATHOLIC RIOTS

ONE Saturday morning Mr. Booth sent for me
and asked me if I had quite settled to my new work,
and if I had made up my mind to stick to it. I said,
"Yes, certainly, I have fixed upon this as my life
work." "Very well," said Mr. Booth, "we think
of sending you to Whitby. Are you willing to go?"
I said, "Yes, sir." "Can you go to-day?" I said
"Yes, sir;" and very soon I was at King's Cross
and on my way. I had been given a ticket for Whitby, which had been bought by Mr. Booth's instructions, and the address of the missioner at that town,
Elijah Cadman, afterwards Commissioner Cadman;
but I had no money. This was my first long railway journey. When we once started I thought we
should never stop. I had never travelled at such
a rate before, and I had no idea the world was so
large. I left King's Cross at three and got to York
at eight, where I had to change. I discovered that
there was no train for Whitby until five o'clock in
the morning. I was cold and hungry, and I had
nothing to do but wait. I had nine hours of that,

and I spent the time in conversation with the railway porters and preaching the gospel to them. I walked up and down the platform, and once or twice I found a group of people in a public waiting-room and I had a chat with them about the Christ I had found, and of whom I was ever delighted to speak.

I reached Whitby at nine o'clock on Sunday morning. Nobody came to meet me, but I found my way to Mr. Cadman's house at 16 Gray Street. He greeted me with the words: "I have been up nearly all night waiting for you." I replied that since three o'clock on the previous afternoon I had been trying to get to him. After a hurried breakfast, I went out with Mr. Cadman and took part in six meetings that day, three out-door and three in-door meetings. The in-door meetings were held in St. Hilda's Hall.

I was now cut off from my first surroundings. I had to stand on my own legs, and I was made to feel that I must launch out for myself. I developed an older feeling and a greater independence of spirit. I did more speaking in the meetings than I had done in London. My singing was always a great attraction, but especially in Whitby among the fishermen. I became a great favorite in the town, and much good was done. Some of the most prominent and most useful local preachers in Whitby at the present day were brought to God under my ministry in the town. Not a few of the converts were rough people, very sadly in need of instruction in Christian ethics. I remember one peculiar case well. A man who had been a drunkard and a fighter was converted. Soon afterwards he was met by one of his old chums from whom he had borrowed a sovereign.

"I say, Jack," said the lender, "I hear you have got converted."

"Yes, I have, and joined the Church."

"Ah well, do you remember some time ago I lent you a sovereign?"

"Yes, I remember."

"Well, I shall expect you to pay it back. When people get religious, we expect them to do what is right."

"Oh," said Jack, "the Lord has pardoned all my sins, and that is one of them."

We had to put Jack right, and to tell him plainly that conversion meant restitution as well as amendment. The jailer when he was converted washed the stripes of the disciples whom he had beaten the same hour of the night, and Zacchæus when he was brought to God made a fourfold restitution to those whom he had defrauded. And we persuaded Jack to do the right thing.

Among my converts at Whitby was a Miss Pennock, whom I afterwards became engaged to, and who is now my wife. As soon as Mr. Cadman knew that I was sweethearting, he communicated with Mr. Booth, and I was removed from the town.

The scenes of my next labors were Bradford, London, and Sheffield. I never preach in Sheffield now without a dozen or more people telling me that it was through my ministry in their town over twenty years ago that they gave themselves to Christ. It was in

Sheffield, too, that my first salary was paid to me, eighteen shillings a week. Fifteen of these went for board and lodging, so that I had three shillings a week for clothes, books, and anything I wanted for the improvement of my mental powers. My three shillings per week did not go far when I had to visit the sick and the needy.

I spent six happy and fruitful months at Bolton. My fellow-workers, with whom I lived, were Mr. and Mrs. Corbridge, who treated me like a son. Mr. Corbridge was a very able man, a deep student of Scripture. Mrs. Corbridge was an educated and refined lady, and a noble helpmate to her husband in his mission work. While staying with Mr. and Mrs. Corbridge, I laid the true foundations of all the educational equipment that I ever possessed. Upon that corner-stone I have been striving to build ever since. I owe more to Mr. and Mrs. Corbridge than to any other person in the Salvation Army or the Christian Mission.

The out-door services at Bolton were held in the Market Square on the steps of the Town Hall, where from two to three thousand people gathered to hear addresses by Mr. and Mrs. Corbridge and myself.

We had some difficulties with the Roman Catholics. Several of them were converted, and two young women brought their beads and rosary to Mrs. Corbridge and gave them up. This roused the anger of other Roman Catholics in the town and of the priests. One night Mr. Corbridge was not feeling well and stayed

at home, Mrs. Corbridge remaining to nurse him.   So
I had to conduct the open-air service in the Market
Square alone.   The crowd was larger than I had ever
seen it before.   My workers rallied round me and I
was provided with a chair.   As the service proceeded
the crowd grew.   Until the benediction was pronounced everything had gone on in peace and quietness, but the moment the benediction was said the
crowd began to sway menacingly.   My band of
workers and myself were in the centre.   The swaying
grew more powerful and the people more excited.
Then they set up one of those wild Irish Catholic
yells and closed in upon us.   My workers gathered
round me for my protection.   One ferocious woman
in the crowd took off her clog and struck at me with
the heel.   But just as she was driving the blow home,
her companion came between me and the heel and
was felled to the ground.   There were a few policemen near the spot, and when they heard the yelling
and perceived what it meant they worked their way
into the crowd and came to my rescue.   I was pushed
into the nearest shop—a drug store.   One of the
policemen came with me and got me out through the
back door of the premises.   We climbed over three
or four walls and eventually reached a side street
which led to quite another part of the town, and so
reached home in safety.   There is no doubt that if
the mob could have got at me that night, my life
would have been ended there and then.   The news
of the riot had already reached Mr. and Mrs. Corbridge, and their anxiety about my safety had been

painful.   They were very glad, indeed, to see me safe
and sound in every limb.

On the following morning, Mr. Corbridge and I
went to see some of the leading townsmen who were
in sympathy with our work, and asked their counsel.
Together we all called upon the Mayor, stated our
case to him, told him that we thought this disturb-
ance had arisen because of the conversion of some
Roman Catholics, and that the opposition plainly
came from an Irish and Catholic mob; and asked
him what he advised us to do—whether to stop our
work or to go on.   He said: "By all means go on.
You are not fighting your own battle merely.   You
are fighting ours as well.   You have as much right
to the square as the priests."   And so that night
we again held our open-air meeting in the Market
Square.   Mr. Corbridge had recovered and his wife
came with us.   The crowd was bigger than ever,
and, as on the night before, there was the most perfect quietness and good order until the benediction
was pronounced.   Then the swaying and yelling
began.   But in the crowd there were sufficient policemen in uniform or in plain clothes to form almost
a chain round us, and, under the escort of this force,
we were marched off to our home at No. 4 Birmingham Street.   The mob followed us all the way, yelling like furies, and when we were safe in our home
a number of policemen were put on duty to watch
the house until all was quiet.

The riots were, of course, the talk of the whole
town, but the feeling and sympathy of all respect-

able citizens were all on our side. The local papers took the subject up and championed the cause of free speech. When the powers behind the scenes realized that their wrath was going to be unavailing, the tumults subsided as suddenly as they had arisen, and there was never another voice or movement against our work in the Market Square. These commotions brought us many friends and sympathizers that we should never have known of, and, instead of hindering our work, greatly helped us. We grew and flourished exceedingly, and the Lord daily added to the church such as should be saved.

CHAPTER XII

" The Word of the Lord Grew and Multiplied."

BALLINGTON BOOTH — MY MARRIAGE — THE CHATHAM FOSSILS

MY next station was West Hartlepool. During these months I was teaching myself reading and writing. I had to prepare a good many discourses. I soon came to the end of my own native mental store, and I had to seek replenishment for my mind in study and thinking. And one cannot well study unless one knows how to read. I taught myself writing from a copybook, and like everybody else who has pursued this method of self-instruction, I found the first line I wrote under the copy was always the best. As I got farther away from the model, the worse my writing grew. The thoughtful reader will see a lesson here for himself. The nearer we keep to our model, Christ, the more like will our life be to His. Should not this be our daily prayer:

> " A heart in every thought renewed
> And full of love divine,
> Perfect and right and pure and good,
> A *copy*, Lord, of Thine "?

My days were spent somewhat after this fashion : I rose about seven and breakfasted at eight or half-

past. Some of the time before breakfast was always
spent in devotional exercises, and occasionally also
in a little study. Then I went out to visit the most
urgent cases. If there were no such cases I spent
most of the morning in reading, writing, and preparing my addresses. The afternoons were occupied
in visiting. I had a service every night, and the
service was almost invariably preceded by an
open-air meeting. On Sunday we had three
services.

My stay at West Hartlepool was brief. Soon I
received instructions to go to Manchester to work
under Mr. Ballington Booth, the General's second
son. An address was given to me at which I might
find him in Manchester. When I got there he was
absent and was not expected home for many days.
The woman who occupied the house told me that
she did not know where I was to stay. I left a short
note with her for Mr. Ballington Booth, saying that
as he was not there, as operations had not begun, as
the hall was not to be opened for some days, and as
I had been working hard and wanted a rest, I would
go and stay at Mr. Howorth's, Blackburn Road,
Bolton, and that that address would find me the moment he needed me. That same night I went to
Bolton and attended a meeting of the Christian Mission there. I was, of course, well known to all the
people. The missionary in charge, a Miss Rose
Clapham, immediately asked me what business I
had in her meeting. The people, naturally enough,
were making something of a fuss of me as an old

friend. I told Miss Clapham that I felt that I had a perfect right to be present; I should do her no harm. I attended these meetings regularly every night for a few days.

On the Saturday afternoon a telegram reached me ordering me to Manchester at once, and saying that I was announced to preach the next day. I had a very sore throat, and I knew that we had no station in Manchester. I replied by another wire that I was not fit to preach or sing, and that I should stay in Bolton until Monday, resting myself. On Monday evening I again attended a meeting of the mission in Bolton. To my surprise, whom should I see there but Mr. Ballington Booth. Miss Clapham, it appeared, had gone to Manchester to consult Mr. Ballington Booth and his mother, who was in Manchester at that time, and to complain of my presence at her meetings. Throughout the whole of the meeting Mr. Booth made no reference to me, never spoke to me, and seemed determined to go away without speaking to me. I placed myself against the door, resolved to bring him into conversation, and when he saw that he must say something, he took hold of me by the arm, and pulling me a little aside he said, "Gipsy, we can do without you." I replied, "Very well, so you shall." I am quite willing and ready to admit that I blundered there. I had no right to take any notice of what Mr. Ballington had said to me. He was not the superintendent of the mission. He did not engage me to work in it, and he had no power or right to dismiss me. But I was a boy and

inexperienced and I felt deeply hurt. Sorrowfully
I went home and sent in my resignation.

The incident caused a great deal of excitement in
Bolton, and many of my old friends, some well-to-
do people among them, besought me that I should
preach to them before I left the town. I preached for
six weeks to crowds of people in the Opera-house.
But I was very miserable all the time. I knew I
had done wrong and I felt it. I knew that the step
I had taken was not the right step, and I felt that I
was not in the place I ought to be. I resolved to
bring matters to a head, and travelled to Newcastle
to see Mr. Booth. I asked for an interview with him,
which was granted readily. I told him I was sorry
for the step I had taken and for the pain I knew I
must have given him. I might have had provoca-
tion, yet I had acted wrongly, and I asked him to
forgive me. Mr. Booth, from whom I personally
had never received anything but kindness, treated
me like a father and forgave me freely. He advised
me to leave Bolton at once, to go home to my father
for a few days, and then to report myself at headquarters, where I should receive further instructions.

I was reinstated as Lieutenant Smith, and stationed at Plymouth. My superior officer was Captain Dowdle. Just about this time, early in 1879,
the Christian Mission was in a transition state and
was being transmuted into the Salvation Army. The
old *Christian Mission Monthly Magazine* had been
replaced by the *Monthly Salvationist*. The new
name for the movement meant new methods and

titles for the workers. While at Dovenport I was promoted to the rank of captain.

I was married to Miss Pennock, daughter of Captain Pennock, of the mercantile marine, at Whitby, on the 17th of December, 1879, at a registry-office. I started my married life with an income of 33s. a week, but I had besides a furnished house rent free. I do not think I shall ever know in this world how much of my success is due to my wife, her beautiful Christian life, and the unselfish readiness with which she has given me up to leave her and the children for the work to which my Master has called me. She knows and I know that I am doing my life's work. When He comes to reward every bit of faithful service done in His name and to give out the laurels, my wife and children will not be forgotten. God has given us three children. The eldest is Albany Rodney, who was born in Newcastle the last day of 1880; then Alfred Hanley, born on the 5th of August, 1882; and Rhoda Zillah, born on the 1st of February, 1884. My eldest son is a sailor boy; my second is a student at the Victoria University, Manchester, a local preacher on trial, who hopes to become a candidate for the Wesleyan ministry; Zillah is at home. When she was somewhat younger, she once said to me: "Some little girls have their daddies always at home; mine only comes home when he wants clean collars." On another occasion she said to me, "Daddy, if you really lived with us you would be happy." My wife and children feel that my work is theirs, and that they must not for a moment say a word or do anything that would in the slightest degree hinder me. Wisely and lovingly have my dear ones carried out this principle.

My first charge after my marriage was at Chatham. This station, which was several years old, had never been a success. If it had, then it had fallen very low. I was sent down to end it or mend it. The General had visited the town and knew the situation exactly. I shall never forget the reception that my congregation, numbering thirteen, gave me on the first night. There had been dissension among them, and each of them sat as far away from his neighbor as possible. I saw there was something the matter somewhere, and resolved to set it right if it were possible. I sat down and looked at my frigid congregation for quite a number of minutes. The thirteen isolated items were meanwhile exchanging glances, mutely inquiring of each other what was the matter, and what they were waiting for. At length one man more bold than his neighbors arose to tackle me, wanting to know what I meant by not beginning the meeting. "I am getting to know," I said, "what is the matter with you. I am studying the disease—am feeling your pulse. A doctor does not prescribe until he knows what the disease is." There was another dead silence, and at length I began the service. But my troubles were still to come. One old man, who had gazed at me in consternation and suspicion all through my address, said to me:

"Who sent you here, my boy?"

"The Rev. William Booth, the superintendent of this mission."

"Well, you won't do for us."

"Why, what have I done? Why do you not like me?"

"Oh," said the old man, "you are too young for us."

"Is that it?"

"That is it."

"Well," I said, "if you let me stop here awhile I shall get older. I am not to blame for being young. But if I have not any more whiskers than a gooseberry, I have got a wife. What more do you want?"

I held up the book containing the names of the members, and I told the people that I had authority to burn it if I liked. But I had no desire to do this. I wanted their sympathy, prayers, and co-operation.

I showed the people that I meant business—that I was eager for the help of those who were of the same mind, and as for the others, they must cease their troubling or betake themselves elsewhere. The result was as satisfactory as it was sudden. Harmony was restored. The individual members of the congregation no longer sat far apart. The people of the neighborhood got to know of the change in the relation of our members to each other, and came to our chapel to see what was happening. The congregation grew apace, and when I left, after nine months' service, the membership had risen from thirty-five to 250.

At Chatham we had some difficulties with the

soldiers and sailors. They took a strange and strong aversion to our work, expressed by throwing things at us. I believe that the publicans were at the bottom of the mischief. The civilian population did not help us, but simply looked on enjoying the fun while we were being pelted and otherwise molested. But one day a gentleman came from London to see me and discuss the situation. He refused to give me his name, and I have never been able to discover it. He asked me if we were conscious of saying anything to aggravate the trouble, and I said no, we had no desire to pose as martyrs and we were not seeking a sensation. The result of the interview was soon manifest. We had soldiers and sailors among our members, and great was our joy when some of them came to us one Sunday morning and told us it would be all right now. Early that morning the soldiers were called out on parade, and a letter from headquarters was read stating that if any soldier was found interfering with the open-air services of the Salvation Army in the town he would be tried by court-martial. Something similar must have happened in the case of the sailors, because from henceforth we had no trouble at all. This was particularly gratifying to me, because I had never complained to the authorities of the treatment we had received. I recognized it as part of the cross we had to bear, and was resolved to face it out and endure it to the end for the sake of the Master.

I could narrate many incidents of my Chatham work. There was one case, at once sad and comical.

A poor, ignorant man—very ignorant—attended the services regularly for weeks. One night, as he was passing out, he said to me: "I am fifty years of age, and have served the devil all the time. But I am giving him a fortnight's notice." I reasoned with him, and urged immediate decision. "Oh no," said the poor man, "I would not like to be treated like that myself. I am going to do to others as I would like to be done by. But I have given the devil a fortnight's notice." When a week had passed, as the poor fellow was again passing out of the hall, he held up one finger to signify that the devil had just one week longer of him. When the notice had expired the devil was dismissed, and the man who had been in his service for fifty years entered a service which he liked much better, and which he has never left. He was for years a true and humble disciple of another Master.

At Newcastle, which was my next station, we had many conversions, as we always had. I remember well the case of a man whom his mates called "Bricky"—he was such a hard, tough customer. Bricky, with some companions, came to our meetings—not to be edified, but to scoff and sneer. I picked him out among the crowd and went to speak to him. He said:

"I am a good churchman; I say my prayers every night."

"Do you know the Lord's Prayer?"

"Of course I do."

"Let us hear it, then."

"The Lord is my Shepherd; I shall not want," etc.

I did not seem to have made any impression on Bricky. I invited him back, and he came this time without his companions. I regarded that as a good sign. He came again, and yet again. I saw that a work of grace was proceeding in him. He began to feel the burden of his sins and to hate them and himself too. Finally he gave himself to Christ. He was changed from a drunken, swearing, gambling sot into a new creature, and was used as an instrument for the salvation of many others.

A few weeks after his conversion, as he was coming one night to the meetings, he passed the theatre, where a pantomime was going on, a theatre that he had been in the habit of attending. At the door he met a good many of his old companions, and they said to him:

"Bricky, we have not seen you for a long time. Are you coming in to-night?"

"No, I cannot come. I am serving a new Master."

"Oh, but have you seen the transformation-scene this year?"

"No," said Bricky. "I have not seen it, but I have felt it."

A man and woman who had lived together for many years unmarried came one night into our meeting at Newcastle. They did not know of each other's presence there. Neither knew what was passing in the mind and heart of the other. At the end, in response to my invitation, they both came forward among the penitents and I dealt with them.

Even while they knelt there before God, confessing
their sins and seeking His salvation and strength,
each was ignorant that the other was among that
little company. But presently, of course, the situation was revealed to them, and the look of surprise
and joy on their faces was a sight that will never be
forgotten by me as long as I live. They told me their
story, and I asked what they meant to do. They
said, "We cannot go home together to-night; that
is certain." I asked them if they knew of any reason why they should not be married. They said
there was none; and they ate their wedding-break-
fast at our house. After this both led beautiful lives,
adorning the grace that had wrought this miracle
in them.

CHAPTER XIII

HULL AND DERBY—A GREAT SUCCESS AND A PARTIAL FAILURE

MY next sphere of work was Hull. The success which we enjoyed there surpassed anything that had hitherto fallen to my lot. The Salvation Army had two stations at Hull, one at Sculcotes and one which was called the Ice-house. I was present, along with General Booth and some leaders, at the opening of this second station. All the money except £1,000 had been promised. Mr. T. A. Denny, however, offered to give £200 if the people would raise the other £800. A deputation of local gentlemen told the General that if they could have Gipsy Smith as their captain, they would raise the other £800 during his stay. By this time I had become known by the name of Gipsy Smith. At the beginning of the work I had been advertised as "Rodney Smith, the gipsy boy." The people talked about me as the Gipsy, and very soon that became my popular appellation. But in order to be quite distinct from my father and his two brothers, who were always spoken of as "The Three Converted Gipsies," I resolved to call myself "Gipsy Smith."

The General consented to the request of the local friends of the army, and I took charge of the Ice-house. Never before had I seen such crowds and such wonderful results. It was quite a common thing for us to have gathered together a thousand people who had been converted at the services, and what is perhaps even more marvellous, an attendance of about fifteen hundred at the prayer-meeting at seven o'clock on Sunday morning. Very often the building was filled, and the street in which it stood, Cambridge Street, completely blocked. Many a time I have had to get to the platform over the seats, as the aisles were so crowded that nobody could walk up them. During the whole six months I spent in Hull we needed two policemen at every service to manage the crowds at the doors. Some conception of the magnitude of the work may be gained from the fact that the Ice-house and the other branch of the mission, which was much smaller, sold every week 15,000 copies of *The War Cry*.

One of the most notable of my converts at Hull was a woman who afterwards came to be known as "Happy Patty." Poor Patty had plunged deep into the sink of impurity, and for eighteen years had been living a life of the foulest sin. She came to the Ice-house and, to quote her own words, "stripped off her old filthy rags and jumped into the fountain filled with blood drawn from Emmanuel's veins." She went home to her house rejoicing, but she had still a hard battle to fight. Her former life continually kept coming back and facing her, and she had to cut off her right arm and pluck out her right eye. The mistakes of her life had been many, the sins of

her life more, but she became a child of God and a
great force for good in Hull. Many weather-beaten
seamen, too, were brought to God by my ministry in
that old town.

From Hull I went to Derby. I do not recall my
work there with much satisfaction. It was a partial
failure. I do not say that I had no success, because
there was success, and great success, but I felt that
I had not the success I ought to have had, and certainly not the success I longed for. There were
palpable evidences of worldliness among the members of the local corps. I rebuked them. They did
not like my rebukes and they did not stand by me.
I fought the battle practically single-handed, and although I had some fruit among outsiders and great
sympathy from them, my labors were not nearly so
happy or so fruitful as they had been at Hull. I
became uneasy about my work, and I told the General, taking upon myself for once to dictate to him,
that I should hold my farewell meeting on a certain
date. He made no objection.

CHAPTER XIV

HANLEY—MY GREATEST BATTLEFIELD

I WAS instructed to go to Hanley, and reached the town on the 31st of December, 1881, accompanied by my wife and one child. The baby was just a year old. It was a Saturday when I arrived. The General had said to me some days before, "Where do you want to go to next?" I answered, "Send me to the nearest place to the bottomless pit." When I got to Stoke station, and began to make my way on the loop-line to Hanley, the pit fires came in sight, and I could smell the sulphur of the iron foundries, and see the smoke from the potteries; I began to wonder if I had not got to the actual place whither I had asked to be sent. At Hanley station we engaged a cab, got our trunks on it, and went off in search of lodgings. For two hours we drove over the town, knocking at many doors. But when we said that we were a contingent of the Salvation Army, the portals were shut against us. At last a poor old Welsh body took compassion on us and took us in.

I went at once to see the battlefield—namely, the building in which the services were to be held. Three young men had been sent to the town to commence operations two or three weeks before our arrival, but they had utterly failed to make any impression

on the people. The meetings were held in the old
Batty Circus, a cold, draughty, tumble-down sort of
place, the most uncomfortable meeting - house in
which I had ever worked. The ring of the circus had
been left just as it was when the circus people cleared
out, and any one who ventured therein was soon up to
the knees in sawdust and dirt. There were no seats
in this portion of the circus. On this Saturday
evening I found two young lieutenants standing
inside the ring, making it a sort of pulpit. Sprinkled
over the seats of the building, rising tier upon tier,
were from twenty to thirty people, looking for all
the world like jam-pots on a shelf, and singing as I
entered, "I need Thee, oh, I need Thee." Believe
me, I stood and laughed. I thought it was true
enough that they needed somebody. After a brief
talk with the people I asked them to meet me in the
Market Place at ten o'clock next morning.

The two young lieutenants, my wife, and myself
duly took our stand in the Market Place on Sunday
morning. Not a soul came out to support us. I
played a little concertina which had been given to
me on leaving Devonport by my friends there, many
of whom were converts. We sang some hymns,
and people living above the shops in the Market
Place, thinking we were laborers out of work, threw
us pennies. I had no uniform on—in fact, got out
of wearing the uniform when I could, and, indeed,
never in my life did I wear a red jersey. I used to
dress somewhat, although not markedly, in gipsy
fashion. Nobody stopped to listen to us. It was

rather wet, and the people who passed by on their way to church put their umbrellas in front of their faces so that we should not see them.   But we went on as though we had been addressing a crowd.   In the afternoon, the four of us were in the open-air again.   At night, about eighty people attended our services in the circus.   The building seated 2,500 people, but these eighty people huddling themselves close together, to keep warm I suppose (for the building was very cold), sat in the midst of the most appalling and depressing desolation.   It was a very dismal beginning, without hope, without cheer, without anything that gave promise of success.

But I was resolved to do what I could in this difficult situation.   On Monday morning we went to the building to see if we could do something to stop the draughts and get the windows mended.   We found a hammer, some nails, and some pieces of timber in the empty stable of the circus, and we worked with these instruments all day, doing our best to make the place habitable.   My wife assisted by holding a candle when we had to creep into dark corners in the course of our labors.   I sometimes nowadays marvel at the great mechanical skill which we discovered among ourselves.   It is wonderful what a man can do, even a man who knows himself to be unskilful, when he is put to it.   For two weeks we went on hammering and plastering, and then I secured the help of my brother-in-law, Mr. Evens, a joiner by trade.   He spent a few days with us, and in that time we made some seats for the ring.

We got hold of some old chairs, knocked the backs off, and planked them together.

In the mean time we continued our services in the Market Place and our audience grew quickly to large proportions. The people listened attentively, and joined heartily in the singing. But we had never more than a hundred people in the circus. After a month's hard labor I asked the General for help—something in the way of a special attraction. I felt we were not making progress quickly enough. The first month's collections just managed to pay the gas bill. There was no money for the poor evangelists, and no money for the rent. We did not apply for pecuniary assistance, because every station was supposed to be self-supporting, and we had made up our minds that Hanley would pay its way too. The General gave us the services of the "Fry family," a father and three sons, splendid musicians, for a few days. They could sing beautifully and play almost any instrument. It occurred to me that if I could get somebody of local reputation to preside at their first meeting we should have a good congregation. I was advised to call on the Mayor of Burslem, who that year was Alderman Boulton, and ask him to preside. It so happened that the Rev. John Gould, who was then Wesleyan minister at Hull, had just been with the mayor, and had told him about my work in that great city. On the strength of Mr. Gould's report, Alderman Boulton promised to preside at the first of the Fry meetings.

I at once got out a huge poster, announcing that a great public meeting in connection with the Salvation Army was to be held in the Batty Circus; that the Mayor of Burslem would preside; that various speakers would address the gathering, and that the singing would be led by the Fry family. The alderman was kind enough to invite a good many of his friends, substantial business men, to accompany him to the meeting, so that the platform was filled, and there was a crowded attendance. The alderman plainly discerned what had been our purpose in organizing this meeting, and his speech was indeed a master-stroke. He told the people tersely, though fully, all about my work at Hull, and then he said, "We have not heard Gipsy Smith, and we all want to hear him. I am not going to take up your time. The gipsy will address the meeting." I was ready and willing, proud, indeed, to face such a magnificent audience. My sermon was very short, for I desired to get the people back again, and so I sent them away hungry. I never wanted a congregation after that meeting. As long as we occupied this old circus it was crowded at every service. The mayor had placed the local hall-mark on our work, and we at once entered into the good-will of the whole town.

The work in Hanley, once well begun, went on increasing in success and fruitfulness. The revival which had its centre in our meeting-place spread over the whole of North Staffordshire. There was no Nonconformist church within ten or twenty miles

of Hanley that did not feel the throb of it. At the
end of every week hundreds and thousands of persons
poured into Hanley, the metropolis of the Potteries,
to attend our meetings. From 6.30 P.M. on Saturday
to 9.30 P.M. on Sunday we had nine services, in-doors
and out of doors. I conducted them all. We sold
ten thousand copies of *The War Cry* every week.
No other station in the Salvation Army has ever
managed to do this, as far as I know. I cannot go
into any congregation in the Potteries to-day without seeing people who were converted under my ministry in that great revival. In America and in Australia, too, I have met converts of those days. I
preached every Sunday to crowds of from seven
thousand to eight thousand people, and every night
in the week we had the place crowded for an evangelistic service. The leaders of the churches in
the Potteries were impressed by the work, and being
honest men and grateful for it, they stood by me.

CHAPTER XV

DISMISSAL FROM THE SALVATION ARMY

AT the end of June, having been six months in Hanley, the General informed me that he wanted me for another sphere of labor. Mrs. Smith was in delicate health at the time, and the ladies of the town sent a petition to Mrs. Booth, appealing to her, as a wife and mother, that for the sake of my wife's health I should be allowed to stay in the town a little longer. The General readily gave his consent. When the leaders of the free churches knew that I was likely to be removed from their midst, a committee was formed, representing all the churches in the town and neighborhood save the Roman Catholics. This committee, a leading member of which was a churchwarden, impressed by the striking work of grace which had gone on under my poor little ministry, felt that I should not be allowed to leave the district without some expression of their love and appreciation, and presented me with a gold watch, bearing this inscription:—" Presented to Gipsy Rodney Smith, as a memento of high esteem and in recognition of his valuable services in Hanley and district, July, 1882."

My wife and my sister, Mrs. Evens, each received a gift of £5. These presentations were made at a public meeting, presided over by Alderman Boulton, who was supported by many of the leading persons in the town. The gifts came from people who were outside the Salvation Army. The soldiers of the army had some intention of making us a gift, but we stopped that movement, as we knew that the General did not approve of such presentations.

To my surprise, about two weeks after, Major Fawcett, my superior officer, called on me about these presents. He said that he was sent to ask me what I had to say about these testimonials. I said that the gifts had not come from soldiers of the army, that they came entirely from outsiders, that I had done no more than many other officers, and that a little while ago an officer in Birmingham had received a silver watch. I added that when I received the gifts I rather felt that head-quarters would be delighted that we had made such an impression on the town, and that outsiders were showing appreciation of our work. The major told me that I should hear from London shortly. On August 4th a telegram arrived for the two lieutenants, who had received silver watches from the same committee, summoning them to London. There was no communication for me that day. These young men had been with the Salvation Army for six months, and I had been for five years. The young men came to seek my advice. I urged them to obey the summons at once. They reached London early next morning, and on their arrival at the Training Home in Clapton, they were told that if they did not give up their watches they must leave the army.

On Saturday morning, August 5th, about six o'clock, my second baby was born, a son. The morning post, a few hours later, brought me the following letter from Mr. Bramwell Booth:

" We understand on Monday, July 31st, a presentation of a gold watch was made to you at Hanley, accompanied by a purse containing £5 to your wife, and the same to your sister.

" We can only conclude that this has been done in premeditated defiance of the rules and regulations of the army to which you have repeatedly given your adherence, and that you have fully resolved no longer to continue with us. The effect of your conduct is already seen to have led younger officers under your influence also astray.

" Having chosen to set the General's wishes at defiance, and also to do so in the most public manner possible, we can only conclude that you have resolved to leave the army. Anyhow, it is clear that neither you nor your sister can work in it any longer as officers, and the General directs me to say that we have arranged for the appointment of officers to succeed you at Hanley at once."

I was greatly upset by this letter. Some of the statements in it were wholly inaccurate. In the first place, I had never given my adherence to any rule forbidding the officers of the army to receive presents. I knew that at a conference of officers the General had made a statement in regard to this matter. He strongly disapproved of the practice, for the reason that some officers, leaving their stations in debt, went off with costly gifts. Moreover, the tendency was that while successful officers received presents, those who had not been successful got none. This, of course, was not conducive to good feeling and discipline. I ought to say that throughout his speech the General was referring to gifts from soldiers of the army—at least this was my impression. It did not apply to presents, such as mine had been, from outsiders. Another grossly inaccurate statement in the letter was that I had led astray two younger officers. The two young lieutenants accepted their watches without consulting me and without receiving any advice from me.

None of us had ever dreamed that trouble would come from these presentations. The letter was totally unexpected, and gave me a painful shock. I was utterly overwhelmed, and such a communication reaching me a few hours after the birth of my second son, was in the greatest degree depressing. The letter was not only inaccurate, it was ungracious. There was no word of appreciation for my five years' hard work, for I had held some of their most important commands, and had succeeded as few others of their officers had done. During that summer I had often secretly thought that some day I might leave the army, but I never gave expression to these sentiments except to my wife. I had written out my resignation twice, but my wife had prevailed upon me not to send it, and so the letters were put in the fire. I knew in my own heart that I was not a

Salvationist after their sort. I felt thoroughly at
home in the Christian Mission, but rather uncomfortable and out of place in the Salvation Army.
I did not like the uniform, I did not care for the titles
nor for the military discipline. My style was not
quite Salvationist enough. Still I succeeded, and
the army gave me a splendid sphere for work and an
experience which no college or university could have
supplied me with. But I had never had any desire
to leave in this abrupt fashion. I had hoped to
withdraw in the most friendly manner and to remain on good terms with the movement and its
leaders. But this was not to be. My heart was
heavy as the prospect of parting from beloved
friends and comrades opened, blank and bare, before
my soul.

I took the letter to my wife and read it to her. She
felt greatly hurt, because she had been very loyal
to the army and its leaders, but she bore it bravely
and was very ready to stand by me. My first impulse was to take the letter to the editor of the local
paper, and then I thought, "No, Sunday is before
me; I will keep the matter to myself till the end of
the Sunday services." I determined in this way
to communicate the news to all those who sympa-
thized with me and my work. There were great
congregations all day. I required no small amount
of strength to go through my work, but I was wonderfully sustained. I preached the gospel as faithfully as I could, despite the burden on my heart.
At the evening service the building was crowded

to suffocation. I had stated at the morning and afternoon services that I had a very important intimation to make at the close of the evening service. I arose in a stillness that could be felt to read the letter from Mr. Bramwell Booth. When I had finished, there was an extraordinary scene. I needed all the self-possession and tact that I could summon to my aid to quell the anger of the people. They began to hiss. But I said, "That is not religion. We have preached charity, and now is the time to practice what we have preached." And they dispersed quietly, but in a state of great excitement.

In the mean time I had replied to the letter from Mr. Bramwell Booth. I concluded my answer thus: "I need not say how sorry we all are in reference to the steps taken in the matter. You know I love the 'army' and its teachings, but, as you wish, I shall say 'farewell' on Sunday. But I shall reserve the right to say that you have turned us out of the 'Army' because we have received the presentations. I can hold the world at defiance as regards my moral and religious life. If I leave you, I do so with a clear conscience and a clean heart. Of course, my sister and myself hold ourselves open to work for God wherever there is an opening."

Early the next morning the testimonial committee was called, and meetings were held every day of that week up to and including Thursday. They sent communications to the General, stating how sorry they were that my dismissal had arisen out of their act, an act which was one of good-will and in loving

appreciation of Gipsy Smith's services.   They said
that if they had known what the result would be,
they would rather have lost their arms.   No good
was accomplished by the letters, and so a deputation
was sent to London to see the General.   It was arranged that they should send a telegram to the meeting at Hanley on Thursday night announcing the
final decision,   The place was crowded to receive
it.   The telegram said: "Dismissal must take its
course."   Immediately there was a scene of the
wildest confusion.

At the close of my last Sunday's services as an
officer of the Salvation Army we found two brass
bands outside waiting for us.   I had no desire for
demonstrations of this sort, and had no knowledge
of these elaborate preparations.   Two big Irishmen
seized me and lifted me on to their shoulders, my sister
was politely placed in an arm-chair, and the bands,
accompanied by great crowds, carried us all round
the town, and finally took us home.   From five thousand to ten thousand people gathered outside the
house on a piece of vacant land.   They shouted for
me again and again, and I had to address them from
the bed-room window before they would move away.

And so ended my connection with the Salvation
Army.   It has given me anything but pleasure to
set forth the story of my dismissal, but I have felt
—so important and cardinal an event it was in my
life—that it must be told in full.   I have not the least
desire, and I am sure that my readers will believe
this, to damage in the slightest degree the leaders

and workers of the Salvation Army. I consider it
one of the greatest and most useful religious movements of the last century. Its great service to the
Christianity of our country was that it roused the
churches from their apathy and lethargy, and awoke
them to a sense of their duty towards the great
masses who were without God and without hope in
the world. I shall always be grateful for my experiences in the Salvation Army, and I look upon
the dismissal as providential. God overruled it. If
I had carried out the intention that I had formed
some time previously and had resigned quietly,
nothing would have been said or heard about me in
that connection at any rate; but the dismissal gave
me an advertisement in all the papers of the land
which cost me nothing and procured for me hundreds and thousands of sympathizers.

I have the warmest feelings of love and admiration
for General Booth. He gave me my first opportunity as an evangelist, and he put me in the way of
an experience which has been invaluable to me. I
think that William Booth is one of the grandest men
that God ever gave to the world. His treatment of
me was always kind and fatherly. I do not myself
share the frequently expressed view that Mrs. Booth
was the real founder and leader of the army. General Booth is too gracious and chivalrous, and, besides, he has too profound a sense of what he owes
to his beloved and lamented wife, to contradict this
view. But, for my part, I believe that William Booth
was both the founder and the leader of the Salvation

Army.   Catherine Booth was undoubtedly a great
woman, a great saint, and an able preacher, but even
as a preacher she was in my opinion greatly inferior
to the General.   I always feel when I read her printed
sermons that I know very much what is coming, for
there is a sameness about her addresses and sermons.
But the General, on the other hand, never gave an
address or preached a sermon without introducing
something quite fresh.   He is more original and
more ready than his wife was, and had he given his
time solely to the pulpit he would have been one of
the greatest preachers.   But for many years he was
fully occupied in the defence and explanation of the
methods and aims of the Salvation Army.   I have
heard him talk for nearly a whole day at officers'
conferences in a simply marvellous fashion—without intermission, full of ideas, practical and possible,
and full of common-sense.   He was splendidly seconded in his work by Mrs. Booth, and has at the present time able coadjutors in his children.   The officers of the Salvation Army are men of intelligence
and zeal.   I have the happiness to number a good
many of them among my friends to-day.   Some of
them, indeed, were brought to God under my ministry.

CHAPTER XVI

HANLEY AGAIN

THE excitement in the Potteries over the dismissal was simply indescribable. I received letters of sympathy from all quarters. Among the kindest of them was one from the Rev. Thomas De Vine, vicar of Northwood. Mr. De Vine, writing from Great Smeaton, near Northallerton, on August 8, 1882, said:

"MY DEAR SIR,—I have just heard in this distant place, where I am staying for a little while, seeking rest and change after my recent bereavement, of the very severe and uncalled-for enforcement of discipline by your commander, and desire to express my deep sympathy with you under it, and to urge you to look up to the Great Commander, the Lord Jesus Christ, in the interests of whose cause and kingdom I believe you to have labored since your coming to Hanley, and He will cheer you and comfort you, because He knows the spring from which all our actions flow. I should be glad if something could be done to retain your services in Hanley, where evidently the Lord hath blessed you. Were I at home, I could talk on the matter with you. Suffer me to commend you to God and the word of His grace. "Yours faithfully,

"THOMAS DE VINE."

For about ten days I remained in Hanley, holding meetings in the neighboring towns arranged by the testimonial committee, in whose hands I was. From every one of these meetings I was carried home shoulder-high and accompanied by a brass band, a distance of from one and a half to two miles. There was no escaping from these demonstrations. The people were simply irresistible. If I took a cab they pulled me out of it. I was riding on the crest of the wave. But I felt that this excitement could not keep on long, that it must soon spend itself. Accordingly, I went to Cambridge for a week, in order to secure quiet, to realize myself, and to think calmly and prayerfully over the situation. I was made to promise that when I came back I would hold meetings on the Sundays, wherever the committee decided upon. In my absence at Cambridge the Imperial Circus, a building capable of seating over four thousand people, was secured for next Sunday's meetings. It had been built at a cost of £14,000, but the circus company had failed, and the structure, which stood on three thousand square yards of land, was in the hands of the National Provincial Bank.

When I returned for a Sunday's services the congregations were overwhelming. At these meetings the committee made a strong appeal to me to remain in Hanley for the sake of the work, of the hundreds of people who had been rescued from sin and misery, and of the hundreds more who were ready to listen to me. Mr. William Brown, a miners' agent, very well known in the district, made a speech in which he asked my sister and myself, "for the sake of the suffering poor and the cause of Christ," to reconsider our determination to labor as general evangelists and to confine ourselves to the Potteries and the neighboring towns. The committee disclaimed any intention of acting in opposition to the work of the Salvation Army. I had told the people that since General Booth had dismissed me from the army I had received letters every morning inviting me to conduct special missions in different parts of the country. I said to the vast congregation that I must have time to consider my decision, and intimated that we intended leaving Hanley again at once for a week to recruit our health. There were at least twelve thousand people in these three Sunday meetings. I felt that I must really get away from these crowds and the excitement.

In my absence my friends and sympathizers were busy. The Rev. M. Baxter, editor of the *Christian Herald*, and the promoter of "The Gospel Army" movement, took a leading part, along with the local men, in the deliberations. At first there were some doubts about taking the Imperial Circus, but Mr. Baxter stated that if the committee did not see their way to do this, he would himself hire the building for religious services. Accordingly the circus was secured by the committee for three months. It was arranged that two ladies connected with the Gospel Army movement should conduct the services until I could make my own arrangements. Alderman W. Boulton, Mayor of Burslem, a Wesleyan

Methodist, was elected president of the committee; the Rev. T. De Vine, Vicar of Northwood, and Councillor Nichols, Wesleyan Methodist, vice-presidents; Mr. R. Finch, a Wesleyan local preacher and former treasurer of the Salvation Army local corps, was elected treasurer; Mr. James Bebbington, corresponding secretary; and Mr. Hodgson, financial secretary. The other members of the committee included Mr. Tyrrell, a churchwarden; Mr. W. T. Harrison, a Congregationalist; and Mr. Bowden, a New Connexion Methodist, and this year (1901) Mayor of Burslem. It was altogether a very strong and representative committee, and remains so to this day.

My committee, you will see, was thoroughly representative of the free churches, of the townspeople, including business men and the hundreds of working people who had been converted during our stay in the town. Besides, many joined us out of mere love of fair play and sympathy with those whom they thought to have been uncharitably dealt with. I had promised to stay a month, but the month grew into four years in all. The fact is, that when the month was up the work had become so important and so large that I felt it would have been sinful to leave it just then. Under the control of my strong committee, it went on with an ever-increasing volume and force. They paid me £300 a year for my services. The building for nearly two years was crowded every night and at the three services on Sunday. We had the largest congregation outside London. The result of these labors

is to be found in many homes. In hundreds of
churches and Sunday - schools to-day all over the
land and in other lands are found officers, teachers,
superintendents, class leaders, local preachers, and
Christian workers who were converted under my
preaching, while many others who were at that time
turned unto God have passed in triumphant deaths
to their reward. Our mission was an inspiration to
the churches. It will be remembered that when I
first started my open-air work at Hanley the people
threw pennies to us, thinking that we were laborers
out of work. But very soon I beheld the leaders of
the free churches, their ministers even, engaged in
open-air work. And even the incumbent of St.
John's, with his white surplice and his surpliced
choir, began to conduct open-air services in the
Market Place, marching through the streets, after the
service was over, to the old church, singing " Onward,
Christian soldiers." I regard the action of the vicar
in some ways as the greatest compliment that was
ever paid to me in Hanley.

It was our custom to meet at 5.30 on Sunday night
for a prayer meeting, preceding the large public meeting at 6.30. The place of gathering was a large side
room, which had been used by the circus people
as a dressing-room, and was situated over the stables.
Late in October, 1882, three hundred of us were in
this room, singing praises to God and asking for
His blessing on the coming service. While we were
singing a hymn the floor opened in the centre and
dropped us all down into the stables, a distance of

ten or eleven feet. Seventy-five persons were injured; arms and legs were broken, a few skulls were fractured, and there were bruises galore. But not a life was lost. The people, gathering in the large hall, heard the crash and were terrified, but there was no panic. Some of the stewards were on the spot, giving all the help they could. Doctors were sent for, and the injured were taken home in cabs. As soon as I could extricate myself from the falling *débris*, it occurred to me that the people in the great building would be in fear as to my safety. I rushed to the platform, explained in a few simple words what had taken place, told the people that all possible help and attendance was being rendered to the injured, and begged them to keep calm and cool. And then I retired to pass a few minutes of acute agony. I was urged to give up the service that night, for though my body bore no bruises, my nerves had sustained a severe shock. However, I insisted on taking my place.

But our troubles were not yet over. When I reached the platform I quietly asked the caretaker to turn on the lights full, and he, poor fellow, in his nervousness and excitement, turned them out. Immediately there was a scene of confusion and fear. Mr. Brown, the miners' agent before mentioned, saved the situation by his presence of mind. He at once began to sing " Jesus, Lover of My Soul," and sang it with great effect, for he was a very good singer. The people presently joined in the hymn, and very soon all were calm. In the mean time the lights had been

put full on and the service swung on its way. I
preached as well as I could, but at the close of the
service—so much had the nervous shock weakened
me—I had to be carried home. Months passed
away before I really quite recovered. I went on
with my work, but not without fear and trembling.
Even now, occasionally, when I am face to face with
a great crowd, something of the feeling of that night
comes back to me.

None of these things—not even my dismissal from
the Salvation Army—at all hindered our work of
saving and redeeming men. The revival swept on
like a mighty river, carrying everything before it.
Strangers to the town seldom went away without
paying a visit to the mission and witnessing for
themselves the work that we were doing. And so,
when I visit towns to-day, people frequently say to
me, "Oh, Mr. Smith, I heard you at Hanley in the
old days."

In March, 1883, my friends in Hull invited my
sister and myself to conduct a fortnight's mission
in their town. I had many spiritual children in
Hull, and I was naturally eager to see them. My
Hanley committee granted me leave of absence.
We were welcomed at Hull Station by from ten thousand to twenty thousaod people. A carriage, with
a pair of gray horses, was waiting for us to convey
us to our hosts. But the people unyoked the horses
and dragged us in the carriage all over the city. The
meetings were held in Hengler's Circus, a building
with accommodation for over four thousand people.

This was all too small for the crowds that gathered every night. When the fortnight came to an end the committee who had arranged the mission determined that the work should not cease, and resolved to establish a local mission of their own. It was settled there and then that my sister and Mr. Evens, to whom she was shortly to be married, should take charge of the Hull Mission, and that they and I should change places pretty frequently for a week or a fortnight. Mr. Evens, who was by trade a joiner, had been a captain in the Salvation Army, and, I may say here, has for the last eight or nine years been engaged along with his wife in the Liverpool Wesleyan Mission. For nearly two years our arrangements for the Hull Mission continued and worked well. At the end of that period Mr. Evens took up the work of a general evangelist, and Rev. G. Campbell Morgan, who has since acquired a world-wide reputation, succeeded him. It was thus I first met Mr. Morgan, and from the beginning I formed the highest opinion of him. My expectations of his usefulness and eminence have been fully realized, but not more fully than I anticipated. After eighteen months' good service at Hull he settled at Stone; thence he was transferred to Rugeley; thence to Birmingham; thence to London. The rest is known to all the world.

In the summer of the same year I had my first experience of foreign travel. I went on a trip to Sweden, as the guest of Dr. and Mrs. Kesson and of the late Mrs. Poulton. They were members of the Hull Mission committee. I had some delightful

experiences during this pleasant holiday. My first
Sunday morning in Sweden was spent at Stockholm.
I went to the meeting of the Salvation Army. The
captain was a Dane, who had been trained at the
army home in London. I had not been five minutes
in the building, where some five hundred people were
gathered, before they found me out, and asked me to
sing. I gave them ' Oh, Touch the Hem of His Garment." The captain told the people the number of
the hymn in the Swedish army hymn-book, and while
I sang in English they took up the chorus in their
own tongue. There were tears in the eyes of many
strong men as the sweet hymn found its way to their
hearts. I sang again in the evening meeting. At
both services I spoke a few words, which were
translated to the listeners.

One day I went to the King's palace and saw the
splendid furniture and the beautiful rooms. As we
stood in the corridor the King himself passed down
and graciously nodded to us. On another occasion
we went to see the King reviewing his troops. Amid
all the military show one little incident touched me
most. A little sweep came running past the spot
where the King was on his horse. His face was
black and his feet were bare, but as he passed the
monarch of Sweden he raised his dirty hand and
saluted his sovereign. The King smiled upon the
little fellow and returned the salute. Immediately
afterwards a dashing officer came galloping up on a
fine horse. His uniform shone like gold and his
sword rattled as he careered bravely along. He also

saluted his King. The King saluted back with all the dignity of a sovereign, but I thought I missed the kindly gleam of the eye with which he had greeted the waving of the little sweep's dirty hand, and I said to myself: " This King loves the little sweep as much as the fine officer. And I love him for it."

The work in Hanley went on without any abatement of interest, attendance, or result. Having to face the same huge congregation so constantly, I began to feel acutely the need of wider reading. I had read very little outside my Bible until I left the army. My time had been fully occupied in teaching myself to read and write and in preparing my addresses. Remaining, at the longest, only six or seven months in each place, my need of more extensive knowledge had not been brought straight home to me. But now my stay in Hanley was extending into years, and I must have something fresh to offer my congregation every time I met it. And so I set myself to study. My first reading outside my Bible consisted of Matthew Henry's *Commentaries*, the lives of some early Methodists, the Rev. Charles Finney's *Lectures on Revival Sermons to Professing Christians*, and *The Way to Salvation*, and the books of Dr. Parker, Dr. McLaren, Robertson of Brighton, something of Spurgeon and of John Wesley. At this time, too, I began to taste the writings of Scott, Dickens, Thackeray, Tennyson, Whittier, Byron, Longfellow, George Eliot, and just a very little of Carlyle and Ruskin.

I read for two things—ideas, and a better grip of
the English language. As I toiled through these
pages—for my reading was still toiling—I lived in a
new world. What an ignorant child I felt myself to
be! I felt confident, too, that some day the people
would find out how little I knew and get tired of
coming to hear me. But they were kind and patient
and put up with my many blunders and limitations,
for they loved me and they knew I loved them. I
was to multitudes of them a spiritual father, and even
to some of them a grandfather. Whenever I was
announced to preach the people came and God gave
the blessing. This was my comfort and encouragement. Without these supports I should have utterly
failed. My soul was possessed of a deep thirst for
knowledge, and I greedily drank in my fill during
the few hours I could find for reading. For I had nine
public services a week, each preceded by an open-
air meeting, and I had much visiting to do. Consequently the time for reading, even with a view to
my work, was short. When I look back upon those
days I humbly and gratefully marvel at the great use
God was able to make of me, with all my manifold
imperfections.

This hard grind at Hanley, and the constant preaching to congregations mainly composed of the same
people, was an invaluable schooling for me. I was
getting ready for the wide-world field of evangelistic work, not knowing, of course, that this was
before me. As Moses was forty years in the desert of
Midian, being trained for the work of leading forth

the children of Israel, so was I, a poor gipsy boy, moulded and disciplined in Hanley during this time for my life's work in the churches of England, Australia, and America.

A few words about our church polity—if I may use this impressive phrase—in Hanley may fittingly come in here. When I began my work in the town the army had not enlisted more than twenty soldiers. Before my term as an army officer came to an abrupt end we had raised the number to between five hundred and six hundred. Our services in the Imperial Circus had not continued long before we had enrolled over a thousand members, all converted under my ministry. We had never any celebrations of communion in the circus, but at regular intervals we repaired in a large procession to one of the Nonconformist churches, and there took communion. I should say that not a few persons who were brought to God in the Imperial Circus left us immediately after this great event in their lives, and joined themselves to the churches with which they had been formerly, in some more or less loose way, associated. Saving that there was no dispensation of the holy communion (except during the later part of my stay), we were in all respects a regularly organized congregation, with Sunday-schools, classes, and the usual societies. I say this in order that no one may regard the Hanley work simply as a prolonged mission, although it is true that all my services were evangelical and most of them evangelistic. I was in the "regular ministry" during these years at Hanley, if ever a man was.

In my congregation were seven or eight members of the town council. The mayor, the magistrates, and all the members of the municipality were in sympathy with us and would do anything for us. The mission was a geat fact in the life of the town, a force that had to be reckoned with. I do not think I exaggerate when I say that my congregation held in the hollow of their hands the fate of any candidate for municipal office. I had a devoted, enthusiastic, and hard-working band of helpers, who relieved me of the great multitude of lesser duties which a church has to perform, and left me free for my platform work. My people were very liberal. We had a collection at each service. The British working-man is not at all afraid of the collection-plate. Several times, in moments of absent-mindedness, tension, or excitement, I have forgotten to announce the collection, but I was promptly reminded of my negligence from many quarters of the building. "The collection has not been made, sir!" was the cry of many voices. I had taught the people that giving was as scriptural as praying or hymn-singing, and that the collection was part of the worship.

In October, 1885, the autumnal sessions of the Congregational Union of England and Wales were held in Hanley. The free-church ministers of the town prepared an address of welcome, and arranged that a deputation of their number should address the Union. I had seen most of these ministers come into the town and had seen their predecessors depart. Although I represented by far the largest congregation in Hanley, a congregation that would have made more than half a dozen of most free-church congregations in the town, I was not invited to join the deputation. When the secretary of my church inquired the reason why, he was answered, "Oh, he's not an ordained minister." That was to them reason enough for passing me over. I was hurt, but I said nothing.

However, one of these ministers, the Rev. Kilpin Higgs, a Congregationalist, was my very good friend, and had helped me from my first day in Hanley. I suspect that Mr. Higgs had spoken to some of the Congregational leaders about this slight to me, for after the deputation had addressed the Union and before Dr. Thomas, the chairman, replied, Dr. Hannay rose and said: "We cannot allow this interesting occasion to close without recognizing in Gipsy Smith a co-worker and a brother. I hear that he is in the church. Will he kindly come to the platform and address the assembly?" I was sitting in the gallery, and so utterly taken aback by this gracious invitation that I cannot recall now whether I walked up the aisle to the platform or got round by the vestry. However, I soon found myself, happy but confused, standing among the leaders of the denomination and beside the deputation of Hanley free-church ministers. I told the delegates that I was not prepared to address them, but I ventured to say a few words which they graciously received with applause. They were acute enough to see that there was some little sore feeling between myself and the local free-

church deputation and that I had been slighted.
After thanking the Union and the chairman for their
recognition, their brotherly sympathy, and the chance
to be seen and heard, I turned to the Hanley ministers who were standing beside me and said:

"Brethren, I did feel hurt that you did not invite
me to accompany you on this occasion. I know I
have not been ordained, but I am your brother. I
have not had the hand of priest or bishop or archbishop laid upon my head, but I have had the hands
of your Lord placed upon me, and I have received
His commission to preach the everlasting gospel.
If you have been to the Cross, I am your brother.
If you won't recognize me, I will make you know I
belong to you. I am one of your relations." The
delegates applauded loudly while I said these words,
and I continued: "You see what you have done.
If you brethren had invited me to come with you I
should have quietly appeared like one of yourselves,
but since you ignored me, you have made me the
hero of the day."

The *Christian World* published an interesting
article of some length on this incident, from which
I may be permitted, without offensive egotism, to
extract a few sentences: "Few incidents outside
the serious proceedings of the Congregational Union
meetings at Hanley excited deeper interest than the
appearance on the platform of Gipsy Smith. Till
Dr. Hannay announced him, but few, it may be
presumed, had ever heard of him. When the young
man rose, presenting a dark but not swarthy counte-

nance, there was nothing, save a flash of fire in his
black eyes as he gazed round upon the assembly,
that would have indicated that he came of a gipsy
tribe, or that he was anything different from an
ordinary youth of the middle class. He certainly
had never stood up in such an assembly before.
His manly tone, his handsome presence, his eloquence, and his earnestness procured him a flattering
reception from the assembly."

The working people's meeting in connection with
the sessions of the Union was held on the Thursday
night in the Imperial Circus, and in this gathering I
sang a solo. "There can be little doubt," says the
writer I am quoting, "that if he did nothing else
the multitudes would crowd to hear him. Accompanied by a small harmonium, he poured forth, with
great taste and skilful management of voice, which
was subdued by the deepest emotion, the most exquisite strains of sacred song. The burden of it
was an exhortation to pray, praise, watch, and work,
the motive to which was urged in the refrain that
followed each verse, 'Eternity is drawing nigh.'
So far as we had the opportunity of judging, the
young gipsy's speech is as correct as his singing.
We saw nothing coarse in the young man's manners,
and heard nothing vulgar in his speech. 'He is
doing more good than any other man in Hanley,'
said an enthusiastic Methodist couple with whom
we fell in—of course, they meant as an evangelist
among the masses. All the ministers we met with
who had come into personal contact with him were

as astonished at the amount of culture he displayed
as at the simplicity and force of his address.   The
many ministers and other men of intelligence who
during last week were brought into personal contact
with Gipsy Smith would one and all express for him
the heartiest good-will, coupled with the sincerest
hope that the grace given to him will be to him as
a guard against fostering any feeling in his heart
opposed to humility, and to the manifestation of
any spirit such as the enemy loves to foster, that
thereby he may mar a good work."

And now invitations to evangelistic work began
to pour in upon me, mostly from Congregational
ministers.   These invitations I at first uniformly
declined, but I was prevailed upon to go to London
in December for a mission at St. James' Bible Christian Church, Forest Hill, of which the pastor was
the Rev. Dr. Keen.   I remember this mission very
vividly, for it marked the beginning of a new era
in my life.   It opened my eyes to my true gifts and
capacities, and showed me clearly that I was called
to the work of a general evangelist, the work in which
for sixteen years I have been engaged and in which
I fully expect I shall continue to the end.   Dr. Keen
wrote an account of the mission for the *Bible Christian Magazine*, under the title, " A Tidal-wave of
Salvation at Forest Hill."   On the first Sunday
evening the building was packed, more persons being
present than when Charles H. Spurgeon preached
at the opening of it.   On the second Sunday evening
scores of persons were outside the church doors

three-quarters of an hour before the service was announced to begin. When I appeared in the pulpit
every inch of standing ground in the church was occupied—vestries, pulpit stairs, chancel, lobby, and
aisles. Hundreds of persons had to be turned away.
Dr. Keen concluded his account with these words:
" There has been no noise, confusion, or undue excitement throughout, but deep feeling, searching
power, and gracious influence. The whole neighborhood has been stirred. Gipsy Smith is remarkable for simplicity of speech, pathetic and persuasive
pleading, and great wisdom and tact in dealing with
souls. His readings of the Word, with occasional
comments, are a prominent feature in his services,
and done with ease and effect. In his addresses he is
dramatic and pungent, while the solos he sings are
striking sermons in choicest melody. He is a gipsy,
pure and simple, but God has wonderfully gifted
him with the noblest elements of an evangelist, and
made him eminently mighty in the art of soul-winning."

The mission made a deep impression upon my
own soul. I perceived clearly that my voice and
words were for the multitude, that I had their ear,
and that they listened to me gladly. I now took
occasional missions, and wherever I was announced
to preach the people flocked to hear me. I had great
joy in preaching to the multitudes and some little
power in dealing with them. The people were calling
me, the churches were calling me, and, above all, God
was calling me to this new field of work, in which,

indeed, the harvest was plenteous and the laborers were few. Every day brought me more and more invitations to conduct missions, and the conviction that here was my life work took such a hold upon me that I could not get away from it. After much prayer and many struggles I resigned my position at the Imperial Circus, Hanley. My people felt the blow very acutely, so did my many friends in the town, and so did I. But, as I was still to have my home in Hanley and give all my spare time to the mission, the wrench was not so severe as it might have been.

I cannot conclude this chapter on the dear old Hanley days without the deepest emotions of love and gratitude to my troops of kind friends in that town, and without expressing my thanks to Almighty God for His tender guidance of me in those times of stress, difficulty, and crisis. Never was more love bestowed upon mortal man than was showered on me by my friends in Hanley, and never have I worked among a people whom I loved more deeply and more devotedly. They were very good to me, and I did my best for them. No one knows as I know in my heart of hearts how poor the best was, but God was pleased to make it His own and to bring forth much fruit out of it to His praise and glory. Hanley and my Hanley friends have a peculiarly tender place in my heart. The very mention of the name makes my spirit rejoice with great joy in God my Saviour, who filleth the hungry with good things, while the rich—those who are conscious of gifts and graces and powers above the common—may be sent empty away. Only the resurrection morn shall reveal the great things that God wrought in that town by the hand of that unworthy servant of His who pens these poor, faltering lines of praise and love.

CHAPTER XVII

MY FIRST VISIT TO AMERICA

FROM 1886 to 1889 I was busy conducting missions among the churches. My experiences from the beginning convinced me that my decision to do the work of an evangelist was right. But during these three years I spent some months full of fear and dismal apprehension. In 1886 I was seized by a painful and distressing throat ailment, which rendered it impossible for me to preach or sing. Sir Morell Mackenzie, whom I consulted, said that the vocal cords had been unduly strained. I had been using my voice in public singing and speaking without a prolonged rest, or any rest at all, for years, and the efforts now began to tell on me severely. For about nine months I was forced to abstain altogether from singing or preaching. I do not desire to spend such another nine months again.

My readers, considering the busy full life I had led for years, will easily understand how sore and heavy a cross these passive nine months were. It was, besides, a severe test of faith. Our little stock of savings very quickly diminished, and we had started on our last £5 before I was able to take up my work again. I was recommended to consult the Rev. Mr. Sandilands, the Vicar of Brigstock, who was a specialist on voice production, and on the diseases of the throat to which clergymen and other public speakers are subject. I spent a fortnight in the Brigstock Vicarage. Mr. Sandilands' treatment was so successful that in a day or two I was reading the lessons in church for him. I believe that the long rest had all but cured me of my ailment, but I was nervous and depressed on the subject, and Mr. Sandilands did me the great service of establishing my confidence in my voice. Before I had left him I was using my voice for five hours every day, and I was soon at work again. Never did I feel more thankful. I was busy during the latter part of the year in the West of England. An influential journal in that district made me the subject of a leading article, as amusing as it was flattering. My literary friends tell me that I must work in as many picturesque touches as I can, and that is my only excuse for making some extracts from this article. An autobiographer cannot directly write about his personal appearance and personal peculiarities, nor is he as competent an authority on these subjects as an outsider may be. Yet these are the very things, I am told, which perhaps most interest readers.

With these apologies, then, let me say that this leader-writer described me as "elegant in form and manner, and as genuine and unsophisticated a son of nature as ever the mother of us all gave to the world." My eyes were described as "rather large, darkly hazel, bright and liquid, wells of light and life," and my countenance was labelled "agreeable and winsome," "The secret of his power," continued the writer, "is his simplicity, pathos, eclecticism, concentrativeness, and intense earnestness. Besides these, he is aided by freedom from all the meretricious airs and graces of pedantry which stick like excrescences to a studied and unnatural rhetoric. He is as simple as a child, as tender as a sister, and as mellow and merry as a nightingale." The writer concluded by saying that I had the power of maintaining "that reverence and attention for the truth in an unconsecrated building crowded with good, bad, and indifferent characters which only a few ecclesiastical authorities could maintain in a sacred edifice. And a man who in himself can so elevate the gipsy as to be deservedly envied by an archbishop, is the man for the masses." I confess it had never occurred to me in my wildest and most sanguine dreams that I might be the envy of an archbishop!

The story of my first visit to America begins in this wise. In 1886 I made the acquaintance of Mr. B. F. Byrom, of Saddleworth, near Oldham, a cotton spinner and woollen manufacturer. Mr. Byrom was residing in Torquay for the benefit of his health while I was conducting a mission there, and that is how we came to meet. A close friendship was soon formed between us, a friendship to which I owe a great deal more than I can ever tell. No man has been more fortunate than I in the number and the stanchness of his friends. Mr. Byrom took a holiday in Palestine and Egypt in the early months of 1887, and while on his travels became intimate with two American Congregational ministers and Dr. R. S. Macphail, the well-known Presbyterian minister of Liverpool.   He spoke to them about his friend, the gipsy evangelist, and told them all that he knew about my life and my work.   They were deeply interested, and the American ministers expressed a strong desire that I should undertake an evangelistic tour in their country.   Mr. Byrom, on his own responsibility, gave some sort of pledge or promise that at some future time I should.   When he came home to England he told me he felt I ought to go; but I was finding abundant and fruitful employment for all my energies in England, and I did not feel that I was called to go to America.   In short, I shrank back altogether from the enterprise.   In the meantime, letters were passing between the two American ministers, Mr. Morgan and Mr. Kemp, and Mr. Byrom.   It was Mr. Byrom's firm faith that I should not only be made a means of blessing to the American churches, but also that the visit would be to me a further education and would supply me with help, material, and suggestion for my own work in the old country.   I could hold out no longer, and in the autumn of 1888 I decided to go to America.   Mr. Byrom generously guaranteed me against loss.

But at the last moment obstacles rose up in front of me, like great rocks out of the ocean.   When all the preparations had been made and my passage taken, word came that Mr. Kemp had suddenly passed away and that Mr. Morgan found some local difficulties which prevented him carrying out his proposals on my behalf just then. And so the way seemed blocked by obstacles which we had not anticipated. But having once made up my mind to go, I was resolved that nothing should hinder me. I had still time to secure letters of commendation and introduction from some of the leading Nonconformist ministers and other persons who knew me and my work. I felt sure that these would procure me a good starting opportunity on the other side.

Among those who supplied me with letters were the Rev. Charles Garrett, Rev. D. Burford Hooke, Rev. S. F. Collier, Rev. Andrew Mearns, Dr. Henry J. Pope, Mr. William Woodall, M.P., the Mayor of Hanley (Mr. Henry Palmer), the Hanley Imperial Mission Committee, Dr. Charles A. Berry, Rev. T. Kilpin Higgs, M.A., Dr. Keen, and Mr. Thomas W. Harrison, Secretary of the Staffordshire Congregational Union. The words that touched my heart most were those of my Hanley Committee. "We cannot," said the signatories, "allow you to leave for America without expressing our deep gratitude for the noble work you have done among us during the last seven years. You came a stranger but soon worked your way into the hearts of the people, and hundreds of the worst characters in the town were converted to God. Hundreds of once wretched but now happy homes thank God that Gipsy Smith was ever sent to our town. The work has spread, the churches have been quickened, and at the present time, in most of the towns and villages of the district, successful mission work is carried on."

I set sail from Liverpool on board the *Umbria* on the 19th of January, 1889. A gipsy uncle—a brother of my mother—who, having no children of his own, was very fond of me, travelled a hundred miles that morning from his wagon to see me off. I took him, attired in his gipsy costume, on board the vessel, and at once all eyes were on him. When the simple man felt the movement of the vessel and saw the water, his eyes filled with tears, and turning to my wife he said, " Annie, my dear, I shall never see him again." He had never been on a ship before—he may, indeed, never have seen one—and he feared that it could not live in the great mighty ocean. The thought in his mind was not that he might die before I came back, but that I should probably be drowned. He asked me, too, if I thought I should have enough to eat on the way, and I managed to assure him on that point. Presently I took farewell of him (the tears rolling down his cheeks), my wife, my sister and her husband, Mr. Byrom and several other friends. I felt as we slowly sailed away that I was venturing out on a great unknown, but though my confidence in myself was poor and weak enough, I was very sure of God.

The voyage was without incident. I am a poor sailor, and during the passage across the Atlantic I was *deeply moved !* I landed in New York on a miserably wet Sunday morning, a perfect stranger, not knowing, to the best of my belief, a single soul on

the whole vast continent. I took up my quarters
at the Astor House—Mr. Byrom had advised me to
go to a good hotel—and sat down to think what I
should do. I cannot say I was feeling at all happy
or confident, but I girded up the loins of my mind
and plucked up some little courage.

On Monday morning I presented myself at the
New York Methodist Episcopal Ministers' Meeting,
a gathering which is held on that day every week.
I had a letter of introduction to the President, Dr.
Strowbridge, from the Rev. Charles Garrett. I was
received most cordially by the assembled brethren,
who all rose to signify their welcome. On Wednesday morning I went to see Dr. James Buckley, the
editor of the *Christian Advocate*. Dr. Buckley was
absent, but Dr. Clark was acting as editor for the
time. I explained to him who I was, what was my
object in coming to America, and asked him to look
at my letters of introduction. He read a few of them
and inquired whether I was ready to begin work at
once. I replied that I was ready, but that I had no
desire to start right away because I thought a rest
would do me good and give me time to look round.
"Well," said Dr. Clark, "Dr. Prince, of Brooklyn,
was asking me the other day if I knew of a man who
could help him in some special services." Dr. Prince
was the pastor of Nostrand Avenue Methodist Episcopal Church, the second largest in Brooklyn, a
brilliant scholar and preacher. Dr. Clark offered
to send me with a note to Dr. Prince. I was greatly
pleased and delighted by the editor's kindness, be-

cause Dr. Clark was known to have very little sympathy with the ordinary professional evangelist. I flattered myself that he had taken to me. The note to Dr. Prince ran thus: " The bearer of this note is Gipsy Smith, an evangelist from England. His letters are all that can be desired. You were asking me about a man to help you in your church. If I were in need of a man I would engage him on the strength of his papers." Dr. Clark was continuously kind and fatherly to me during this American campaign. His little comments on my work in the *Christian Advocate* helped me as much as any of the press notices I received in America.

When I went to see Dr. Prince in his handsome parsonage, adjoining his church, the door was opened by Mrs. Prince. The busy doctor was in his study, and his wife—faithful guardian of his time and energies—put me through a set of questions before I obtained admission. When at last I was ushered into the presence of Dr. Prince, I felt somewhat awed and hushed. I handed him the note from Dr. Clark. He put on his gold pince-nez and, after reading the note with a rather severe expression of countenance, he took them off, and looking me hard and full in the face, said in a decisive voice:

" Well, brother, I guess I don't want you."

I returned his gaze calmly, and replied, " Well, doctor, I think you do."

He smiled, pleased rather than offended at my " cheek," and I went on. " I am no adventurer. I ask you to read these before I leave you," handing

him my letters of introduction. Finally he promised to talk to some of his official brethren that night
about the matter at the close of a service which was
to be held.

That service was attended by from two to three
hundred people (of whom I was one), gathered in
the lecture-hall. I was told that this was the third
week of nightly prayer-meetings, that a great spirit
of supplication had taken possession of the Church,
and that neither the pastor nor the officials felt that
they dare close the meetings. They were praying
for a revival. The service that night was most earnest, solemn, and impressive. Dr. Prince came in towards
ards the close of the meeting and spied me among
the congregation. Without speaking to me or giving me any warning he said: "Friends, we have a
real live gipsy in the house to-night." The people
at once looked round in search of this presumably
desperate character, and Dr. Prince continued: " But
he is a converted gipsy. I will ask him to talk to
you." I addressed the people very briefly, just long
enough to know that they were thoroughly interested and anxious for me to go on. While they
were bowing their heads for the benediction I slipped
out. They sought for me, but I could not be found.

While at breakfast the following morning the colored waiter informed me that Dr. Prince and two
gentlemen desired to speak to me. They told me
they wanted my help, and I must go forthwith and
stay with Dr. Prince in the parsonage, for they believed that God had sent me across the seas specially

for their Church.   And I believe with all my heart that it was so.   The prayer-meetings had started before I left England, and by supplication and consecration the people had been getting ready for my coming.   They did not know it, and I did not know it.   But God, who brought us together, did.   This interview took place on Thursday morning, and it was arranged that I should begin on the Sunday. An announcement to that effect was put in the papers, including also a few extracts from my letters of introduction.   The letter which helped me most was that from the late Dr. Charles A. Berry, for he had only recently refused the call to succeed Henry Ward Beecher at Brooklyn.   These short newspaper notices were all the advertisement that was employed.

Mr. Ira D. Sankey, of never-dying Moody and Sankey fame, took me for a long drive on the Saturday before my first service.   I asked him if he remembered that during the campaign at Burdett Road, Bow, he was driven out one day to a gipsy encampment in Epping Forest.

"Yes, I remember it very well, and I remember meeting the converted gipsy brothers who were doing a good evangelistic work up and down your country."

"One of these brothers, Cornelius Smith, is my father, and he is still doing the same work."

Mr. Sankey was pleased to hear this.

I further asked him: "Do you remember that some little gipsy boys stood by the wheel of the trap in which you were driving, and that, leaning over, you put your hand on the head of one of them and said, " ' The Lord make a preacher of you, my boy '?"

" Yes, I remember that, too."

" I am that boy."

Mr. Sankey's joy knew no bounds.

A little incident illustrating the famous singer's true kindness and solicitude on my behalf took place on this same drive. In those days I wore a frock-coat of unimpeachable cut, I hope, and a white shirt and front of unblemished purity and snowy whiteness, I know, but no tie. The reason of this omission I cannot tell. I suppose I felt that I was dressed enough. Said Mr. Sankey to me all at once:

" Brother Smith, why do you not wear a white tie?"

" I really do not know."

" Well, Brother Smith," said Mr. Sankey, " I guess you would do well to buy some to-night, and wear one to-morrow."

Mr. Sankey was very anxious that my first impression upon the people should be as favorable as possible, and even a white tie would count for something.

The mission was successful from the beginning. The Nostrand Avenue Church, which seated fifteen hundred people, was crowded at the first service and at every service during the three weeks. Between four hundred and five hundred people professed to have found the Lord. The Methodist Episcopal churches do not use the inquiry-room. The penitents are invited to come forward to the communion rail and there settle the great transaction. My way was made in America. I next proceeded to the Central Methodist Episcopal Church, Seventh Avenue, New York, the church of which General Grant was a member while he lived, and which is now the centre of the New York Methodist Forward Movement over which the Rev. Dr. Cadman presided for so many years. The same scenes were repeated here. Then I went to Trenton, New Jersey, where I had the exquisite happiness of meeting a great many persons from the Potteries who had settled there, who knew me well, and some of whom had been among my personal friends.

I saw a congregation of colored people for the first time in Philadelphia. It was a communion service, and about eight hundred of my ebony brethren were present. As far as I could observe I was the only other-colored person in the audience. The opening prayer of the dear old pastor contained many passages characteristic, I believe, of his class: "O Lord, thou knowest dat this be a well-dressed congregation; help 'em to remember dat when de offerings ob de Lord are made. O Lord, bless de official bredren. Sometimes at their official meetin's they fall out and they quarrel. And, Lord, before they take these emblems dis afternoon, Lord, they want reconverting. Come down and do it, Lord." At this stage, one big black brother, not one of the official bredren, cried out in a loud and zealous voice:

"Amen, amen! Press hard on dat point, bruder; press hard dere!" And the pastor went on: "Lord, go up into the choir and convert the organist!" The organist, who was sitting just behind me, sniffed and said, "Umph!" It was whispered into my ears that he was the pastor's son-in-law. No one took offence at these very direct petitions, not even the official brethren, or the choir, or the organist. They all heartily responded "Amen." They loved and trusted their old pastor, and did not think less of him for the faithfulness of his dealings with them.

I was greatly delighted and impressed by the singing of the congregation. I heard the Fisk Jubilee Singers, who came to this country and enraptured us all, but this negro congregation excelled even that famous band in the sweetness and grandeur of their performance. I shall never forget how they sang the hymn, "Swing low, sweet chariot, coming for to carry me home." It seemed to me at the moment as if the roof of the church must open and the chariot descend into our midst, the singing was so grand and yet so artless—as natural as a dewdrop. I shall carry the memory of that service with me into eternity.

Some of my most interesting experiences during this trip befell me in Cincinnati. One little incident, trifling in itself—one of those trifling things which one does not soon forget — occurred at the house where I was a guest. On the morning after my arrival, when I came down-stairs, I found a little daughter of the house lying in a hammock swung in the hall, daintily dressed and waiting to receive me. Her father and mother had talked about me to her, and she knew I was coming. I talked as sweetly as I could to the little maiden. I said, "What a nice girl you are!" She answered nothing. Then I said, "What nice hands you have! what beautiful hair, what lovely eyes!" Still she did not speak. I could not make it out. I knew she was very intelligent, because I could see the brightness of her spirit in her eyes. I tried once again. "Oh, my," I said, "what a nice frock you have! what a lovely dress!" Still not a sound. At last, looking at me with impatience, not unmingled with disgust, she pushed her little feet prominently out of the hammock and said, "Ain't you stuck on my new slippers?" This was the compliment she was waiting for.

During my stay in Cincinnati I visited a gipsy encampment close at hand, the Cumminsville Colony. An account of this visit given in a local paper was so interesting that I reproduce it:—

A ROMANY RYE.

Gipsy Smith, the Evangelist, in the City. A Romantic Scene at the Cumminsville Colony.

" There was a rare and decidedly romantic scene enacted at the gipsy encampment at Cumminsville yesterday afternoon. Shortly before five o'clock a dashing team of bays, with bang-tails, landed upon the street leading into the centre of the Romany village, with much life. They drew

behind them a handsome landau occupied by four gentlemen, and as they came to a halt in front of one of the several
tents of this nomadic race there was a shout in the weird
language of the gipsies. Instantly there was a warm
note of recognition from several men with the brown-hued
countenance peculiar to that race standing near by, and a
number of female heads, bedecked with gay colors, a weakness of the Romany woman, appeared from the folds of the
canvas home.

"A neatly-dressed gentleman, with dark complexion
and raven-black hair, leaped from the carriage, hat in
hand, and for a few minutes the air was full of the nattiest
kind of conversation in that strange tongue which men
have for years tried to collect, as he shook hands most
enthusiastically with those about him.

"The new arrival was Gipsy Smith, the famous British
evangelist, who twelve years ago gave up the wandering
life of his family and turned his attention to preaching the
Gospel in his native land, and is now conducting a revival
at the Trinity M. E. Church.

"There was a striking contrast between this civilized
Romany Rye and the untamed ones that soon gathered
around him. He was attired in a three-button cutaway
black coat and black and gray-striped pantaloons, and a
white tie peeped out from under a turned-down collar. Sur-
rounding him was a motley gathering of men, women, and
children. All gazed upon him with great curiosity, but he
soon relieved them, and each eagerly tried to talk with him.
The young men wore rather shabby attire, with the never-
absent colored handkerchief about their necks. They
had but little to say, but one middle-aged, stoutly-built
man, as fine a type of the gipsy as mortal man ever looked
upon, was unusually friendly.

"'I belong to the Smiths,' said the evangelist.

" ' What, from England?'

" ' Yes, my father was Cornelius Smith'; and he rattled off a list of the James Smiths that completely threw in the shade the long line of the same noted family in this country.

" ' Well! well!' replied the big fellow, 'I am a Lovell, and my mother was related to the Smiths. Here is my wife,' as he pointed to a matronly-looking female, enveloped in a faded calico dress, with a white cloth about her head. She took great interest in the stranger, and was soon questioning him about various members of her family.

" ' We have been in this country twenty-three years, but we hear continually from the old 'uns. Times among us over there wasn't very good. My poor mother stood it nearly three years in this country, when she died,' said he of the Lovells.

" Peeping into the tent, the evangelist espied a dark-hued woman sitting tailor-fashion upon the ground. She was a perfect specimen of the gipsy fortune-teller of romance. Her ears were ornamented with lengthy pendants of gold, to all appearance; long braids of rich black hair hung over her shoulders. Her head was covered with a wide hat with a brilliant red lining, and in her lap was a young baby with a complexion the richness of which was in striking contrast to the dark olive hue of the mother.

" Laughing loudly, Smith said in Romany tongue, ' What a thorough Gentile baby!'

" The mother smiled, and a sturdy man who stood near by did not relish the utterance a bit. He was the father, and was marked in not having the least resemblance to the race.

" Smith explained that it was the title always given a child born of the gipsy wife of a husband not a Romany.

" Lovell and his wife were the only ones in the colony who had ever been abroad, and gradually the talk was confined to them. The others, naturally retiring gradually dropped out of sight and disappeared either into the shambly tents or walked away to Cumminsville. The little children —and there were two-score of them—several of whom were perfect beauties, with their dark features and curly hair, returned to their play, and soon had forgotten the distinguished caller.

" ' Where are all your horses?' was asked of Lovell.

" ' Oh, the camp is lighter this week than it has been for a long time. Most of our folks are out on the road, and many of our boys and girls will not be back for an hour,' was the reply.

" ' Won't you come down and take a bite with us?' was asked of the evangelist; and he looked anxiously at the iron crane stuck in the ground under which was the smouldering embers of a fire.

" ' Oh, yes.'

" ' Make it Sunday?'

" ' I would like to, but I have three meetings that day.'

" ' All right; we will try and get some of the boys to come down and hear you.'

" ' Say, Lovell, did you ever hear the people say we dyed our faces?" continued the evangelist.

" ' Oh, yes.'

" ' What foolish talk! I can account for the dark complexion. It is due to the long-continued contact with the sun and elements. The poor gipsy is a much-maligned individual.'

" The trio rehearsed many interesting matters about old forests, celebrated Romany retreats in England, and noted leaders who had passed to their long rest, and after an affectionate farewell the evangelist got into the carriage, in which were Dr. Henderson, of Trinity, and T. A. Snider, of Clifton, and was driven away.

" He was highly delighted with the visit, and said that such meetings gave him new zeal in his work.   Referring to the baby, he said: ' A birth in camp is made the occasion of great festivities.   The new arrival is baptized, a minister is always summoned, and the whole ends with a fine meal.' Just then two gaudily attired gipsy girls passed on their way to the camp.

" ' Where have they been?'

" ' Out fortune-telling ; and I want to tell you a funny part of the talk I had with the women at the camp.   I was explaining to Lovell's wife about the death of my mother, and said the only thing that she regretted was about her telling fortunes, which were all false.   It worried her.

" ' Yes, that is so; they are all lies,' replied she.   ' But then,' continued Smith, ' the women will do it, the money temptation being too great for them.'

" ' What did Lovell mean by saying that business was bad abroad?'

" ' Oh, you see, the British government is very severe with our women in the matter of fortune-telling, and fines and imprisons them.   This has driven hundreds of them to this country, and there are not as many families over there as of old.' "

Back I went to New York, where I enjoyed the rare privilege of hearing Dr. Talmage in his own church.   From all I could gather from friendly and unfriendly critics, Dr. Talmage is never heard at his best in England, either as a lecturer or as a preacher. His power over his great audiences in America is simply enormous and overmastering, and I felt at New York, for the first time, what a priceless gift the American churches had in this mighty preacher.

I could fill many interesting pages, I think, with extracts from the American papers concerning me. Some of them afforded me the greatest amusement. They were all kind and helpful. But though I am not shy now, I could hardly read them, even in private, without blushing deeply. My readers, I think, may be interested with a few specimens of American journalism. One Cincinnati paper said: "Gipsy Smith speaks as if composing cable despatches at a cost of a dollar a word for transmission. As a forest tree laughs at the pruning-knife, so he would be spoiled if trimmed into a decent uniformity by grammar and rhetoric. His words are vascular; cut them and they would bleed. Sometimes, like an auroral light, he shoots up a scintillating flame of eloquence, and is always luminous. At times his voice mellows down until his words weep their way to the heart."

Another journal dealt with me in a more critical, yet not unkindly manner. It informed the world that I was "not very beautiful, and not of commanding presence," but "modest and unassuming." The writer further said that I was a very quiet preacher, though not an ordained minister of the gospel. He informed his readers that I had never read any book but the Bible, but that I knew that by heart from cover to cover. I wish the last statement had been, and even now were true. The writer further spoke of General Booth as Field-Marshal Booth. He said that I had been presented to such men as Mr. Gladstone, John Bright, the Prince of Wales, and other celebrities; and while a stanch English patriot, I was neither a Jingo nor a Chauvinist. I need not say that the journalist gave me too much honor. I was never presented to Mr. Gladstone, John Bright, or the Prince of Wales. It is true that I have been the guest of the last mentioned, but not an invited guest. It was in the days when we sometimes stood our wagon and pitched our tent on a piece of land on the Prince's estate at Sandringham.

I was quite a known character before I left Cincinnati, and my name was used—without my authority, of course—as an advertisement by the keepers of stores. One advertisement ran thus:

" He has good taste.

"Gipsy Smith is creating a great sensation in church circles just at present, and wherever he holds forth the edifices are crowded. He is a great entertainer, and that he is posted in city affairs is shown from the fact that when he attends a church festival he always wants the ice-cream and strawberries to come from ——."

During this first tour in America I visited Philadelphia. Among other places of interest there, I was shown through Girard College, a college for the up-bringing and education of one thousand five hundred boys. This, I was told, is the wealthiest corporation in the whole city.[1] The will of the

---

[1] Girard College is not a corporation but a part of the estate of Stephen Girard, who was, in his time, the wealthiest man in America. The city of Philadelphia is trustee for the estate.—*Note by American Editor.*

founder stipulated that no minister of the gospel should enter it, but that the highest code of morals should be taught. The trustees decided that the highest code of morals was taught in the Bible. Hence, every day these boys read the sacred scriptures and engage in prayer. I was shown over the whole building, but in accordance with the trust deeds, I was not permitted to address the boys.

I had also during this trip a brief interview with Mrs. Parnell, the mother of the famous Irish leader. The Pigott forgeries had just been exposed, and the old lady, very proud of her son, was delighted to talk about this matter, and was eager to hear news from England. Two American ministers accompanied me on this visit, and the old lady at once asked impatiently when we entered the room, " Which is the one from England?" We talked with her only a few minutes, because she soon became excited, and her friends thought it advisable to bring the interview to a close. She was a sweet, gracious lady, with a face that bore tokens of much suffering, and I shall never forget that interview.

The American people treated me in a very kind way, and from the time of this first visit I have always cherished the warmest feelings towards them. They are a religious race, a nation of church-goers. Their religious life is marked by a fervor and an outspokenness that one would like to see more of in our churches at home. The men of America are in the main well read, educated gentlemen, with whom it is a liberal education to associate. I was

much struck by the almost sacred regard that is
paid to prayer-meeting night and the week-night
services in America.   It is to me one of the saddest
and most depressing features of church life in England that the week-night prayer meeting is so
painfully neglected. Many ministers whose Sunday services are attended by congregations of
from eight hundred to one thousand people,
find themselves face to face at the weekly prayer
meeting with a congregation of from a dozen to
thirty and would be mightily surprised and delighted
if the attendance should one night reach a hundred.
It is not so in America. The week-night services
are almost as well attended as the Sunday services.
Religious Americans would not think of accepting
invitations to social functions on that night.[1] Not
only does absence from the week-night service offend
the religious feelings, it is also contrary to their
sense of good form. Many people in this country
seem to think that it would be bad form to attend a
prayer-meeting. There is more friendliness, more
brotherliness, in the church life of America. You
will see more hand-shaking after one service in America than after ten in this country. In England,
when the benediction is pronounced, we rush for
the door; in America they rush for one another.

[1] Most Americans will regret that Mr. Smith's account of the
American week-night service now holds good in very few instances.
The picture that he gives of the prayer-meeting attendance in England
tallies pretty closely with average conditions in America also—
although there are glorious exceptions.—*Note by American Editor.*

They are very good to their ministers. If a worship-
per in an American congregation feels that he has
derived special benefit from a sermon he tells his
minister so.

They have beautiful churches, beautifully furnished. The floors are laid with Brussels carpets
—no shabby strips of cocoanut matting in the aisles
of American churches. The school-rooms, church-
parlors, and vestries are all in keeping in this respect
with the church. I once asked a lady and her husband how it was that they spent so much money
on their churches in making them luxurious. They
replied: "We make our homes beautiful; why should
we not make the house of God beautiful?" The
equipment of their Sunday-schools is much superior
to that of ours. The children are studied in every
possible way. The schools are often divided into
many class-rooms, and the children are given seats
in which they can listen in comfort to what their
teacher has to say. The Americans, in short, have
caught the spirit of the age. They believe in adapta-
tion, and they believe that the church ought to have
the best of everything. We are now learning the
same lesson in this country. We are giving our
best men, our finest buildings, and our sweetest
music for mission-work in the great centres of population, and the results are justifying these methods.

CHAPTER XVIII

THE MANCHESTER WESLEYAN MISSION

My tour in America had been somewhat curtailed by an affection of the eyes, the result of passing from a heated room—and they do stew you in their rooms in America!—to a cold outside atmosphere. My Hanley friends gave me a most cordial welcome home again. My readers will not forget that during all this time I was the honorary head of the Imperial Mission, Hanley. My people paraded the town with a brass band, braying out jubilantly on account of my return, and in the evening welcomed me home. The Sunday scholars gave me a handsome Bible. While in America I had the pastorates of two fine churches offered to me. But I declined them, and when I got back among my dear people at Hanley I felt so glad I had declined.

Before my American trip, I had conducted a few missions in connection with the great work of the Rev. S. F. Collier in Manchester. I found when I returned home that Mr. Collier's committee had taken over the Free Trade Hall for a great Sunday night service. I was invited to work with Mr. Collier for a year. I accepted the call, and removed my home from Hanley to Manchester, where I have now lived for twelve years. At my first service in the Central Hall I had an experience that was very trying to the temper and mettle. As I was describing what took place between Christ and the two thieves at Calvary, an old gentleman, whose hair and beard were almost as white as snow, and who was sitting close to the platform, uttered a loud cry of dissent. I stopped for a moment, then tried to proceed, but was again interrupted. The audience became excited, then impatient, then angry, and voices were heard crying, "Put him out! Put him out!" But this I would not have. "No, there is nobody going to be put out of this hall this afternoon. Leave our misguided brother to me. It is for such as he that this hall has been opened. When this meeting is over I shall go and pray for him. Hundreds of you will do the same, and our erring brother will be brought into the way of truth." Then, to put the audience into a good temper, I told them a story of a certain converted prize-fighter. He was present at a meeting where a man would persist in interrupting the speaker, and, taking off his coat, he was asked what he was going to do. "Oh, I am going to ask the Lord to let me off for five minutes until I settle with that fellow who is spoiling our meeting." I told the people that I myself had for a moment felt a little like that prize-fighter that afternoon. Then I offered up a prayer on the old man's behalf. That prayer called forth many "Amens," the loudest of which came from the old man himself. When the service was over, the white-haired old gentleman made his way to the platform, and shook hands with me in the most friendly manner.

During this year I conducted services occasionally at the Free Trade Hall and the Central Hall, besides holding special meetings in the various chapels of the mission. I was also sent on visits to Lancashire and Yorkshire towns in behalf of the mission. My year of service was so successful and so helpful, both spiritually and financially, to the mission, that the committee unanimously invited me to stay a second year. And I did. I consider that my connection with the Manchester Mission opened my way among the churches in England more effectually than any work I had yet undertaken. I was cordially received in many Methodist centres into which otherwise I should not have penetrated for years to come. But as a fellow-worker, though in a humble way, with Mr. Collier, I was received with open arms in every Methodist chapel I visited.

One of my richest possessions to this day is the friendship of Mr. Collier. He is my pastor, and I do not think any two men in the kingdom have ever taken so many meetings together as we have during the last twelve years. Mr. Collier preaches in the Free Trade Hall to the largest Methodist congregation in the world. A very able, practical preacher he is, too—a preacher who makes every man feel that he is his friend. As an organizer he is, as far as I know, unequalled, and is, to my mind, the wisest statesman in the religious life of this country. His mission is now the greatest thing of its kind in the world. I have known, in some degree at least, the forward movements in America, Australia, and Great Britain, but not one of them can compare with the Manchester Mission. Mr. Collier's first congregation consisted of forty-two people. Now fourteen thousand persons are gathered every Sunday in the various chapels of the mission. The membership at the beginning was forty-five; it is now between five thousand and six thousand. The income necessary for the work is £10,000 a year, and three-quarters of this is raised by the mission itself. If the income was trebled or quadrupled, Mr. Collier would easily find beneficent and profitable use for it. The membership of the Manchester Mission includes many persons who have had strange careers. There are some converted burglars in the congregation, and I know of at least one converted murderer, a man who was saved from the hangman's rope solely on account of his youth.

During ten days' special services that I conducted at the Central Hall we had forty meetings, four a day—a meeting for business men; an afternoon Bible-reading, conducted by the Rev. F. B. Meyer, B.A., Rev. G. Campbell Morgan, or other eminent minister; an eight-o'clock service, and a midnight service conducted by Mr. Collier. This midnight congregation was the most wonderful assembly of people I ever saw. At ten o'clock two hundred and fifty workers, accompanied by two brass bands, proceeded from the Central Hall to visit every beer-shop in that neighborhood of Manchester, every music-

hall, and every theatre.   At the doors of these places
bills were distributed announcing the midnight service, and as many persons as possible were given
a personal invitation to attend.   The congregation, numbering from three hundred to six hundred people, consisted of bookmakers, gamblers,
drunkards, harlots, and thieves.   Many of them
had been found walking the streets after the
beer - shops and theatres were closed.   Not a few
were drunk, many half - drunk.   I do not know
of anybody except Mr. Collier who could have managed such a congregation.   His method was to give
them a lantern lecture; to seize their attention by
means of the pictures, and get in the Gospel when he
could.   It was pathetic to observe how a favorite
hymn thrown on the screen—say, " When I survey
the wondrous Cross"—would move these hardened
drunkards and lost men and women to tears.   So
overcome were some of them that they had to be carried out.   The service was so impressive that it actually sobered not a few of them, at least to the extent
of making them understand what was being said.
During that mission six hundred persons passed
through the inquiry-room.

Some of those who were won to God during my
ministry at this time are now Methodist preachers.
At a mission in Burnley one of the converts was a
lad called George McNeal.   George McNeal became
the Rev. George McNeal, and, curiously enough, was
until quite recently the third minister of the Manchester Mission, and, as such, my class-leader.   It

was Mr. McNeal's duty to take the overflow meeting from the Free Trade Hall, held across the street in the Grand Theatre of Varieties. One Sunday night, as he was going into the theatre, he saw a young man standing at the door smoking a cigarette.

"Won't you come in? We are going to have a very bright service, and we shall be glad to have you with us." He replied, "No, that is not for the likes of me. I will not come in to-night." Mr. McNeal urged him to think better of it and to come in, and then himself passed into the theatre. At the close of the service one of the workers came to Mr. McNeal and said, "There is a young man here who would like to speak to you." It was the same with whom he had spoken at the door. He was completely broken down. This was his story: "I came to Manchester yesterday. I have been a traveller for a firm in Huddersfield, and I have been tampering with my master's money. I knew that by yesterday I should be found out, and I had not the courage to face the exposure. So I bolted and came here, hoping to hide myself and my crime in this great city. But God has found me out. What shall I do?" Mr. McNeal said, "If you mean to be a Christian you must play the man. You must face your master, tell him you have done wrong, and throw yourself on his mercy." And the young man went away, arranging to meet Mr. McNeal next morning at the Central Hall.

Monday morning came and the young man, fulfilling his appointment, told the preacher that he was fully determined to take his advice, and asked him to communicate at once with his employer. Mr. McNeal telegraphed. The employer did not answer, but took the next train to Manchester. He told Mr. McNeal that on Saturday, when he discovered the guilt of his employé, he went to the police station to obtain a warrant for his arrest, but he was too late that day. On Sunday he attended the church of Dr. Bruce, which, having been converted at a mission conducted by Gipsy Smith in the town, he had joined. The sermon was on "Forgiving my Brother," and the employer, cruelly wronged as he had been, felt that he could not issue the warrant. On Monday morning Mr. McNeal's telegram came, and he had proceeded at once to Manchester. Mr. McNeal told the manufacturer that he, too, was converted under Gipsy Smith, and this created a strong bond of sympathy between them. The master and employé had a private interview in a room at the Central Hall, and as a result the young man was reinstated in his former position. He is living to wipe out the past and to forget it.

Rev. S. F. Collier has been kind enough to send me the following notes about my work for the Manchester Mission:

" It was in the year 1883 that I first saw Gipsy Smith. Wandering down Anlaby Road, in Hull, I came across the Wilberforce Hall. Entering in, I was at once attracted by the remarkable voice and earnest manner of the speaker.

A dark young man was delivering an impassioned appeal which stirred the audience to its very depths. On inquiry, I found it was Gipsy Smith, of Hanley. I did not come into personal contact with the gipsy until about three years later. Then began a friendship which has been continued with increasing warmth and strength to this day. We have been on closest terms of intimacy, and probably no two men have occupied the same platform together more frequently. I have the highest opinion of him as a man, as a friend, and as an evangelist.

" In the early days of our friendship, Gipsy Smith several times conducted services in the Manchester Mission. I was so persuaded that he ought to be free to take special missions in the large centres, that I urged him to leave his settled pastorate at Hanley, and undertake evangelistic work in the wider sphere. Gipsy was naturally reluctant to leave the place where he had been seven years, and saw difficulty in leaving the work of which he had been the founder and mainstay. But at last he yielded, and I have always felt thankful that I had any share in leading Gipsy out into the great work God has enabled him to accomplish in Great Britain, America, and Australia.

" Gipsy joined the staff of the Manchester Mission as special evangelist in 1889. Applications soon came to hand for his services, and it was not long before it was evident that the Gipsy was in great demand. For two years Gipsy conducted special missions, with intervals, when he preached in the large halls of the Manchester Mission. No place was large enough to seat the crowd whenever his name was announced.

" It may be of interest to many to read the following paragraphs, printed in our magazine, and giving the impression of Gipsy's work at that date :—

" ' Many friends wonder why our special evangelist is so seldom with us during the winter months. This is not difficult to explain. There is such a great demand for Gipsy Smith as special missioner, and he is so richly blessed in this work, that the Manchester Mission Committee think well to grant many of these requests. So it comes to pass that our friend has been conducting missions at Hull, Barrow, Droylesden, Norwich, Lynn, Stockport, and Oakengate during the past four weeks. Showers of blessing have come upon the churches connected with these places. The letters written by those in authority in the various centres tell of immense crowds, great spiritual power, and inquiry-rooms full of penitents. At several of the places men and women came forward unasked while the evangelist was preaching.

" The speaker is gifted with marvellous power of pathetic appeal, mingled with terrible denunciation of sin of every kind. He displays a very clear insight into human nature, and deals consequently with deceit and hypocrisy. It is most refreshing to hear the law of God so faithfully expounded and enforced in its relation to the atonement. The result is that the inquirers dealt with at the services are generally in deep penitence over a sense of sin. The chapel is filled every night.

" On Gipsy's return from America, five years ago, it was my intention to make arrangements with him as evangelist on our staff. But the thought occurred to me that if the National Council of the Evangelical Free Churches would take up evangelistic work, and engage Gipsy Smith as the evangelist, the free-church movement would benefit, and with Gipsy as evangelist success would be assured. I spoke to two or three of the leaders of the movement, and as soon as Gipsy arrived in England made the suggestion to him, and begged him to consider the matter favorably. The result is well known, and throughout the nation thousands thank God that Gipsy was called to this work.

" I have watched with the greatest interest Gipsy's increasing popularity, and have rejoiced to see the growth of his power as a preacher and his success as an evangelist. Above all, one cannot but be struck with the abundant grace of God that has kept him true at heart and sound in judgment amid such great popularity. God has bestowed on the Gipsy great gifts, and he uses them for the highest purpose.

" As a member of our church Gipsy is highly esteemed, and as a preacher every visit is welcomed and greatly appreciated. In his own church he is as popular as anywhere. Loyal to the mission, he is ever ready to help it, and on many a platform has pleaded on its behalf."

CHAPTER XIX

MY SECOND VISIT TO AMERICA

BEFORE I became connected with the Manchester Mission I had made an engagement with friends on the other side of the Atlantic that I would soon visit them again, and accordingly in August, 1891, I set sail on board the *Etruria* for my second trip to the great continent. I was again furnished with many valuable letters of introduction. Most of them were from friends who had helped me in this way when first I crossed the Atlantic, but some were from new friends, such as Dr. Bowman Stephenson, Rev. Hugh Price Hughes, M.A., Rev. W. L. Watkinson, and Rev. Dr. Moulton, who was president of the Wesleyan Conference for 1890–91. Mr. Watkinson's letter was particularly characteristic. "I earnestly hope," he said, "that your visit to America may be made a great blessing to you, and that you may prove a great blessing to the American people. Your work with us has been deep and genuine, and I am persuaded that it will remain. Much evangelistic work here of late has been very superficial, but you appeal to the conscience and intelligence of the people, which renders your ministry specially valuable. Nothing will tempt you, I feel sure, to forsake this path. Allow me to say how much I appreciate the

purity of your style and your instinctive taste, and
nothing is to be gained by compromising this. I
feel sure that the American churches will be greatly
edified by you, and I only hope they may not like
you too well."

I went straight to the camp meetings at Ocean
Grove, which are held from August 21st to 31st,
inclusive. I had timed my departure from England
so as to be present at these great gatherings. My
intention was merely to be a witness of them. Ocean
Grove is a city with a population of from five thousand to ten thousand people, managed entirely by a
Methodist association. The banks, post-office, and
all the institutions of local government are in the
hands of this society. There is not a beer-shop in the
town, and if one buys a building-site one is obliged
to subscribe to a clause providing for the forfeiture
of the property if the owner is detected selling spirits.
The gates of the town are closed on Saturday night.
Neither postman nor milkman is allowed to go his
rounds on a Sunday, and I believe that while the
association cannot prevent trains from passing
through the town on that day, they at least prevent
them from stopping there. I did not observe a single
policeman in the place during my visit, and only one
uniformed official was employed to keep the great
crowds in order.

The town was founded by a few Methodist preachers
who years ago went there for their holidays and
camped in the woods. Their idea of making Ocean
Grove a great camp-meeting ground became so

popular that now it is the largest camp-meeting place in the world. In the auditorium, which seats nearly ten thousand people, three gatherings are held each day during the camp-meetings. Just across the road is a building called Ocean Grove Temple, seated for about 2,000 people, and here two meetings for young people are held daily. The young people are of all ages, from thirteen or fourteen up to anywhere under ninety! In the height of the camp season, the hotels, cottages, and tents of the town are crowded with a population of from seventy thousand to eighty thousand people, from all parts of America. I have seen sometimes as many as two hundred and fifty ministers on the platform. Indeed, Ocean Grove is a favorite holiday resort for American pastors. People from most cities of America at some time or other attend these meetings, and take home with them a zeal and an evangelical spirit that spread throughout all the churches. The enthusiasm and the fire of Ocean Grove live all over the continent, maintaining alert the revival spirit. Ministers have told me that but for Ocean Grove many a church in America would have been closed.

To me the most interesting feature of the meetings were the testimonies. Brief, bright, crisp, and clear statements they were from Methodists, Baptists, Presbyterians, and Episcopalians, for though Ocean Grove is a Methodist institution, the meetings are attended by members of all the Churches. The Americans, rich and poor, old and young, male

and female, are more ready than we are to state
publicly the reasons for the hope that is in them.
The Ocean Grove audiences consist for the most
part of well-off people, people who can afford a holiday
of from a month to six weeks.   In 1891, the president
of the meetings was the Rev. Dr. Stokes, whom I
had met once before and who had shown me much
kindness.   He introduced me to many of the ministers
present whom I did not know, explaining who I was
and why I had come to the States.   In this way,
before I left Ocean Grove I had practically completed
the programme of my autumn and winter's work.
I had made a good impression on the ministers by
two addresses I had given at the Young People's
Meetings.

My first mission was in Old Jane Street Methodist
Episcopal Church, New York, of which the Rev.
Stephen Merritt was the pastor.   Mr. Merritt was a
truly wonderful man.   He carried on his pastorate
and the business of an undertaker at the same time.
His work in the latter capacity was very extensive.
He stood high in the trade, and to him had been
intrusted the obsequies of General Grant.   While
still a layman, he preached with so much success
that the bishop of the diocese gave him the charge
of Old Jane Street.   When I was in New York, Mr.
Merritt was one of the best-known men in that city.
He had turned the old church into what was described as a tremendous converting furnace.   My
mission there was held during the month of September, a very hot month in New York, and yet

the crowds came and hundreds were turned into the Lord.

One Sunday evening, while the people were gathering, a couple came into the vestry to the pastor and asked him to marry them. When the ceremony was over, the bridegroom said to the minister, "You seem to have a large congregation?" "Yes, we have the evangelist Gipsy Smith from England here taking a mission for us." "Oh, we have heard of him, and I should like to hear him." The upshot was that the bride and bridegroom, having no friends with them, decided to stay for the service. The marriage ceremony took place at 7.30, and within two hours the newly married couple knelt with a number of others at the communion-rail, and gave themselves to Jesus Christ. And so they commenced their new life under the very best of all bonds.

At Washington I attended the Œcumenical Conference, and for the sake of the venerable William Arthur, who introduced me, and who was the most revered man in the conference, I was allowed to sit in the body of the hall, was treated as an honored guest, and was invited to a great reception at the Arlington House. That night I was introduced to Frederick Douglas, the great negro orator, who, in that assembly, seemed to tower above everybody else. I told Mr. Douglas that I had read the story of his life and was charmed by it. He was greatly pleased, congratulated me on my success as an evangelist, and wished me God-speed.

My readers may remember that my first mission

in America was held in Nostrand Avenue Methodist
Episcopal Church, then under the pastorate of Dr.
Prince. I worked at this church again during my
second visit, when the reins of government were in
the hands of Rev. Arthur Goodenough. I was told
that many of those who had been converted during
my former mission were now splendid workers in
the church and in the Sunday-school.

One night, as soon as I got into the pulpit, my
eyes fell upon a gipsy and his wife. At the close of
the service I went to speak to them. Gipsies are
always delighted to meet one another. We had never
met before, but we were *tachino romany chals* (true
gipsy men), and that was enough. I found that
they had pitched their tents a little outside Brooklyn,
and I made an appointment to visit them. They
were a fairly well-to-do couple. Six ladies of the
church begged to be allowed to accompany me,
and I had great pleasure in taking them to the gipsy
camp. The gipsy wife had prepared for us a nice
little tea in the tent. There were only three cups
and three saucers in the "house," and some of us
had to drink our tea from cups and some from saucers. My lady friends were fascinated and charmed
with the novelty of the experience, and with their
handsome host and hostess, for they were a handsome pair indeed. The gipsies were more than delighted to have as guests in their tent a *romany rashi*
(a gipsy preacher) and his friends. It marked a
red-letter day in the experience of the ladies and of
the gipsies. I have made it a practice whenever

I am in the neighborhood of a gipsy encampment to pay it a visit. One reason for this is that I never know whether I may not discover some of my relatives there.

The greatest mission I conducted in New York was at Calvary Methodist Episcopal Church, Harlem, of which the Rev. James Roscoe Day, D.D., was the pastor. The church was seated for two thousand three hundred people. All the seats were let, and Dr. Day was accustomed to preach to crowded congregations every Sunday. The pastor and his officers had thoroughly prepared my way, and the members of the church seemed to rally round me almost to a man. Night after night for a whole month the building was crowded. There were many conversions, including whole families. Little children and old men knelt side by side seeking the same Saviour. Sunday scholars for whom their teachers and parents had sent up many prayers to heaven were brought to the saving knowledge of the truth, and were led to confess their Lord. This month passed away all too quickly. I would gladly have prolonged the mission, but I had made other engagements that I was bound to fulfil. On leaving this church a set of embossed resolutions, signed by Dr. Day and all the twenty-four members of the official board, was presented to me. "We believe Gipsy Smith," wrote the signatories, "to be an evangelist particularly called by God to his work, the possessor of rare gifts as an expounder of the truth and as a winner of men. We believe our membership has been greatly quickened spiritually, and through our brother's instrumentality many souls have been added to the church." I was handsomely remunerated for my services here, and the ladies sent a gift of £20 to my wife, in England—the wife who had so generously allowed me to cross the Atlantic to help and bless them.

My work in New York was not at first looked upon with friendly eyes by all the Methodist Episcopal ministers of the city. During my mission in the Harlem church I attended the usual Monday meeting of the New York Methodist ministers in company with Dr. Day. Dr. Day told his brethren something of the revival at his church, saying that it was a revival on old-fashioned Methodist lines. Whereupon a certain Dr. Hamilton rose and said: "I do not believe in evangelists. I have been in the ministry many years, and I have never had an evangelist in my church, and I never shall have. When the wind blows the dust blows, and when the wind settles the dust settles. I believe in hand-picked fruit, in conversions which result from the ordinary work of the ministry. But I am glad to see Gipsy Smith present this morning, and I shall be glad to hear him." The brethren called out loudly for "Gipsy Smith! Gipsy Smith!" I had no desire to address the ministers, and unless called upon by the president I had no right to do so, but the cries for me were persistent, and I was invited to have my say. I began: "Mr. Chairman, gentlemen, and brethren,—If I were at home in England, among my brethren and the ministers who know me, who have watched me, and who know my manner of work, I would venture to reply to Dr. Hamilton. But as I am a stranger in a strange land, and your guest, I prefer to be silent. If I am only a gipsy boy, I know what belongs to good breeding." Then I sat down.

The brethren present shouted in American fashion, "Good, Brother Smith! Good, good, good!" and urged me to go on. "Very well," I said, " very well, if you will hear me, you shall. It may be a very smart thing to say that when the wind blows the dust blows, and when the wind settles the dust settles, but it is not a Christ-like thing to say of a brother and his work," and, turning to Dr. Hamilton, "if God has given to the church evangelists it is because you need them. What God has called clean, do not you call common." There was a cry of, "Good, good, that's so, Brother Smith!" "Well," I added, "you say you believe in hand-picked fruit; so do I. It fetches the highest price in the market; but what are you to do when the fruit is too high for you to reach it, and you have no ladder? Everybody knows, too, that some of the best fruit is on the top of the tree. Are you going to lose that fruit because you are not tall enough or strong enough to get it? I won't! I will ask the first godly brother who comes along to help me to shake that tree, and we will get the fruit though we bruise it in the getting. I would rather not have said this. I do not believe in defending myself, or setting myself against my brethren in the ministry. I have tried always to be the pastor's help, and I never allow myself in public or in private to say one disparaging word of my brethren. It hurts and grieves me when I hear a pastor speaking disdainfully of the work of the evangelist, remembering as I do that God has given to the church some apostles, some prophets, some evangelists, as well as pastors and teachers." It was plain that the ministers were with me and not with Dr. Hamilton. On the following Sunday afternoon Dr. Hamilton was a member of my congregation. In due course we both appeared together at the ministers' meeting on Monday. He told me that he had greatly profited by my sermon of the day before, and said he liked it so much that were he going to preach from the same text, he would incorporate some of my sermon into his own discourse.

To me the most memorable incident of my two weeks' mission at Old Bedford Street, New York, was the conversion of a Roman Catholic priest. As I was speaking one night to the penitents at the communion-rail a man with a handsome, clean-shaven face looked up to me through the tears that were streaming down his face, and said, "Do you know who I am?" I said, "No, sir." He answered, "I am a Roman Catholic priest. My church has failed to give me what I am hungry for." My theme that night had been " Jesus, the only Cure." The priest said to me, "I am seeking the Cure, the only Cure!" I remembered that I had seen in the audience the Rev. Father O'Connor, an ex-priest, well known in New York for his work among Catholics.   I called him to my help, feeling that he would be better able to deal with this man than I could, and when I told him what I had just heard at the communion-rail, he said: "Yes, I know all about it.   I brought him here."   The priest had been ignorant of the plan of salvation, but there and then, renouncing his church and his old religion, he gave himself to Jesus Christ. The next day I dined with him at the Rev. Father O'Connor's.   I discovered that the priest, having become dissatisfied with his church and his profession, had gone to Father O'Connor and sought his aid.   Father O'Connor said to him, "Come and live with me, and see how my wife and children live, and what simple faith in Christ has done for us."   The priest went to stay at Father O'Connor's house, and at his suggestion came to my meeting. He sent in his resignation to the bishop, and soon was preaching Christ as the only way of salvation. Not a few Roman Catholics have been converted at my missions, but this man was the only priest, as far as I know, who came to God under my ministry. This was the last mission of this visit.

I called on Mrs. Bella Cook, the author of *Rifted Clouds*, at New York, and each time I visited America I have gone to see her.   Mrs. Cook has been bedridden for thirty-five years.   She lives in a humble little cottage.   When she first rented it, it stood in the fields, and the cattle were grazing about the doors.   Now it stands in the backyard of a large store.   Mrs. Cook, though she suffers much pain, is

always active. Hundreds of people come to see
her, and there have been the greatest and most sacred
transactions in her room. She lives by faith. She
has no money, except what the Lord sends her, and
she wants for nothing. Many rich people make
Mrs. Cook the dispenser of their charity. The last
time I called upon her was on the eve of Thanksgiving Day, and she was sending out the last of two
hundred turkeys to make the Thanksgiving dinner
of some poor family. I asked her if she had peace
in the midst of all this loneliness and suffering.
"Peace!" she said, "peace! I have the Author of
peace." "How do you live?" I asked. "How
do the angels live?" she answered; "my Father
knows my needs, and supplies them." Her face
was one of the most beautiful I have ever seen. Although she is advanced in years she has no wrinkles
or blemish of any sort. The peace of Heaven plainly
rests upon her. She lives in the cloud that over-
shadowed the disciples and their Lord on the Mount
of Transfiguration.

The more I knew of America, the more I came to
love her and her people. I was greatly struck during
this visit by the entire absence of drink from the
tables of the houses where I stayed or visited. Writing now, after five trips, I can say that I have never
seen drink in any shape or form on any private table
in America. The home-life of America has a great
charm for me. I should think that the Americans
are the most hospitable people under the sun. There
is no touch of reserve or suspicion in their kindness.

They are eager to serve others, and they are also eager to acknowledge the services of others. It is quite a common thing for a member of a congregation to go to the minister at the close of the service and say, "Thank you for that sermon; it has done me good." I am sure that this helps the American ministers to do their work better, and I am equally sure that if English preachers got more of this encouragement their people would save them many heart-pangs, and would help them to preach better.

About five hundred friends and converts came down to the steamer to see me off. As the stately ship sailed away they sang, "God be with you till we meet again!" I was never more eager to get home in my life. I had been parted from my wife and children for seven months—it seemed more like seven years to me. As we sailed up the Mersey I thought to myself that no city ever looked so grand as Liverpool did that day. Very soon I was in the midst of my friends in the dear homeland, glad to have been away, more glad to have got back.

CHAPTER XX

WITH THE CHILDREN

I HAD been away from my wife and three bairns for the long period of seven months. How sweet and merry their faces seemed to me on my return! Naturally they interest me more than another man, but still I hope some of their quaint sayings and doings may amuse my readers. That is my excuse for a few anecdotes about them.

Mr. Collier was having a great bazaar in connection with his mission work. My wife and I took our children to the function, and there I encountered my good friend Mr. Byrom—a bachelor he then was. My daughter Zillah was hanging around me, and I was delighted with her love and sweet attentions. But I was afraid that she might worry my bachelor friend, unaccustomed to children; so I took some money out of my pocket, and displaying it in the palm of my hand said to my little girl, "Zillah, take what you like and go and spend it!" Her big, dark eyes filled with tears. She looked up wistfully at me, and said, "Daddy, I don't want your old money; I want you! You have been away from us for seven months; do you know it?" I felt that my little girl had justly rebuked me, and I felt at that moment how different she was from many people in the world who are willing to have the gifts of God, and yet do not recognize Him as the Father. I also called to mind these lines:

> " Thy gifts, alas! cannot suffice,
>   Unless Thyself be given:
> Thy presence makes my paradise,
>   And where Thou art is heaven."

One day, when we were living in Hanley, my two boys came home for dinner at half-past eleven instead of half-past twelve. I asked them what they had been doing.

"Oh, we have been playing."

"Yes, you have been playing truant. I never played truant in my life."

"No," said Albany, the elder, "because you never went to school!"

"My boys, you will have to be punished."

I loved my boys, and I was a very young father, and I did not well know how to begin, so I said: "Albany, you go to one room, and Hanley, you go to another. You will have to stay there all day and have bread and water for dinner." The youngsters marched off, Albany singing, "We'll work and wait till Jesus comes." Hanley followed in silence. He was too deeply ashamed of himself to speak or sing. When dinner-time came, some bread and water was taken up to them. Albany ate his eagerly and asked for more. Poor Hanley did not touch it. He could not bear to look at it, and his dinner stood on the table beside him all day. Presently Albany fell asleep, and began to snore loudly. Hanley could not sleep. As darkness came on he heard my step along the landing and called me to him. For I had quietly climbed the stairs a good many times that afternoon to see what my boys were doing. The punishment was more to me than to them. When I reached him I made a grab at him and lifted him up, bed-clothes and all; for my young father's heart was full of tenderness towards my boy.

Weeping bitterly, he said to me:

"If you will forgive me this once, I will never play truant any more."

"Forgive you?" I said, at the same time trying to keep back his tears as they fell. "Yes, I forgive you fully."

Then he said, "Do you really love me?"

"Yes, you know I do."

"Are you quite sure?"

"Yes, I am quite sure."

"Well, then," said Hanley, "take me down to supper."

The boy naturally expected that I should show my love by my deeds. This is what our God expects from us. "If ye love Me, keep My commandments."

Albany and his mother on one occasion were among my congregation at a mission service. That night I sang, "Throw Out the Life-line." Albany and I went home hand in hand. He stopped me underneath a lamp. He said, "Father, I believe that I am converted."

"How do you know, my son?"

"Well, while you were singing 'Throw Out the Life-line,' I seemed to get hold of it."

The boy had been deeply impressed, and for a time he really tried to be a good boy. When the day came for our going home he was full of his conversion. When the cab pulled up outside the door of our house he jumped out in hot haste, rang the bell, and when the maid came to the door at once asked to see his sister and his brother. "Hanley," he said, "I am converted!" Hanley was always a bit of a philosopher. He looked at his brother quietly for a moment and said, "Are you? I think I shall tell your schoolmaster; for he has had a lot of trouble with you." Then plunging his little hands deep down into his pockets he meditated in silence for a few seconds. "No, I won't; I will leave him to find out, because if you are really converted the schoolmaster will know it, and so shall we."

Albany, at another mission service, was sitting beside his aunt, Mrs. Evens, and seeing some people going forward to seek the Lord, he said:

"Aunt Tilly, can I be saved?"

"Oh yes, of course you can."

"Shall I go and kneel down there?"

"Yes, my boy, if you are in earnest and really mean what you say."

Forthwith he marched boldly forward and knelt down at the penitent-form. He came back to his aunt and said:

"I have been down there. I have knelt and it is all right now. Of course it is; I am saved."

14

A few days later entering the house, I found a great commotion was proceeding. Albany and the maid had fallen out, and he was giving her a very lively time. His brother said to me, "Albany says he was converted a few days ago; see him now!" I called the little rebel to me and said—

"Albany, what is the matter?"

"I am in a fearful temper."

"So it seems, but you must not get into a temper. They tell me you went forward to the penitent-form the other night: were you saved?"

"Yes."

"I am afraid, then, you are a backslider to-day."

"No, I am not; I am not a slider at all."

"But when people are converted their temper gets converted, too. Come, let us consider the matter. How do you know you were converted? Where were you converted?"

The poor little fellow looked at me for a long time in deep puzzlement, casting his eyes up to the roof, then down to the floor, and round the room, racking his little brain to discover in what part of him conversion took place. At last an inspiration visited him. "Daddy, I am saved all round my head!" I am afraid that Albany's case is the case of a great many people; their religion is in their heads; and that means that it is too high.

My children were always holding meetings in our home, the audience consisting of tables and chairs. One night I had come home from a service as the children were being sent to bed. They came to bid

me good-night.   But they had arranged a little ruse
for getting to stay up longer.   I was reading in my
room, and as they approached me I heard Albany
say to his brother, "Hanley, let us have a meeting."
"All right," says Hanley.   The meeting started as
soon as they came into my room.   Albany gave out
the hymn, "Jesus loves me, this I know," saying,
"Brother Gipsy Smith will play the accompaniment."
After the hymn was sung, he said, "Brother Gipsy
Smith will pray."   Glad was I of this opportunity
given to me by my children to pray with them and
for them.   I knelt down and besought God to take
them into His keeping, and to make them His.   After
that we sang a hymn.   Albany then said, "We
shall now have Brother Hanley Smith's experience."
Hanley at once rose and said—

> "I am only a little sparrow,
>   A bird of low degree,
>   My life's of little value,
>   But there's One who cares for me."

When Hanley sat down Albany called upon me,
saying, "Now we shall have Brother Gipsy Smith's
experiences."   I spoke a few words to my children,
and I can truthfully say I never spoke more earnest
words in my life.   I told them what God had done
for me, how he had taken me out of the gipsy tent
and made me a herald of His own gracious Gospel.
And I added that these and even greater things He
would do for them if they surrendered their lives to
Him.   Zillah was not present at this meeting, and

the only person who yet remained to speak was Albany. After my little sermon Albany stood up, and with a mischievous twinkle in his eyes, said: "Friends, the meeting is over!"

Zillah usually took part in these meetings as the soloist, but she would never sing unless she was properly and ceremoniously introduced to the chairs and tables as Miss Zillah Smith: "Miss Zillah Smith will now oblige with a solo!"

On one occasion Albany, sitting beside his mother at a mission meeting, saw a man kneeling at the penitent-form, but only on one knee. "That man won't be saved," said Albany; "he is not earnest enough, or he'd get down on both knees."

Albany and Hanley one night were preparing their lessons for school, and were engaged in a parsing exercise. The word to be parsed was "Oh!" Hanley said it was an interjection, Albany said it was an "indigestion." I interfered in the controversy, and asked Hanley if he knew the difference between interjection and indigestion. "Of course I do," in tones of indignation; "a pain in the stomach!"

I always have on the mantelpiece of my study a spray for the throat and nose. One night Hanley came into my room, and picking up the bottle, said, "I think I will have some of this to-night." "What is the matter with you," said Albany, "have you got banjo or guitar?" The boy had heard me speak of catarrh.

We had observed that Albany, on taking his seat

in church, always bowed his head, like his elders, and seemed to be engaged in prayer. One day we persuaded him, after much coaxing, to tell us the words of his prayer: "For what we are about to receive, O Lord, make us truly thankful!"

My two boys went to school at Tettenhall College, Wolverhampton, and attended, as all the boys of the college did, Dr. Berry's church on Sunday. I once conducted a ten-days' mission in that town, and my sons were allowed by the headmaster to spend the two Sundays with me. They sat beside me on the platform during an afternoon meeting, and in telling some simple little story about my home life I referred to the fact that my boys were beside me and that they attended a school in Wolverhampton. On the way home Albany said to me, "Look here, if you are going to make me conspicuous like that, I'm not coming any more. I don't like to be made conspicuous in public." While we were drinking tea Albany kept nudging me, asking me what I was going to preach about at Queen Street that night. "Our chapel, you know"; and saying, "remember it must be one of your best sermons to-night." My stern monitor was about fifteen years of age at this time. The boys said "good-night" to me before they entered the church, because they had to return to school immediately the service was over. When I had finished my sermon Albany leaned over the pew in front of him and was heard to say to one of his school chums—Dr. Berry's son or nephew it was—"I think he has made a good impression!"

And presently the boy who did not want to be made conspicuous walked up the pulpit steps before the whole congregation to kiss his daddy "good-night." I said, "Hallo, who's making me conspicuous now? You must not make me conspicuous!" But the boy was too proud of his father to take any notice of my little sally.

It is the sweetest joy to me that my children have a great love for my people. They are never happier than when visiting the gipsies. A meal in the tent has a great charm and delight for them. This love for the gipsies is a natural growth in their lives. I have never sought to drill it into them. The natural outcome of love for their father has been love for their father's folk. Zillah was recently chosen to recite Tennyson's "Revenge" at the Exhibition Day of the Manchester Girls' High School. She was asked to appear in costume, and, as her own idea, chose the garb of a gipsy girl. Zillah was not always fond of this character. When she was a little thing I sometimes called her "little gipsy girl," and she would answer quite hotly and fiercely, "No, Zillah not gipsy girl; gipsy daddy!"

Nor was Albany, in his earliest school-days, proud of being the son of a gipsy. One afternoon he brought home from school a boy whose nose was bleeding profusely. The following conversation ensued:

"What is the matter?" I asked.

"I've been fighting."

"So I see. I'm ashamed of you."

"I'm ashamed of myself."

"What were you fighting about?"

"That thing called me 'gipsy kid!'"

"But, my son," I said, earnestly, "it is quite true you are the son of a gipsy. Your father is a real live gipsy and you ought to be proud of it. It is not every boy who has a gipsy for his father."

"Oh, that's all right, I know all that, but I was not going to have that thing call me 'gipsy kid'— not likely!"

One day, when Zillah was about nine years of age, she was walking with me to church. I found two little lambs straying upon the road. I knew where they came from, and I put them back into the field, saying as I did so, almost to myself, "All we, like sheep, have gone astray."

"I think," said Zillah, "that will be a good text to preach from."

"How would you treat it?" I asked.

"I think I would begin by saying God was the shepherd and we were the sheep, and that He has a fold, and we have got out of it. Then I should try to make it very plain that Jesus comes to find the sheep and bring them back again to the right place, just as you did just now."

I think that was a very beautiful speech for a girl of nine.

At a certain church where I was conducting a mission there was a very sour-looking office-bearer, so sour that he kept everybody away from him. The church was crowded at every service, but the

aisle of which he had charge was always the last
one to be filled up.   The people went to him as a
last resort.   Zillah, who attended the services, noticed
the man, and said to me one night:

"Daddy, is Jesus like that man?"

"No, my dear," I said, for I could not libel my
Lord to please an official.   "Why do you ask?"

"Because if He is, I shall run away; but if He is
like somebody I know, I shall put my arms round
His neck and kiss Him."

Children know when Jesus is about.   They seldom
make a mistake.

My sister, Mrs. Evens, has a boy who was accustomed when he was little to go to meetings.   He
thought the world of his uncle, and the greatest
punishment that could be inflicted upon him when
he had done wrong was to tell me about it.   By-and-
by he got into the habit of saying to his parents,
when they did anything to displease him, "I will
tell my uncle about you."   On one occasion his
mother and he were waiting for Mr. Evens in the
vestry of a church in which he was taking a mission.
Bramwell, as he is called, had been naughty, and his
mother said to him:

"Your uncle must know, and you are not far from
him now."

"Oh, mother," said little Bramwell, "will you really
tell him?"

"You know very well, Bramwell, if you are a
naughty boy he must be told."

"Mother, can I be saved?"

"Yes, my son, certainly you can if you are in earnest."

"Will you kneel down and pray for me?"

"Yes, I will."

Just as she got on her knees the vestry door opened, and a little boy, with whom Bramwell had not been able to get on well, entered. At once he rose, and pushing his little fist in the face of his enemy, said, "Go away; can't you see I am getting saved?"

Bramwell was like not a few; he wanted to be saved on the sly. But the whole object of his manœuvre was to gain time, and by contriving to be converted, as he thought, to induce his mother not to tell me of his naughtiness.

Children have more sense than we give them credit for. One night I observed a little girl walking up and down the inquiry-room as if in search of somebody, but her search seemed fruitless. I asked her whom she was looking for. "I am looking for nobody," she answered. "I have come in to see how you convert them."

A little girl, eight years of age, attended my mission at Bacup. She was deeply impressed, and rose to go towards the inquiry-room, but was dissuaded therefrom by her parents. I was their guest, and in the morning the little maiden told me that she was trusting Jesus as her Saviour, but she had not gone into the inquiry-room. I said, "Never mind that. It is all right if you are trusting." But I saw she was uneasy. When I addressed the converts at the close of the mission she was present.

I told them that they would never regret the step they had taken, by which they had definitely and publicly committed themselves to God. The little girl told her school-mistress that she had become a Christian, but she had not entered the inquiry-room.

"That does not matter," said the teacher.

"Oh, yes, it does," persisted my sweet maiden; "I should like to have come out publicly!"

Several months later I was conducting a mission at Rawtenstall, in the same Rossendale Valley. If the impression on that little girl's spirit had been merely superficial, it would have passed away during that period. But when she heard that Gipsy Smith was conducting a mission at Rawtenstall, she persuaded her parents to allow her to attend, accompanied by a maid. When I invited the penitents to come forward, she at once walked into the inquiry-room. It was for this purpose that she had come to Rawtenstall. Her soul was not satisfied until she had made a public confession of her Lord. The thoughts of children are often much deeper than we imagine. Their hearts and spirits are often exercised in a way we know not of.

A mother coming home from one of my meetings went in to see her little girl of six or seven.

"Where have you been, mother?"

"I have been to hear Gipsy Smith, my dear."

"Who is he?"

"Gipsy Smith is an evangelist."

"Oh," said the little girl, her eyes lighting up with

joy, "I know; that is the man who led Pilgrim to the Cross, where he lost his burden."

The answer was so beautiful, and in the deepest sense so correct, that the mother said:

"Yes, my child, that is right."

Children are often told very wild and foolish things about the gipsies. The little son of a house where I was going to stay heard about it and said:

"Is Gipsy Smith going to live here, mother?"

"Yes."

"Is he a real gipsy?"

"Yes."

"I mean, is he one of them real live gipsies that have tents and wagons and live in them?"

"Well, he used to be."

"Oh, well, I am not going to stay here; I'm off to my granny's!"

And I never saw him.

Accompanied by a lady, I was one day walking up a street in a provincial town where I was conducting a mission. A little boy on the other side of the road shouted, "Aunty, aunty!" The lady did not hear, and the boy, though he kept calling, remained at a safe distance. At length I asked her if that boy was calling to her. She looked round and said, "Oh, yes; that is Sydney," and beckoned Sydney towards her.

Sydney approached shyly, keeping as far from me as possible and clinging tenaciously to his aunt.

"Sidney," she said, "this is Gipsy Smith."

"How do you do, Sydney?" I said.

Sydney looked up at me with some wonder and more fear in his eyes. I expect he was astonished to find me so well dressed.

"Sydney," I said, "are you afraid of me?"

"O—h, no; but it isn't true, is it?"

"What isn't true?" I asked.

"That you are one of them gipsies that get hold of little boys and takes away all their clothes?"

"No, I am not; no, certainly not," I said.

"I thought it was not true," said Sydney, drawing a deep sigh of relief.

"Who told you that story?" I asked.

"Nurse."

Nurses should be instructed never to tell children fables of that sort, or anything that frightens the little ones. Prejudices poison.

CHAPTER XXI

MY MISSION TO THE GIPSIES

My readers may remember that Mr. B. F. Byrom had met Dr. Simeon Macphail in Palestine and had spoken to him about my work. This, later on, led to an intimate friendship between me and Dr. Macphail, who has been very kind and helpful to me; indeed, it was to Dr. Macphail that I owed an invitation to conduct a fortnight's mission in Edinburgh in May, 1892. The place of meeting was Fountain Bridge Free Church (now United Free Church), of which the minister was the Rev. George D. Low, M.A.[1] This was my first visit to Edinburgh and to Scotland. The church was too small for the crowds who came to hear me, and on the last night of the mission, when I gave the story of my life, the meeting was held in St. George's, of which the renowned Dr. Alexander Whyte is the minister. Dr. Whyte was good enough to preside at the lecture, and at the close he said to me: "I have heard many great men in that pulpit, but I have never felt my heart so moved as it was to-night by your story. I do not envy the man who listened to it with dry eyes."

[1] Mr. Low's congregation has so grown in numbers that a new and larger church has been erected for it, called the Candlish Memorial United Free Church.

I can never forget Dr. Whyte's smile. It is so obviously the effluence of a rich, noble, generous soul. It suggests a quarter of an acre of sunshine.

Mr. Low contributed an account of the mission to the *British Weekly* of June 23d. He said:

" My friend, the Rev. Simeon R. Macphail, M.A., of Canning Street, Liverpool, when visiting me in March spoke of Gipsy Smith, but when he proposed a fortnight's mission to be conducted by him in my church at the end of May and the beginning of June, the proposition did not commend itself to me. Evangelistic services in summer, and just as the sittings of the General Assemblies were concluding, were not likely to prove a success. Mr. Macphail urged me to close with the offer, saying that once Gipsy Smith was on the spot he would speedily make his way among us. And so we arranged to invite him.

" From the outset the attendance was encouraging, and it soon became manifest that a man of no ordinary power had come. The numbers speedily increased until the church was full, a large proportion of the audience being young men. On the evening of the second Sabbath, every inch of available space was occupied and many failed to get admission. So far as I know, nothing like it has been seen in Edinburgh for many years.

" Gipsy Smith is a born orator with great dramatic fire, of singular intensity of spirit. His voice is tuneful and flexible, and lends itself readily to the expression of every mood of mind and every form of discourse. He is specially effective when he illustrates and illuminates some point, or some Gospel truth, by an incident simple, tender, pathetic, from his old gipsy life, to which he frequently alludes as one proud of his origin. His addresses are Scriptural, as might be expected from one who is an unwearied and res-

olute student of the Bible.   In manner he is simple, un-
affected, gentlemanly, and I can speak the more confidently
regarding this as he lived under my roof while in Edinburgh,
and gained the esteem and affection of every member of my
household by his sunny, gracious personality.   IIis singing, which is of great purity and excellence, adds greatly
to his power.   From first to last no fewer than one hundred
and fifty professed their faith in Jesus Christ.

" Gipsy Smith has agreed to come back again to Edinburgh, and we shall hail his return.   Meantime we rejoice
that his first visit has been so signally owned of God.
Many in my own congregation and beyond it will never
cease to thank God for his fortnight's mission at Fountain
Bridge."

Out of this visit to Edinburgh grew my mission
to the gipsies.   I had long had it in my heart to do
something for my people, but the opportunity had
never come to me.   I could not myself undertake
the responsibility of the work, nor could I very well
lead the way.   Still, I had always hoped to see the
time when some missionary would live among my
people in a parsonage on wheels, teaching the children, and preaching the Gospel to them and their
parents.   My last service was on Monday night.
I was to leave Edinburgh early on Tuesday morning.
I remember it was a miserably wet day, raining in
the determined and pitiless way that rain has in
Edinburgh.   In the midst of the rain, a lady drove
up to Mr. Low's manse and asked to see me.   I should
like very much to give her name, but I am not permitted to do so.   She had heard me in Dr. Whyte's

church the night before. Owing to illness, that was the only service that she had been able to attend. For some years she had been deeply interested in the gipsies, and God had been continually urging her to do something for them. I asked her how she first came to be interested in my people. "Some years ago," she said, "I was living near a great Lancashire town, and I devoted all my leisure to visiting the homes of the poor. I was one day summoned to a gipsy wagon where a poor woman lay very ill. I read the Bible to her, I prayed with her, and she seemed grateful." The name of the spot where the gipsy encampment which the lady visited was situated was familiar to my ears. I asked the lady some further questions. I discovered that the poor woman was no other than my aunt, my mother's brother's wife. The distinguishing mark by which I recognized her was the big scar on her forehead that had been observed by the lady, and the way in which she dressed her hair to hide it. I felt my heart open in love and gratitude to one who had so kindly served one of my own folk. The upshot of the conversation was that the noble Scotch lady said to me: "If you will take charge of a mission to the gipsies, I will give you the first wagon, the parsonage on wheels for which you asked in your lecture last night." And so was formed the Gipsy Gospel Wagon Mission.

Dr. Alexander Whyte was good enough to become one of the directors, so also was Dr. Simeon Macphail, of Liverpool. The Rev. S. R. Collier, among all his multitudinous activities, finds time to manage the mission, and my friend, Mr. B. F. Byrom, is the honorary treasurer.   The principal support of the mission has been the collections that are taken at the close of my lecture on the story of my life.   We also get a few subscriptions and a few donations. Our first wagon missioner, who is still with us, was Mr. Wesley Baker, an excellent man and a good evangelist.   He generally has an assistant for company and fellowship.   A lonely life in a wagon would become almost unbearable.   The wagon has travelled all over the country and has been especially useful in the New Forest and at Blackpool.   Evangelistic work among the gipsies is slow and hard. My people have quick eyes, quick ears, and ready tongues.   But for years—nay, for centuries—their hearts have been blinded to the things of God.   There is hardly a race on the face of this globe to whom religion is so utterly foreign a thing.   The gipsies are slow to comprehend the plan of salvation, and even when they have understood they are slow to use it, because, for one thing, their trade is declining; they are depending more and more on the fortune-telling, and they know very well that if they become Christians that lying practice must cease.   Despite these difficulties, Mr. Baker and his assistants have done good work.   They have been cheered by not a few conversions, and they have done not a little to give the children some smattering of an education. The manner of their life makes anything more than this impossible.   However, I am fully confident that the Gipsy Gospel Wagon Mission is the leaven that will, in course of time, leaven the whole lump.

I have only just received a report from Mr. Wesley Baker concerning some work at Blackpool which may give my readers an idea of what the Gipsy Mission is doing. "Some five or six weeks ago," writes Mr. Baker, "Algar Boswell came down to our tent and signed the pledge. Since then he has been most happy, and he has made up his mind to take Christ as his Saviour, intending to make a public confession last night. But in consequence of the sudden death of a relative, who left Blackpool last Tuesday intending to winter at Sheffield, he was called away yesterday morning, and, of course, could not be with us. Before he left home he said to his wife : 'Now, Athalia, you go down to the tent to-day and tell Mr. Baker how sorry I am not to be able to attend the last services. Tell him not to be discouraged, as their faithful work is not without results, as I mean to give up this kind of life and serve God.' Some of the gipsies stayed last night until near ten o'clock, but Athalia did not get the blessing. She came down this morning in great distress. We had prayer with her, and she herself prayed most earnestly, and just before twelve the Lord saved her. We are expecting Algar back this afternoon, and he and his wife are coming down to-night, when we hope to have a prayer-meeting with them.

"Algar has had a most remarkable dream. He dreamt that he was falling into a deep pit, and after struggling for some time, he saw our wagon coming along. It stopped close to where he was, and making a great effort, he succeeded in getting hold of it at the back. Just then Mr. Zebedee and I went to him, took him by the hand, and lifted him out of his misery. We placed him on a rock and told him to stay there. At this point he woke up. It was two o'clock in the morning. He roused his wife and children and related his dream to them."

CHAPTER XXII

AMERICA AGAIN

ACCOMPANIED by my wife, I sailed for the United States again in August, 1892, arriving in time for the Ocean Grove camp meetings, August 21st to 31st. We crossed the Atlantic in the midst of a dreadful storm. I spent a good many hours of the time in the music-room singing hymns to the passengers, who were most attentive.

I was heartily welcomed at Ocean Grove, for now I was no stranger, but a brother beloved. Just as I was about to address the people a minister said to me: "Now, Brother Smith, you have got a crowded meeting. You have a bigger congregation than the bishop had. Go and spread yourself!" I looked at this man hard for a moment and said, "I am not going to spread myself at all. I am going to lift up my Lord!" and I began my address by telling the people what this minister had said to me. We are only too apt to draw too much attention to ourselves. We do not sufficiently hide behind the Cross. At the close of the sermon about three hundred people were on their knees—some seeking to be filled with the Spirit, some offering thanks to God for victory over besetting sin, some backsliders begging to be restored, and many sinners seeking God for the first time.

When I reached the house at which I was a guest, I saw a lady and her husband seated on the veranda waiting for me. Said the lady:

"I wish to speak to you about my soul. I am very anxious. I have been seeking Christ for ten years."

"Well," I said, "there is something wrong, surely. It does not take a seeking Saviour and a seeking sinner ten years to find one another if the sinner is in earnest."

She replied: "I have heard all the best preachers in America. I have travelled from city to city with all the leading evangelists, until I almost know their sermons by heart; but I cannot find what I want. I have read all the best books I can get hold of, and sometimes at the bottom of a page my hopes have been high, and I have thought I shall find what my soul desires when I turn over this leaf, but I have not found it yet."

I showed her where she had failed. The best preachers, the best evangelists, and the best books could not give her what she was seeking. She must take her eyes away from these completely. "Were I you," I said to her, "I would refuse to hear another sermon or read another book, or even another chapter. I would go home now and shut myself up alone with God and settle the matter there, for it is not men nor meetings nor methods that you need, but an interview with the Son of God. And like the woman who touched the hem of His garment, when you pass through the crowds and get to Jesus your present

troubles will be all over, and rest and peace will
come." She went away and did as I advised her.
The next day I saw her with beaming face. I asked
her how it was with her, and she replied:

> "I struggled and wrestled to win it,
>   The blessing that setteth me free,
> But when I had ceased from my struggles,
>   His peace Jesus gave unto me."

I was well known to many of the ministers at the
Ocean Grove camp meetings, and before they were
over I had practically completed my programme for
this visit. Among my audience at Ocean Grove
was a famous negress preacher, Amanda Smith.
Once or twice she called out in the midst of my address, "That's hit the bull's-eye, Brother Smith;
hit it again!" Her face the while was shining like
ebony. There was another colored sister in whose
heart I had won a place. She sat next to my wife
on the platform, not knowing that she was my wife.
Turning to Mrs. Smith, she said: "I like that young
man. I've taken quite a fancy to him. I think he
promises very well. I think I will get him to come
along with me conducting missions among my
people. We should make a very good team." "Oh,
indeed," said Mrs. Smith, much amused; "do you
know he is my husband?" "Oh, if he is, he is all
right for that, and you are all right, too."

At one of the meetings, the Rev. Charles Yatman,
the evangelist, and a well-known character in America, came up to the platform while I was on my feet,

and sat down on my chair. When I had finished reading the lesson there was no chair for me. Mr. Yatman pulled me on to his knee, where I sat in full view of the audience while the notices were given out and the collection was taken. Presently I began to preach, and while in the heat of my discourse I heard a crashing noise behind me, and observed that the congregation was chuckling. Mr. Yatman had fallen through the chair, and lay all of a heap on the platform. The people laughed loudly when I turned round to look at him. I said, "It is very remarkable that that chair did not collapse when both of us were on it; but now that you alone occupy it, you crash through it!" Turning to the audience, who were convulsed with merriment, I said, "A good many more of you will fall before I am through. He is the first one. Who is the next?"

I need not give a detailed account of all the missions I conducted during this tour. But there are some striking incidents still strong and clear in my mind which will probably be of interest to my readers. I conducted a mission at Lynn, Massachusetts, about twenty miles from Boston, at the church of Dr. Whittaker, an able, kindly, scholarly man. At the close of one of the services, when I had come down from the pulpit, a mother walked up the aisle towards me, leading her little boy.

"Will you shake hands with my boy, sir?"

"Yes, certainly, but why do you want me to do so?"

"I think if the Lord spares him to grow up to be a man it will be nice for him to say, 'I shook hands with a gipsy whom God had saved, and taken out of his tent to be a preacher. That gipsy led my mother to Christ.' I think that by shaking hands with you the incident will be fastened on his mind forever."

So I held out my hand to the little fellow, and he pushed his left hand to me.

"My boy, is there anything the matter with your right hand? Is it well and strong like this one?"

"Yes, sir."

"Well, then, I will not shake hands with the left. I must have the right one."

Still he kept his right hand behind his back, and the only thing which moved in his face were his eyes, which seemed to grow bigger and bigger. He seemed firm, and I had to be firmer. Pointing to a group of people, I said: "You see those people? They are waiting for me, and unless you are quick I shall go to them before we have shaken hands." When he thought I was really going he pulled his little right hand from behind his back and pushed it towards me. But now it was shut. I said, "Open your hand." He seemed very loath indeed to do so, but after much coaxing the tight, obstinate little fingers gave way and his hand opened. There in the palm lay three or four marbles. The little fellow could not take my hand because of his playthings. And many a man misses the hand that was pierced because of his playthings. "Little children, keep yourselves from idols," or, as the Scot said, "Wee bairnies, keep yersels frae dolls."

A Lynn newspaper gave the following description of my personal appearance. As it is a characteristic piece of American journalism I quote it:

GIPSY SMITII.

" A short, wiry, thick-set gentleman, with an elastic, springy step, dressed in common every-day suiting, sans style, sans shimmer, sans everything save the stamp of store trade goods; a head well rounded and finely formed; a face of fair finish and clear countenance, brown as the berries of the autumn bush; a heavy, dark moustache, backed by half-cut, well-trimmed English whiskers; dark eyes that glisten like diamonds with the zeal of religious enthusiasm; a magnificent head of hair, black as the raven's wing, and strikingly suggestive of the nomadic race that gave him birth—all this paints a fair pen-picture of the man who, for over two hours and a half, riveted the attention of fifteen hundred people in the Lynn Common Church on Thursday evening."

I conducted a most successful mission at Wharton Street Methodist Episcopal Church, Philadelphia, of which Dr. Vernon was pastor. My work was easy there, because all the people were in sympathy with it. Not infrequently an evangelist finds that a section of the church members, while not definitely opposing, hold aloof, and do not countenance the work. Only those who have experienced it can realize the hindering power of this. But at Old Wharton Street it seemed as though every man, woman, and child in the church had resolved on having what Americans call a good time. The presidential election took place during this mission, and it was thought at first that meetings would be useless on that day. On the night of the election America, at least in the big cities, goes wild. Huge canvases are stretched outside the newspaper offices blazing forth the returns every few minutes. The people are all in the streets that night. However, we decided to meet as usual, and to everybody's astonishment we had a larger crowd than at any other meeting during the mission.

When I think of Old Wharton Street my mind at once recalls a beautiful story of a young girl there. She was a bright creature, fond of society, fond of pleasure. The story begins some weeks before my mission. A dance was to be held at a friend's house, and the girl was anxious to go to it. Her mother said, "Lilly, if you get converted and join the Church you may go to the dance." Shortly after this Lilly joined the Church, and she said to her mother, "Now that I have joined the Church, mother, I may go to the dance, may I not?" "Oh, but, my dear, you have joined the Church, it is true; but you are not converted. You know very well that you are not, and we can see very well that you are uot." Nothing more was said on that occasion. Presently I came to the church to conduct a mission, and Lilly was persuaded to attend. One night her proud, wayward heart was subdued and broken in penitence, and she gave herself to God. There was still a week or two before the dance. Her mother knew of the great change in her daughter's life, and she noticed also that Lilly had ceased to speak about the dance. One day she said, "Lilly, what about this dance; it comes off next week. Are you going?" "Oh, mother dear," said the sweet girl, throwing her arms round her mother's neck and shedding tears of joy, "I have given my heart to the Lord, and I have no longer any desire to go to the dance." Mother and daughter both shed happy tears of gratitude to God.

Most of my missions in America were under the auspices of Methodist Episcopal Churches, but at Yonkers, on the Hudson, I held a really united campaign. All the ministers of the place, except the incumbent of the Episcopal Church, joined to invite me. I was altogether nearly a month in Yonkers, and this mission is among the greenest spots in my life. My wife and I spent one of the happiest months of our lives—away from home, that is—in Yonkers. Hundreds passed through the inquiry-room, rich and poor. An amusing little incident occurred one night. Three ladies rose from their places near the pulpit and asked for prayer. They did not come into the inquiry-room at the close of the meeting, and I stepped down to ask them the reason why. "Oh no, we could not go there; we could not think of it," said one of them.

"Are you a Christian?" I asked.

"No, sir; I'm an Episcopalian."

One night, a boy of ten came into the inquiry-room; the next night he brought his mother, and the night after they two brought the grandfather.

I made some very valuable friends at Yonkers, including Dr. Hobart and Dr. Cole. When I left, the ministers presented me with an address, inscribed " To the 'Rev.' Rodney Smith." "We love you," they said, "with the love of brothers, and we are sure we shall meet when our work and yours is done, and love you through eternal years in heaven." Dr. Hobart wrote to me some time after the mission that he had on his books the names and addresses of sixty people who had joined the church as the result of the mission, and that he could account for every one of them.

The Yonkers' Gleaner published an interesting article on this mission, from which I may quote:

GIPSY SMITH.

" Gipsy Smith is a notable evangelist, notable for what he is, as a warm-hearted, frank, honest, effective preacher. He knows how to persuade men. He deals with great truths. His views of truth are in accord with the best thoughts of those who have had advantages far greater than his. He is an instance of what great wisdom can be gotten from the Scripture by a man who is truly converted. It tells us again by example that in the Scriptures ' the man of God is thoroughly furnished unto every good work.' We honor him as a man sent of God to gather harvests.

" But he is notable for what he will not do. He did not condemn the ministry nor the churches, though he spared not the sins that were found in them. He did not get mad when inquirers were slow to make themselves known. He did not assume to decide who were saved and who were not. He did not put a drop of vitriol on the end of his sen-

tences concerning the wicked or the unfaithful, as if he
rather enjoyed the opportunity to say ' hell.' He did not
spend a whole evening discanting on the sex or gender of
the Holy Spirit, though he holds no uncertain opinion about
it. He did not preach a sermon on the unpardonable sin
(! !), as a flaming sword to drive people into the inquiry-
room. He did not for once make an effort to be funny; he
is too much in earnest. He did not appeal for money, and
did not hurt his cause by telling stories that slurred sacred
things. He came in love; he spoke in earnest. He was
full of sanctified common sense. He won our hearts, he
did us all good. May choice blessings follow his efforts!"

I paid a second visit to Calvary Methodist Episcopal Church, New York, and had again the pleasure
of working under my friend, Dr. Day. The church
seated two thousand three hundred people, and it
was crowded every night during the best part of a
month. I was incapable of work for a few days by
reason of a throat affection. This visit is always
associated in my mind with a certain splendid young
fellow whom I encountered there. He was an intelligent and lovable man, popular with everybody, but
he was not on the Lord's side. He was too good to
be on the other side, but still he was there; and there
are many like him. Nobody can tell what the Church
loses, and what such men themselves lose, because
they do not declare themselves publicly for God and
take up their stand boldly. This young fellow came
to many of the services. One day I met him on
Broadway.

"Will you be at church to-night?"

"No, I have a long-standing engagement to keep."

"Well, then, will you pray for me?"

He looked at me aghast, staring hard for a few moments.

"Do you know what you are asking? You are asking a man to pray for you—a man who has not prayed for himself for years!"

"Never mind; will you pray for me to-night?"

"Oh well, you know I would do anything for you, anything I could, but to pray for you—to pray for you—!"

"Yes, that is what I want. That is the service I want you to do for me."

"I wish you would ask me something else. You know, of course, that if I promise to do it, I will."

"Yes, that is why I am so eager to get you to promise. I know you will fulfil it."

"But you know, as I say, I have not prayed for years. I should not know what to say."

"Oh, I will tell you what to say," and I took out a scrap of paper and wrote, "O God, bless Gipsy Smith to-night, and help him to preach Thy gospel in the power of the Holy Spirit, so that sinners may be converted. For Christ's sake." Then I said, "Will you kneel down and say these words for me to-night?"

He stood as still as a rock for a minute or two, and as silent as the grave. Then suddenly gripping my hand, he said passionately, "I will!" and turning round abruptly, went away.

On the following night, naturally, I kept a sharp look-out for this fellow, and great was my joy when I saw him come into church. He walked straight up to me, with a gracious smile on his fine face.

"You knew what you were up to. You knew what you were doing, you did."

"Well," I said, "did you fulfil your promise?"

"Yes, but when I knelt down to pray for you I felt that I was the meanest man in America. I had neglected my God and Father for years. In the distress of my heart I could not utter the words of the prayer that you wrote for me. I cried, 'God be merciful to me a sinner,' and He was merciful, and He saved me. And then I prayed for you."

We ministers and evangelists must cultivate the greatest skill in throwing the gospel net. In the work of saving men we need to use all the brains we have, and think for God as earnestly and as thoroughly as we think for our business.

Among the congregation at Calvary Methodist Episcopal Church was an intelligent, educated man, who several times asked for prayers on his behalf, but he did not seem to get any further forward. He was earnest, he was sincere, but no light, no joy, came into his soul. I was grieved to the heart to witness his distress. I had a talk with him, and discovered that he had been a backslider for years. He said:

"I have given myself fully to Christ as far as I know, and I have cut myself off from every sinful thing. I have asked Christ in sincerity and in truth to restore to me the joy of His salvation, but still there is no happiness in my heart. I do not understand myself."

"What were you doing in the church when you turned your back on God?"

"I was at the head of a large class of Sunday-school children, and I gave it up in a temper."

"Ah, that explains everything. You wickedly threw up your duty. You must begin work again at once and start where you left off."

After some persuasion he said he would. I lost sight of him for a few days, but when he returned he said to me: "I did as you told me, and all the old joy has come back."

I believe there is a great lesson in this incident for many Christians who have been disappointed in the spiritual life. They sing:

> " Where is the blessedness I knew
> When first I saw the Lord?"

My answer is, "It is where you left it. You have been dropping some of your Christian work. Go back to it, and you will find the blessing there. God is the same. It is you who have changed."

I had been a guest of General Macalpine and Mrs. Macalpine at Sing Sing for a few weeks. This was just before the General became a member of the Cleveland Cabinet. His wife was a Brandreth, a member of the well-known family of manufacturing chemists. Mrs. Macalpine suggested that I should hold drawing-room meetings at Fifth Avenue,

New York. I gladly consented. These meetings were held in one of the largest mansions of the city. There was no advertising, but personal letters were sent to the aristocratic ladies of New York, inviting their attendance. At the first meeting one hundred and seventy-five ladies, including many of the exclusive four hundred, gathered at eleven o'clock to hear a gospel address by a converted gipsy. Mrs. Rockefeller and her daughter, Mrs. Russell Sage, and many other well-known ladies, were present.

My first sermon was on "Repentance." I did not try to adapt myself in any way to the rank of my congregation. I only remembered that they were sinners needing a Saviour. It was just an ordinary service, lasting for an hour and a quarter. At the close one of my congregation said to me, "If what you say is religion, I know nothing about it." Another lady, who was weeping bitterly, sought my counsel. "God has spoken to you," I said, "obey Him; follow the light."

A lady, who had quite recently lost her husband and her child, thanked me at the close of one of the services, and said, "Remember that in every congregation, however small, there is always somebody with a broken heart."

The original plan was for six meetings, but a seventh was held at the request of the ladies, at which the men were invited to join their wives, mothers, and sisters. I remember that Mr. Rockefeller himself was among the congregation. I have had many communications from America regarding these draw-

ing-room meetings, giving conclusive testimony
to the lasting good that was wrought by them.

During my mission at Tarrytown, on the Hudson,
I was helped by my sister, Mrs. Evens, and her husband. We had splendid gatherings for a month
in the church of Dr. McAnny, a beautiful preacher,
not perhaps of the most popular type, but winning,
poetical, and eloquent. I should almost say that
there were too many nosegays in his sermons, but
in the midst of all the beauty of his discourse there
was a strong evangelical note.

One night we had a curious and rather trying
experience. The service had been powerful until
the end, but when the penitents were invited to come
forward to the communion-rail, no one moved. This
has happened several times in the course of my ministry. It means, I think, that God desires first of all
to test our faith, and in the second place to humble
us, to make us realize keenly that the power is in
His hands. However, when the benediction was pronounced the people still sat in their seats. They would
neither go away nor come forward. I concluded that
God was working in their hearts, and that His Spirit
was striving against their hardness and obstinacy.
I began to sign a hymn, "The Saviour is calling
thee, sinner," with the refrain, "Jesus will help if
you try." I do not think I had concluded the first
verse before a young man, seated in a back pew,
arose and walked up the aisle to the communion-
rail. While I was still singing, thirty or forty more
followed him. The fact was, that many of the peo-

ple had been eager to come, and that each was looking to the other to lead the way. The people were
calling out in their hearts, as they are always doing,
for a leader. I often wonder, in the midst of such
experiences, how far it is safe to go in constraining
people, and I have come to the conclusion that we
may legitimately go a long way farther than any
of us have yet gone. Our duty is to bring the people
to Christ, and to do so we must use every expedient.

The Tarrytown mission deeply stirred the little
town. All the stores, and even the saloons, were
closed one night, in order that those employed in
them might have an opportunity of attending the
meetings. I write in October, 1901, and only a few
weeks ago I met at Truro a lady who was converted
in this mission at Tarrytown.

My visit to Denver, Colorado, will live in my memory forever. It meant a journey of two thousand
miles across the continent, occupying three nights
and two days. American travelling is a luxury,
but you have to pay for it. The railway journey
over this great territory impressed me just as much
as did my voyage across the Atlantic, and I enjoyed
it vastly more, because I am a poor sailor. One
cannot take such a journey without being impressed
by the enormous and almost exhaustless possibilities of the country. It is easy to use the words
"exhaustless possibilities," but to realize it, to have
it, so to speak, burned into one's mind, one has only
to undertake a long journey in the States. Some
of the country was flat and dull, but other parts of

it were richly wooded. We passed through miles and miles of magnificent forests. Colorado is very high, and is often for months without rain, but it is irrigated from the Rockies, and so great is the natural fertility, that people say, "You tickle the earth, and it smiles into a harvest."

Forty years ago Denver was inhabited by Red Indians, and overrun by buffaloes and other wild animals. It has now a population of about two hundred thousand, with magnificent residences, stores, and churches, and is called the Queen City of the West. The town lies on a plateau five thousand feet above the sea-level. The air is dry, bracing, and wholesome. Mrs. Smith, who was suffering somewhat from bronchitis, was cured at once when we entered Denver. On the other hand, the air had such an effect on my voice that I could speak all right, but I could not sing. However, the people told me that they could not get good singers to visit Denver on account of this peculiarity of the air. It was very flattering to me to be told that I was suffering from the same disability as affected eminent sopranos, baritones, etc.

I owed my invitation to Denver to Mr. and Mrs. Thomas, English people from Torquay, who had settled in the Far West. During my stay in the town they were kindness itself to me. The mission was held in a church which had cost £50,000 to build, and which possessed an organ worth £6,000. The pastor was the Rev. Dr. McIntyre, and he was accustomed to address a congregation of two thousand.

I preached every night for a month to daily increasing crowds. Five hundred people knelt at the communion-rail as penitents, one of whom was a Chinaman. Only the other day he sent me his photograph and a five-dollar bill as a thank-offering for the blessing he had received from the gipsy preacher. The church at Denver was very generous to me, more generous than any other church in America. Our travelling expenses, amounting to £50, were paid for us, and our services during the month were handsomely recognized. If one serves the American churches well, they treat you well. I have been five times to America, and I have never once made a fixed arrangement with regard to the financial side of my missions. I have trusted entirely to the generosity of those for whom I have worked, and only in one instance have I been disappointed.

The sheriff of Denver sat near the platform at one of the services. He pointed out to me a young man who had risen to ask for prayer, but whom I had not seen. "Get that man out while he feels like it!" he said. Of course, I took that to be the act of a Christian man. The morning after, I called on the sheriff and began to talk with him about the man. There was another man in the room who had been at the meeting and had sat next to the sheriff. Presently I observed that they were exchanging significant glances, and I asked what it meant.

"Oh," said the sheriff, "you are talking to me as if I were a Christian man, and I am not."

"I am amazed," I said. "Did you not the other

night urge me to get hold of a man who seemed anxious to come out. If you are not a Christian, why
did you do that?"

He answered thus: "When I was a boy I attended
some revival meetings in our town. My father was
a Methodist local preacher for thirty years. During
the service my boyish heart was moved, and I wanted
so much to be a Christian. I left my father's pew
and began to walk to the communion-rail. He saw
me on the way and came to meet me.

"'What do you want, my son?'

"'I am going to the Communion-rail to seek religion.'

"'Wait till you get home and I will talk to you
about it.'

"My young desire was crushed. Obedient to my
father I went back to my seat. When we reached
home he talked to me and prayed with me, but I did
not get religion, and I have not got it yet. It has
been my firm conviction that if I had been allowed
to go to the altar that night I should not only have
found Christ as my Saviour, but I should have been
in the ministry. And so, whenever I have seen a
man or a woman, a boy or a girl, showing a desire
to seek God I have given all the encouragement I
could."

Mr. Andrew C. Fields was my host at Dobbs Ferry,
where I conducted a short mission. At one of the
services, as I was telling the story of Zaccheus, and
had got to the words, "Zaccheus, come down," Mr.
Fields, who sat on a camp-stool at the back of the

church, collapsed on the ground in a heap.   In that
position he remained until the end of the discourse.
At Dobbs Ferry I had the weird experience of hearing my own voice through the phonograph.   I do
not want to hear it again.   It gives me an uncomfortable feeling—that years after my body is mould-
ering in the grave my voice may be alive, speaking
through this dread instrument.   Mr. Fields took
me to Albany, the capital of New York State, where
I was received by the Governor.   I was introduced
to the legislative assembly of the State, and was requested by the president to open the session with
prayer.   I expect I shall have a long time to wait
before a similar invitation is extended to me from
Westminster.

CHAPTER XXIII

GLASGOW

I CONDUCTED a great mission campaign in Glasgow from September, 1893, to the end of January, 1894. The mission was arranged by a committee of twelve free church ministers, and the work was carried on in almost as many churches. The campaign was interrupted for a short time by the Christmas holidays, and by a short vacation that I took. During this visit to Glasgow I met the late Professor Henry Drummond, who was very kind to me. When he and I first conversed together I had been working for seven weeks in seven churches, and I told him in reply to a question, that I had not given the same address twice. This statement seemed to impress him greatly. He asked me some questions about my life, and how I prepared my discourses. I was attracted at once by the sweetness of his spirit and the graciousness of his manner and disposition. Henry Drummond at once appealed to the best in you. I have met many great ministers and preachers in my life, but never one in whose company I felt more at ease than Henry Drummond's. There was no subduing awe about him. One would laugh at oneself for being afraid of him, yet he conveyed to one's mind an unmistakable impression of greatness.

The late Dr. Bruce attended my mission services, and took part in one of them. I was told that never had he done such a thing before. Dr. Bruce was well-known for his frankness of speech, and, addressing his students, he described the inquiry-room work as tomfoolery. "But," said he, "you must all go and hear the gipsy. That man preaches the gospel." Perhaps the most memorable part of my campaign was that in the Free College Church, of which Dr. George Reith was the pastor. Dr. Reith wrote an account of the mission for his church magazine. He said: "We have seen nothing like it since the visit of Messrs. Moody and Sankey in 1874. The speaking was remarkable. We have seldom, if ever, listened to a long series of addresses of the kind so admirable in every respect; effective, pointed, and free from sensational appeals. . . . Our friend, Gipsy Smith, has left memories of a singularly pleasant kind, and what is of more importance, his presentation of the gospel of our Lord will not soon be forgotten by those who heard it." People of all kinds attended the services—old, young, and middle-aged—the fashionable inhabitant of the West-end, the middle-class citizen, the artisan, the domestic servant, the school-boy, school-girl, and soldier. A member of Dr. Reith's congregation wrote in the magazine that " the gipsy's illustrations are usually well chosen and apposite. One evening we observed a fashionable young lady sitting perfectly unmoved through the service, until a touching little story at the close did its work—unlocked at least a spring of emotion. . . . Judicious management of the inquiry-room is admittedly one of the most difficult and delicate departments of evangelistic work, but we are sure no one who remained to confer with Gipsy Smith would ever regret having done so."

It took a long time to break down the caution and reserve of the Scotch character, but once it was broken down it broke down completely. Three thousand people passed through the inquiry-room. A large proportion of these were men. Some of them, indeed, were remarkable triumphs of God's grace. The history of the conversion of some of these men was curious. At first they would be merely interested in the services. Then they would be impressed, and perhaps convicted of sin, and so they were led to follow me from church to church, until, in some cases, they had been listening to me for quite seven weeks before they fully resolved to give their lives to God. At one service, and that the most fruitful, there was no sermon, because the people began to go into the inquiry-room immediately after the hymn. I have no doubt that many of them had already made up their minds, and really came to the meeting with the intention of taking their stand publicly. We spent that whole evening in simply saying to the people, "Come, come!" I think that God taught us a great lesson that night. We are so apt to think that this must be done, and that that must be done, and that a certain fixed course of procedure must be followed, or else we

must not look for results. Too often I fear our
rules and regulations and orders of service simply
intrude between men's souls and their God. We
all need to be taught when to stand aside.

The figures do not indicate with anything like
completeness the total results. When the ministers
of the city came to visit the individual inquirers,
they often found that in the same house there were
three or four other persons who had been brought
to God during the mission. When a Scotsman is
once set on fire, he blazes away at white heat. And
so it came about that among the best workers during
the closing week of the mission were the converts
of the early weeks. I have never met people in my
life who could sing Sankey's hymns better than the
folks of Edinburgh and Glasgow.

The farewell meeting of the mission was held in
the City Hall, one of the largest public buildings in
Glasgow. It was crammed to suffocation. The
North British Daily Mail gave a good account of
the services, heading its article, " A Glasgow Pentecost." The platform was crowded with Glasgow
ministers, many of whom made very cordial speeches
of thanksgiving and congratulation. The Rev.
David Low said that he had seen nothing approaching the mission since 1873, when Mr. Moody first
came to this country. I was greatly cheered by the
statement of my friend, Rev. J. J. Mackay, now of
Hull, that never had he a worker more delightful
to co-operate with than Mr. Gipsy Smith. He was
as simple and natural as a gipsy boy. My heart

was full of gratitude to God for the great things He had done for us in Glasgow, and to my warm-hearted Scotch friends for their exceeding great kindness. I think it was that night that I enjoyed a little rub at them for their comical and absurd attitude—for so it seemed to me—towards instrumental music. They would not let me have an instrument at the morning service nor at the afternoon service, but I might have one for the evening service. The idea was, I believe, that the morning and afternoon services were attended by staid, sober, decorous Presbyterians, who regarded instrumental music as a desecration of the regular services in the sanctuary. The evening services in Scotland are always more of an evangelistic character, and are intended more particularly to reach the outsiders and the non-church-goers. I suppose it was thought that instrumental music would please these people, and would not offend their less sensitive, less decorous consciences. Since 1894, however, things have greatly changed, even in Scotland, and most of the Presbyterian Churches, I am told, have now organs or harmoniums. I do not believe for a moment that the result has been a diminution in the solidity and gravity of the Scotch character.

CHAPTER XXIV

AUSTRALIA

DURING the last weeks of my stay in Glasgow, my friend, Mr. J. L. Byrom, J.P., brother of Mr. B. F. Byrom, suggested that I should take a tour round the world, spending most of the time in Australia, and coming back by way of America. He most generously bought my ticket for the whole journey, a valuable gift. Accordingly I set sail from Tilbury Docks on board the P. and O. liner, *Rome*, in April, 1894. We sailed *viâ* the Suez Canal, and landed at Adelaide on May 22d. We were five weeks on the sea, and a more dreary, profitless five weeks I do not think I have ever spent in my life. I was heartily glad to get on shore again. I am a bad sailor, and I was infinitely tired of the sea. Besides, the people on board were the most godless set of beings that I have ever mingled with. They spent most of their time in drinking and gambling, and all the forms of worldliness that they could devise. I have seen them make a pool on Sunday morning on the running of the ship, and then go in to prayers.

The voyage was marked by two incidents which still remain in my memory. Some of us went ashore at Port Said. This town is the most desperately wicked place on earth, and we were warned by the captain that we must go about in groups. It was not safe for any one of us to go alone. The place is simply infested with pestering vendors of all sorts of trifles. They knew the names of a few eminent English people, and we were addressed as Mr. Gladstone or Lord Salisbury, or Lord Rosebery, or by the name of some other English notable. The vendor who pursued me called me Mr. Gladstone. His attentions were unlimited. He followed me up and down I do not know how many streets, pressing me to buy some cigarette holders. I told him that I did not smoke, but that had no effect on him, because he did not seem to understand me. Then I acted out my dislike of smoking. I feigned to be putting a cigarette in my mouth, and then taking it out and throwing it away with an expression of disgust. At last it dawned upon the Arab what I had been trying to say, "Ah, oh, eh, umph! You a tottle-ottler! I spend all my speak on you for nothing!" He walked away, looking at me with infinite scorn, but I felt much relieved.

We were diverted at Aden by the feats of the small diving boys. The passengers amused themselves by throwing pieces of money into the water, and seeing the boys dive for them. A coin does not take a straight course to the bottom. Its pathway is rather a wriggling one, and the art of the boys is to get hold of the money while it is still on its course to the bed of the ocean. They are exceedingly smart little fellows. One of them clambered up the side of the ship like a monkey, and taking ten three-penny pieces out of the right side of his mouth, held them up, saying, "Big money for that, please!" He meant: "Give me half a crown for it." When he was given his half-crown he took ten more three-penny pieces from the left side of his mouth and asked for another half-crown. The person who had obliged him before could not do so again, and so I, who was standing by, was asked to accommodate him. I took six half-crowns out of my right pocket, and before I had brought my left hand to the right, he had whisked off four of them, and dived again into the sea. His smartness was much admired, and I was greatly chaffed at being so cleverly done. "You are a fine gipsy, you are!" said the people.

The Sunday before we landed, while I was dressing for dinner in my state-room, there was a knock at my door. A deputation of ladies came to request me to give a little lecture to the passengers that evening. I knew they did not desire to hear the gospel. I knew they had been rude to the good old bishop on board the ship, who had lovingly and tenderly remonstrated with them on their gambling. "It does grieve me," he said, "to see gentle girls gambling like old men." They had actually that morning raffled tickets by auction round the old bishop's chair. The fact is that they were somewhat tickled at having a gipsy travelling with them, first class. They were curious to know all about me, and I had taken care not to satisfy their inquisitiveness. Questions were often put to me with the intention of drawing me on. But a gipsy is usually a shrewd fellow, and I was not to be caught. This had annoyed them, and suggested to them the device of getting me to deliver a lecture to them. Accordingly I graciously declined the invitation, adding: "Most of you are going to Adelaide, Sydney, Melbourne, or other of the large towns of Australia. Now I shall be preaching in these towns, and my meetings will be advertised. If you will come and hear me I shall be very pleased." They went away feeling sore and balked. But the incident greatly raised my reputation, even among those who had been maliciously trying to draw me.

My fellow-passengers were mostly rich people, but some of them were neither courteous nor kind. I was amused one day by the remark of an insolent young fellow. "I suppose, Mr. Smith," he said, "the society on board is very different from what you are accustomed to?" I answered, "If you mean that it is inferior, it *is* different." The supercilious youth said no more to me. On another occasion, when we were having some little innocent sports on deck, a general and myself were elected as judges. Two young men, who were competing in an obstacle race, were disqualified before they started—which meant that the race must be re-run. I told them they had disqualified themselves, but they persisted in running. When the contest was over I declared it was no race. A captain in the army, who consisted mostly of legs, and who was a friend of one of the competitors, said, "Who are you, you little

under-sized piece of humanity?" "Captain," I said,
"my brains are not in my legs." From that moment
the gallant captain treated me with the utmost respect.

My arrival in Adelaide was quite unheralded. My
coming had not been trumpeted abroad, and my
sole human equipment consisted of my letters of
introduction from Dr. McLaren, of Manchester, and
other free church leaders. Dr. McLaren had been
particularly kind to me in connection with this visit.
He called me to his house before I left, and spoke
to me about the various places I should visit. When
I arrived in Adelaide the Methodist General Conference was in session, and I at once placed my letters
of introduction before the secretary. He received
me rather coldly, and, indeed, my reception by the
assembly was anything but hearty and encouraging.
Thomas Cook, the well-known Wesleyan evangelist,
after conducting a month's mission at Pirie Street
Church, Adelaide, had left for the interior of the
colony. I had made up my mind to preach in Adelaide, the first city of Australia I touched, and I
naturally wanted a mission in a Methodist Church.
The Methodist ministers were not at all anxious to
have me. "Why did you not tell us you were coming?" "Why did not your pastor write to inform
us of your visit to the colonies?" I told them that
personally I disliked long preliminary booming,
that I desired to begin quietly, to stand on my own
merits, and that, besides, my trip to the colony was
as much for rest and education as for work. I first
approached the superintendent minister of Pirie

Street Church, and suggested that I should hold a
mission there. My idea was that that would help
those who had declared for Christ during the mission
that Mr. Cook had just conducted. No, they would
not have that at all. Then Mr. Cook had planned
to take a mission in Archer Street Church, and had
not been able to fulfil his engagement. I saw Mr.
Lloyd, the minister, and Mr. Drew, a leading layman,
and I suggested that I should hold a mission there.
They both said that it would never do. The disappointment that the people had suffered when Mr.
Cook failed them would make it useless for me to
try to take his place. I said, "If I am not afraid to
face this disappointment, I think you ought to give
me a chance." I suggested that they should telegraph to Mr. Cook and see what he said. "Mind
you, I am no fraud, no adventurer. I shall abide
by Mr. Cook's answer." But they were not willing
to do this. It was suggested that I should go on to
Melbourne to the Forward Movement and conduct
a mission there. My Adelaide friends were good
enough to say that if that mission was successful
they would invite me to their town. I said, "No,
I am going to preach in Adelaide if I preach in the
street. If my own Methodist Church won't take
me in, there are other churches that will." When
I said this I was not speaking without my book,
because I knew that Franklin Street Bible Christian
Church, of which Chief-Justice Way was a member,
was open to me. I had met Chief-Justice Way in
America. He knew me and my work. When I told

my Wesleyan Methodist friends that this church was open to me they said, "Well, suppose you go there for a mission, and if we want you afterwards, will you come to us?" "Yes," I said, "I will." I was somewhat discouraged by this rather freezing reception, but I did not get angry. I felt confident that God had sent me to Australia, and that presently all would be well.

I called on the minister of Franklin Street Bible Christian Church, and told him that I knew Gipsy Smith was in the colony, that he was willing to conduct a ten days' mission for the Bible Christians, and that he was prepared to start work on Sunday. It was now Thursday. The minister asked me what authority I had to speak for Gipsy Smith, and I replied by saying, "Look into my face and see if you can discover any sign of dishonesty." And he took my word for it, and without any evidence produced, he accepted my statements. We went off together to see the editors of the two newspapers in the city to arrange for notices of the mission. When we were discussing the matter I took my letters of introduction from my pocket, and, handing them to the editor, said, "Perhaps these may be of some use to you." The minister looked at me gaspingly, and said, "Are *you* Gipsy Smith?" I confessed that I was, whereupon the old man embraced me tenderly.

Franklin Street Church was seated for about seven hundred or eight hundred people, and it was crowded every night during the ten days of the mission. Sixty or seventy boys from the Way College, who all attend the church, passed through the inquiry-rooms. The great things that were being done in Franklin Street were soon known all over the city, and when the ten days were up Archer Street Church, the congregation that Mr. Cook had disappointed, was ready for me. My feet had been established on a rock in Adelaide. I preached for six weeks in the city to ever-increasing congregations. If my Wesleyan Methodist brethren had received me with warmth and cordiality, I should perhaps have stayed only a fortnight in the town, but I stayed six weeks, because I was determined before I left to make myself thoroughly felt.

During my stay in Adelaide I visited the prison and preached to the convicts, addressing them as I should have addressed an ordinary congregation. I sang to them:

> " There's a hand held out in pity,
> There's a hand held out in love,
> It will pilot to the city,
> To our Father's house above.
> There's a hand held out to you,
> There's a hand held out to me."

Some of the poor fellows wept bitterly. I always feel very tenderly towards convicts. When I look at one, I say to myself, like the old Puritan, " There am I, but for the grace of God." Besides, I always reflect that there are a great many persons outside prisons who are worse than those inside.

Mr. Drew, a leading layman of Archer Street Church whom I have already referred to, was a director of the Children's Hospital, and persuaded me to tell the story of my life on behalf of the institution. Chief-Justice Way presided over an assembly which crowded the Town Hall, the largest building in the city. All the tickets were sold several days before the meeting. After deducting all expenses, about £100 was handed over to the hospital. The authorities, in gratitude, decided that for five years two of the little cots should bear the name "Gipsy Smith's Cot." I was very glad to be of some help to the little sufferers as well as to the older sinners.

Chief-Justice Way did all he could to make my visit to the town, of which he is a distinguished ornament, bright and pleasant. The Chief-Justice is one of the most able men on the Australian continent, and one of the most esteemed. His opinions always command the greatest attention and respect. Before I left Adelaide he invited me to a farewell breakfast, but, unfortunately, I could not attend. I took the liberty of sending him my photograph, and in return he sent me the following letter:

" CHIEF-JUSTICE'S CHAMBERS, ADELAIDE,
" *June*, 29, 1894.

" MY DEAR MR. GIPSY SMITH,—Thanks for the likeness. It is excellent. I was sorry you could not come to breakfast, but I know how busy you must be preparing for your departure.

" Pray accept the enclosures—with my kind regards and best wishes for your happiness and usefulness.

" Believe me,
" Yours faithfully,
" S. J. WAY."

When the Chief-Justice came to England in the Diamond Jubilee year I had some further communication with him. He told me that my work in Australia was not, and never would be, forgotten.

The last meeting I attended in Adelaide was the service which Mr. Cook returned to hold as his farewell to the colony. Pirie Street Church was packed to the doors, and a more enthusiastic service could hardly be conceived. Many letters and telegrams were sent from places where Mr. Cook had held missions. Next morning, Mr. Cook and I left Adelaide by the same train, he for Melbourne and I for Ballarat. The railway station was crowded with people who had come to say good-by to us.

By this time news had reached me from England that my wife was very seriously ill. In consequence I had to shorten my visit considerably, and my plans were altogether altered. I could not get a boat for three weeks yet, and I spent this agonizing period in work at Ballarat, Melbourne, and Sydney. I joined Mr. Cook in the midst of his wonderful mission at Melbourne in connection with the Forward Movement. I had written to him telling him that my wife was seriously ill, that my plans were changed, that I was on my way to Sydney, and that I should like to spend a Sunday with him. He replied by telegraph, asking me if I would take his service on Sunday morning, and I gladly consented. It was the closing Sunday of his mission. Mr. Cook, in his interesting book, *Days of God's Right Hand,* quotes the following account of that wonderful day's services from a Melbourne paper:

"Gipsy Smith took the morning service to relieve Mr. Cook. The building was quite full, an event which has not happened for many a long year at a morning service. The whole sermon bristled with tersely-put truth, straight home-thrusts and earnest appeals, varied in a most natural and easy manner by irresistible flashes of humor and the tenderest pathos. The description of the punishment of his two boys for playing truant, the callousness of the elder, and the contrition, repentance, and forgiveness of the younger, how he reassured himself again and again of the fact of his forgiveness, and then abandoned himself to the enjoyment of the restored favor of his father, brought tears to almost every listener. After the sermon, Mr. Smith sang 'Throw Out the Life-line.' He has a beautiful voice, which, moderated and controlled by the heart-feeling be-hind it, finds a response in the hearts of those who listen which words would fail to elicit. About two hundred stood for consecration at the close of this service.

"The afternoon meeting was for men only; and a mag-nificent sight it was, towards three o'clock, to see the great building packed more than full with men, many standing for want of a possible chance to sit down. Gipsy Smith sang 'The Saviour is my All in All'; and then 'Onward, Christian Soldiers,' from that audience, was something to remember. The Rev. Thomas Cook gave the address, a straight-out piece of personal dealing from end to end. At the conclusion, Mr. Smith sang, 'Can a Boy Forget His Mother's Prayers?' and eighteen sought and found the Saviour.

"At the evening service the church was filled to over-flowing in every available spot long before the time of the meeting; so the Conference Hall was again opened, and soon also crowded out; no more could be packed in either. Rev. J. W. Tuckfield opened the Conference Hall meeting while Gipsy Smith sang in the church. As soon as this was over he took charge of the meeting in the hall, and sang the same piece again: 'Come, the Dear Master is Calling.' 'God has given every one of you,' he said, 'a square chance for heaven. He has called you by a thousand loving entreaties, by bereavement, by special invitations, such as these meetings, and now He calls you by the lips of a poor gipsy boy, who, although he never went to school, has crossed the Jordan and given himself to Christ.' At the close of this service, sixteen found the Saviour."

So great was the impression made upon the people by these services that they besought me to conduct more services for them. I told them that I was in Mr. Cook's hands. It was his mission. He must direct. I would only do just what he wished. The outcome of my friends' importunity was an arrangement that I should conduct noonday services on Monday, Tuesday, and Wednesday. On each of these three days I had a congregation of over two thousand people, a large majority of whom were men—lawyers, merchants, and workmen. The crowning gathering was on the Thursday night, when I told the people the story of my life. The meeting was announced to commence at 7.30, but by four o'clock the place was crowded, and there were two or three times as many people outside. Wherever a window could be reached from the ground that window was broken, and whatever could be found to stand upon was seized and utilized. Thirty fainting people were carried into the manse, next door to the church. Mr. Edgar, the minister, told me, when on a visit to Manchester, that he had paid over £7 for broken glass! Had I been on the spot I should have begun my lecture as soon as the place was full, but not anticipating this extraordinary enthusiasm, I had gone into the country to spend the day with some friends, arranging to return in time for my lecture. The crowd bore the long wait of three-and-a-half hours with great patience and good-humor, but it was deemed advisable to put up speaker after speaker to give addresses in order that the audience might be kept orderly and interested.

I spent the last week in Australia at Sydney, in the Centenary Hall, the head-quarters of the Forward Movement. The hall seated two thousand five hundred people, and was the largest building I preached in in the colony; but it was far too small for the crowds who came to the services. A great burden of sadness was bearing me down, but God was my strength and my salvation, and I preached the gospel as well and as faithfully as I could. Another cablegram reached me at Sydney: "Wife very seriously ill. Come home at once." I sailed on the 20th of June. Two thousand people came down to the boat to see me off, and sang, "God be with you till we meet again." I had been barely three months in Australia.

My impression of Australia was that there were

untold possibilities for Christian work in the country.
Many of the people are from England—from home,
as they say—and the moment you begin to talk to
them about the old country they are homesick. Their
hearts become tender and receptive. There are
not a few people in Australia who have been shipped
there by their friends in England, so that they may
redeem their careers and stand erect on their feet
again. Such people gain from their new life not
only new opportunities, but fresh susceptibility to
moral and religious influences. They make the
material among which good evangelistic work can
be done. They come to your meetings, and because
you are from home, you make a particular appeal
to them. You are a link between them and the
people they have left behind, and they think you
are speaking to them in the name of their friends in
the old country. It seemed to me easy to get the
Australians to attend evangelistic services. It fell
that my visit immediately followed their great financial collapse, and it may be that their distress and
difficulties made their hearts more hungry for the
gospel.

It came to my knowledge later that three days
after I left Sydney it was announced in a Ballarat
paper that my wife was dead. Archer Street Church,
Adelaide, in which I had conducted a mission, held
a memorial service for her. The Methodist papers
in Australia copied the paragraph from the Ballarat
paper, and in due course it found its way into the
Methodist Recorder. Rev. S. F. Collier at once wrote

to the editor contradicting the statement. By this time my wife was much better, but a lie once set travelling is very difficult to overtake. The news of my wife's death spread so wide and so fast, that I have in my home at Manchester a whole drawer-full of letters of sympathy and condolence. I never read them, but Mrs. Smith did and replied to them all. There are people to this day who think I am a widower. Not so long ago I conducted a mission at Chatham where, as my readers will remember, I labored in the early days of the Christian Mission. I called at the house of a lady who had been very friendly with my wife and myself in those far-off days, and I told her that I was just going to the station to meet my wife, who was coming from Manchester, and that I should bring her to tea. "All right," said the lady, in cold, indifferent tones, "do as you like." I could not make it out. I wondered whether an estrangement had arisen between my wife and her Chatham friend. Later in the day I again called at this house, making the same statement. "Very well. Do as you like. I do not care." I went to the station and brought my wife to this house. When the two met, the Chatham lady lifted her hands in amazement and exclaimed, "Good heavens! I thought you were dead!"

Of course, I knew nothing of the rumor concerning my wife's death. Travelling *viâ* the Fiji Islands I reached British Columbia, and thence proceeded by way of Montreal to New York. A cable from home was awaiting me, saying that my wife was

better, and that there was no need to hurry to England if work demanded my stay in America. Accordingly I paid a short visit to Ocean Grove, and
conducted a month's mission in Indianapolis. A
local paper said: "No adequate idea of the sermons
of Mr. Smith can be conveyed by literal reports of
his words, which are apt in forcefulness, illustration,
and analogy, for he preaches with greater force and
effectiveness by gesture, manners, and intonation of
voice." Here I met ex-President Harrison in his
own home. I found him a courteous, high-toned
Christian gentleman, deeply interested in all work
for the salvation of men and of the nation. On
returning to the vestry at the close of one of the services, there was an old retired minister, with white,
flowing locks and a grave, dignified appearance,
waiting for me. As I sat down in the chair, he put
his hands on my head. I thought he was going to
give me a father's blessing. But to my surprise he
began to run his fingers through my thick hair and
to feel about for bumps.

"Are you a phrenologist?" I said.

"No, not quite; but I am trying to discover the
secret of your success."

"Well, sir, you are feeling too high. You must
come down here," placing my hand upon my heart.

At the Sunday morning service, immediately in
front of me sat Dr. Clyne, a throat specialist, who
was related by marriage to the pastor of the church.
The doctor could see that I was having trouble with
my throat, and he sent a message to me through the

pastor saying that he wanted to see me at his office
next morning.   The doctor in fifteen minutes gave
me an amazing amount of information about my
throat.   He told me that I had pockets in the tonsils,
which were in a chronic state of inflammation, and
that these pockets needed to be drained out.   I was
to come to him when the mission was over, and he
would set the matter right.   In the mean time he
attended almost every service of the mission.   On
the morning after the mission ended he performed
an operation on the tonsils by means of an electric
battery, deadening the pain with cocaine.   The
only unpleasant sensation was the smell of the singe-
ing produced by the electricity.   I asked him for his
bill, for I would gladly have paid whatever he had
asked, provided, of course, it had been within my
means.   He was a great surgeon, and his fees were
heavy.   In reply to my question he looked at me
quietly for a moment, and said, in deeply moved tones :
" Sir, two of my boys have been converted during
your mission.   Will you give me your bill for that?
Can I ever pay you for bringing those boys to Christ?
How much is that going to be worth to me?   I cannot preach, but if I can help you to preach with ease
and comfort to yourself, I have a share in your business."   Presently the boys came in.   The father
had given each of them a new Bible, and the lads
asked me if I would inscribe their names in them.

I reached home on November 23d.   My tour
round the globe had occupied eight months.

CHAPTER XXV

MY FATHER AND HIS TWO BROTHERS

LET me interrupt my personal narrative for a little to tell my readers some things about my father and his two remarkable brothers that will, I think, interest them.

My father, Cornelius Smith, though in his seventieth year, is still hale and hearty. He lives at Cambridge, and, even in the fulness of his years, spends most of his time in religious work. There are few evangelists better known in the Eastern counties. When he goes to a place that he has not visited before, he always begins his first discourse by saying: "I want you people to know that I am not my son, I am his father."

I wrote my father's first love-letter. This is how it came about. My readers will remember that my mother died when I was very young. My father married again, some time after his conversion, but his wife died in less than a year. When, twenty-two years ago, the last of his daughters (now Mrs. Ball) was about to get married and to leave him all alone in his tent, my father came to me in very disconsolate mood, saying:

"What shall I do now?"

"Will you live with me if I get married?" I said.

" No, I'd rather not; I've always had a little corner of my own."

"Well, why don't you get married yourself?" My father was forty-seven at this time, and he looked younger.

"Oh, come now, whom could I marry?"

"Well, I think I know a lady who would have you."

' Who?"

' Mrs. Sayer."

My father looked both surprised and delighted.

"How do you know that?" he asked.

"Well, when I was working at the Christian Mission, Whitechapel, and you used to come to see me, Mrs. Sayer often came too, and she was forever hanging about me, for you were always in my neighborhood. One day I said to her, ' Do you want any skewers or clothes-pegs to-day, lady?' She was taken aback, seemed to guess what I meant, and smacked me in the face.

"Well," said my father, " it is strange that I have been thinking about Mrs. Sayer too. It is some years since first I met her, and I've seen her only very occasionally since, but she has never been out of my mind."

"Shall I write to her then for you?"

"Yes, I think you had better."

My father outlined what he desired me to say in proposing to Mrs. Sayer, and after I had finished the letter I read it to him. He interrupted me several times, remarking, " Well, I did not tell you to say that, did I?" and I replied, " But that is what you meant, is it not?" Soon after Mrs. Sayer, who at that time was a captain in the Salvation Army, and had been previously employed by Lord Shaftesbury as a Bible-woman in the East End, and my father were married. It has been one of the chief joys of my life that I had something to do with arranging this marriage, for it has been a most happy union. In the year of this marriage my father's brother, Woodlock, died, and two years later the other brother, Bartholomew, died. "The Lord knew," my father has said, "when he took away my dear brothers that I should feel their loss and feel unfit to go to meetings alone; so my wife was given to me. And the Lord is making us a great blessing. Our time is fully spent in His work, and wherever we go souls are saved and saints are blessed."

When my father was converted he did not know A from B. But by dint of much hard battling, at a time of life, too, when it is difficult to learn anything, he managed to read the New Testament, and I doubt whether anybody knows that portion of Scripture better than my father does. I do not know any preacher who can in a brief address weave in so many quotations from the New Testament, and weave them in so skilfully, so intelligently, and in so deeply interesting a manner. My father has an alert mind, and some of the illustrations in his addresses are quaint. During my mission at the Metropolitan Tabernacle he spoke to the people briefly. His theme was "Christ in us and we in Christ," and he said, ' Some people may think that that is impossible; but it is not. The other day I was walking by the seaside at Cromer, and I picked up a bottle with a cork in it. I filled the bottle with the salt water, and, driving in the cork, I threw the bottle out into the sea as far as my right arm could send it. Turning to my wife, I said, ' Look, the sea is in the bottle and the bottle is in the sea. So if we are Christ's, we are in Him and He is in us.' "

Before my conversion, while I was under deep conviction of sin, I used to pray, "O God, make me a good boy; I want to be a good boy; make me feel I am saved." In my young foolishness of heart I was keen on *feeling*. My father had heard me pray, and had tried to meet my difficulty, but without success. However, it chanced that one afternoon we were invited to drink tea at the house of a friend in a village where the three brothers were holding a mission. Attached to the house was a beautiful large garden, containing many heavily laden cherry-trees. My father was as merry and whole-hearted as a boy, and not ashamed of liking cherries, and we all went out to pick the fruit. Presently I was amazed to observe my father gazing up steadfastly at the cherries and saying, in a loud, urgent voice, as he kept the inside pocket of his coat wide open, "Cherries, come down and fill my pocket! Come down, I say. I want you." I watched his antics for a moment or two, not knowing what to make of this aberration. At length I said:

"Daddy, it's no use telling the cherries to come

down and fill your pocket. You must pluck them off the tree."

'My son," said my father, in pleased and earnest tones, "that is what I want you to understand. You are making the mistake that I was making just now. God has offered you a great gift. You know what it is, and you know that you want it. But you will not reach forth your hand to take it."

My father was frequently engaged by a gentleman in Norwich, Mr. George Chamberlain, to do evangelistic work in the vicinity. At the time of this story there was an exhibition of machinery in connection with the agricultural show then being held in the old city. Mr. Chamberlain gave my father a ticket of admission to it, saying, "Go, Cornelius, see what there is to be seen; it will interest you. I'm coming down myself very soon." When Mr. Chamberlain reached the ground he found my father standing on a machine, with a great crowd, to whom he was preaching the gospel, gathered round him. He gazed upon the spectacle with delight and astonishment. When my father came down from this pulpit, Mr. Chamberlain said to him:

"Well, Cornelius, what led you to address the people — without any previous arrangement, too, and without consulting the officials? I sent you here to examine the exhibits."

"That's all right," said my father; "but the fact is I looked round at all the latest inventions, and I did not see one that even claimed to take away the guilt and the power of sin from men's hearts. I knew of something that could do this, and I thought these people should be told about it. There were such a lot of them, too, that I thought it was a very good opportunity."

My father was on one occasion preaching in the open air to a great crowd at Leytonstone. A coster passing by in his donkey-cart shouted out: "Go it, old party; you'll get 'arf a crown for that job!" Father stopped his address for a moment, looked at the coster, and said, quietly, "No, young man, you are wrong. My Master never gives half-crowns away. He gives whole ones. 'Be thou faithful unto death, and I will give thee a crown of life.'" The coster and his "moke" passed on.

I have said before that the three gipsy brothers, after their conversion, always travelled the country together. Wherever they went they never lost an opportunity of preaching. And their preaching was very effective, for the people, knowing them well, contrasted their former manner of life—lying, drinking, pilfering, swearing—with the sweet and clean life they now led, and saw that the three big, godless gipsy men had been with Jesus. They beheld a new creation. When they came to a village the three big men—my father was six feet, broad in proportion, and he was the smallest of them—accompanied by their children, took their stand in the most public place they could find and began their service. The country folk for miles around used to come in to attend the meetings of the three converted gipsy brothers. Each of them had his special

gift and special line of thought.   Uncle Woodlock,
who always spoke first, had taught himself to read,
and of the three was the deepest theologian—if I
may use so pretentious a word of a poor gipsy man.
He was very strong and clear on the utter ruin of
the heart by the fall, and on redemption by the blood
of Christ, our substitute.   Over the door of his cottage at Leytonstone he had printed the words, "When
I see the blood I will pass over."   It was very characteristic.

After Woodlock had made an end of speaking,
the three brothers sang a hymn, my father accom-
panying on his famous "hallelujah fiddle."   Uncle
Bartholomew never to the day of his death could
read, but his wife could spell out the words of the
New Testament, and in this way he learned by heart
text after text for his gospel addresses.   His method
was to repeat these texts, say a few words about
each, and conclude with an anecdote.   My father
came last.   It was his part to gather up and focus all
that had been said, and to make the application.
He had a wonderful power in the management of
these simple audiences, and often melted them into
tears by the artless pathos of his discourses.   But
the most powerful qualification these evangelists had
for their work was the undoubted and tremendous
change that had been wrought in their lives.   Their
sincerity and sweetness were so transparent.   It was
as clear as daylight that God had laid His hand upon
these men, and had renewed their hearts.

Until the marriage of which I have told in this

chapter, my father lived in his wagon and tent, and still went up and down the country, though not so much as he had done in his younger days. I told him that he could not ask Mrs. Sayer to come and live with him in a wagon. She had never been used to that. He must go into a house. I suggested that he should buy a bit of land, and build a cottage on it. "What!" he said, "put my hard-earned money into dirt!" However, he came round to my view. The three brothers each bought a strip of territory at Leytonstone and erected three wooden cottages. But they stood the cottages on wheels!

Uncle Woodlock was not so fortunate in his wife as the other two brothers. She was not a Christian woman, and she had no respect and no sympathy for religious work. When Woodlock came home from his meetings his wife would give him her opinion, at great length and with great volubility, concerning him and his preaching. The poor man would listen with bowed head and in perfect silence, and, when she had finished her harangue, he would say, "Now, my dear, we will have a verse," and he would begin to sing, "Must Jesus Bear the Cross Alone?" or, "I'm Not Ashamed to Own My Lord!" or, "My Jesus, I love Thee." Uncle Barthy's wife was a good, Christian woman, and is still on this side of Jordan, adorning the doctrine of the gospel. When I was conducting the simultaneous mission campaign at the Metropolitan Tabernacle she came to hear me. The building was crowded, and the policeman would not let her pass the door. "Oh, but I must get in," she said; "it's my nephew who is preaching here. I nursed him, and I'm going to hear him." And she was not baffled.

The brothers were not well up in etiquette, though in essentials they always behaved like the perfect gentlemen they were. They were drinking tea one afternoon at a well-to-do house. A lady asked Uncle Woodlock to pass her a tart. "Certainly, madam," said he, and lifting a tart with his fingers off the plate handed it to her. She accepted it with a gracious smile. When his mistake was afterwards pointed out to him, and he was told what he ought to have done, he took no offence, but he could not understand it at all. He kept on answering: "Why, she did not ask me for the plateful; she asked for only one!"

Woodlock and Bartholomew have now gone to be for ever with the Lord who redeemed them, and whom they loved with all the strength of their warm, simple, noble hearts.

Uncle Woodlock was the first to go home. The three brothers were together conducting a mission at Chingford in March, 1882. At the close, Woodlock was detained for a few minutes in earnest conversation with an anxious soul. My father and Bartholomew went on to take the train for Stratford, leaving Woodlock to make haste after them. Woodlock, in the darkness, ran with great force against a wooden post in the pathway. It was some time before he was discovered lying on the ground groaning in agony. To those who came to his help he

said, "I have got my death-blow; my work on earth
is done, but all is bright above; and I am going home."
His injuries were very severe, and though his suffering was great, he never once lost consciousness.
My father stayed by him all night, while Uncle
Barthy returned to Stratford to tell the families about
the accident. When morning dawned, Woodlock's
wife came to see him, and then he was removed to
his own little home in Leytonstone, where he breathed
his last. Within an hour of his departure he turned
to his weeping relatives, and said: "I am going to
heaven through the blood of the Lamb. Do you
love and serve Jesus? Tell the people wherever
you go about Him. Be faithful: speak to them
about the blood that cleanses." Then, gathering
himself up, he said: "What is this that steals upon
my frame? Is it death?" and quickly added:

> " 'If this be death, I soon shall be
> From every sin and sorrow free.
> I shall the King of Glory see.
>   All is well!' "

He had been ill for twenty-eight hours. He lies
buried in Leytonstone church-yard, awaiting the
resurrection morn. He was followed to his grave
by his sorrowing relatives and over fifty gipsies,
while four hundred friends lined the approach to
the church and burying-place. The parish church
had a very unusual congregation that day, for the
gipsy people pressed in with the others, and as the
vicar read the burial service, hearts were deeply

touched and tears freely flowed. At the grave, the
two surviving brothers spoke of the loved one they
had lost, and told the people of the grace of God
which had redeemed them and their brother, and
made them fit for the inheritance of the saints in
light. Woodlock was a hale man, only forty-eight
years of age.

Two years later Uncle Barthy followed his brother
Woodlock into the kingdom of glory. He died in
his own little home at Leytonstone, but most of the
days of his illness were spent in Mildmay Cottage
Hospital. All that human skill could devise was
done for him, but he gradually grew weaker, and
asked to be taken to his own home. A few hours
before he passed into the presence of God he called
his wife and children around him, and besought
each of them to meet him in heaven. In his last
moments he was heard to say, "There! I was almost
gone then—they had come for me!" When asked
who had come, he replied, "My Saviour." Turning
to his wife, he said: "You are clinging to me; you
will not let me go; and I am sure you do not want
me to stay here in all this pain. I must go home;
I cannot stay here. God will look after you. He
knows your trouble, and He will carry you through."
The poor woman was expecting a baby in a few
months. My father tried to comfort her, and to
teach her resignation to the will of God.

"Tell the Lord," he said, "that you desire His
will to be done."

She said, "Oh, it is so hard!"

" Yes," answered my father, " but the Lord is going to take Bartholomew to Himself. It will be better for you if you can bring yourself to submit with resignation to His will."

Those gathered round the bedside then knelt down. The dying saint sat up in bed with his hands clasped, looking at his wife, while she poured out her soul before the Lord and told Him her trouble. God gave her the victory. She rose from her knees exclaiming, "I can now say, 'Thy will be done!'" She gave her husband a farewell kiss. Immediately he clapped his hands for joy and said : "Now I can go, can't I? I am ready to be offered up. The time of my departure is at hand. Lord, let Thy servant depart in peace. Receive my spirit, for Jesus' sake!" And so Bartholomew's soul passed into the heavenly places. The whole bed-chamber was filled with glory. Uncle Barthy rests in Leytonstone church-yard beside his brother Woodlock. In death they are not divided.

It is strange, rather, that my father, the eldest of the three brothers, should live the longest. It is seventeen years since the death of Uncle Barthy. My father is like a tree planted by the rivers of water, still bringing forth fruit. When I go to see him I kneel at his feet, as I used to do when I was a boy, and say : "Daddy, give me your blessing. All that I am I owe, under God, to the beautiful life you lived in the old gipsy wagon." And with a radiant, heavenly smile on that noble old face, he answers, with tears of joy in his eyes, "God bless you, my son! I have never had but one wish for you, and that is that you should be good." Some time ago, when I was conducting a mission at Torquay, I talked to the people so much about my father that they invited him to conduct a mission among them. And then they wrote to me: "We love the son, but we think we love the father more." They had found that all that I had said about my father was true.

CHAPTER XXVI

LONDON, MANCHESTER, AND EDINBURGH

BEFORE setting out on my trip round the world I had made a promise to the Rev. Andrew Mearns, secretary of the London Congregational Union, that I would undertake three months' evangelistic work in the metropolis. Accordingly, on the 17th of December, Mr. B. F. Byrom, who was fixing my engagements at the time, accompanied me to London to settle the final arrangements with Mr. Mearns. When we entered the Memorial Hall on the morning of the 18th Mr. Mearns handed me a telegram. I opened it and read these words: "Mrs. Smith seriously ill. Come home at once." When I left my wife the night before she seemed to be in good health, busy making preparations for a happy Christmas with us all at home together. I returned to Manchester at once. She had been seized with dreadful hemorrhages, which, beginning at ten o'clock on the night of the 17th, had continued at intervals till eleven o'clock on the evening of the 18th. The doctors, on leaving me at three o'clock in the morning of the 19th, said that she was practically a corpse—that it was simply impossible for her to live. When they returned next morning and saw how greatly improved she was they said, "This is a resurrection." The prayers offered for her and for me by hundreds of Christians all over the country had been answered. Slowly but surely she regained her health, though it was five or six months before she was quite well again.

My work for Mr. Mearns in London called me away from my wife early in January. I am not skilled in the formation of diplomatic circumlocutions, and therefore I must say frankly that I do not look back upon this work in London with any real satisfaction. I was sent to several churches which were practically deserted. Indeed, my work was mostly among weak causes—in a few instances causes without a pastor or any organized band of workers. And most of the missions were only for a week. It took one quite a week to make oneself felt in these localities, and just when one was beginning to get a good hold of the people one had to leave and go elsewhere. Good was done, I am sure, and in every case before the week was finished we had crowded congregations. But it was surely unwise to send me to chapels which were without pastors, because there was no one to look after any converts that God gave us. In this campaign I worked at ten or eleven places. The right plan would have been the selection of six or seven of the strongest churches and a fortnight's mission in each. In a live church, with a capable minister and a competent band of workers, something great might have been accomplished. To send a missioner to some deserted, disorganized chapel, situated perhaps in a godless wilderness, and then expect valuable results in a week is like sending a man to gather apples in the Sahara desert.

In this three months' campaign there was a short break which I spent at Manchester. Dr. McLaren had taken the keenest interest in my trip round the world, and as soon as I returned home I went to see him. Immediately he said to me, "I want you to have a mission in my church. I cannot commit myself yet, for I have not consulted my office-bearers; but I do not want you to fix up any engagements for the week February 10th to 17th, 1895, until you hear from me." These words quite took my breath away. I was overwhelmed. I did not know what to say. The honor that Dr. McLaren proposed to do me was too great. There had never before been a mission in Union Chapel. When I could find utterance I stammered out: "Oh, Dr. McLaren, I can never conduct a mission in your church. I can never stand in your pulpit." "Nonsense!" said Dr. McLaren, in his characteristically emphatic and decisive manner. "You must. I won't listen to that sort of thing. Keep these dates clear until I consult my office-bearers." I felt I must give in. There was no withstanding Dr. McLaren. I knew him, trusted him, loved him. He had won my heart years ago, and he had allowed me to call him my friend. I knew that the invitation was given only after much prayer and thought. Dr. McLaren is not a man to settle anything hastily or precipitately. I feel it is impossible for me to make my readers understand how terrible was the responsibility this invitation imposed upon me. I was deeply exercised in my spirit on account of my unworthiness.

The formal invitation from Dr. McLaren and the deacons of Union Chapel reached me about the end of November. Never did a church enter with more thoroughness into the necessary preparatory work. The Rev. J. E. Roberts, B.A., B.D., the co-pastor, superintended the organizing arrangements with great skill, and toiled day and night for the success of the mission. He was ably supported by Mr. Alister McLaren, Dr. McLaren's son, and many other workers. Thousands of visits were made to the people. I was told that in three days a hundred ladies made over six thousand visits. I know that the workers called at our house three times during the week of the mission urging my wife and myself to attend. We faithfully promised to do so. Thousands of printed invitations to the services were issued, all of them signed by Dr. McLaren and Mr. Roberts, a fact which lent weight and power.

The mission opened on Sunday, February 10th. Dr. McLaren preached in the morning from Acts ix. 31, and at the conclusion of his discourse spoke thus:

"It has been to me a very sore trial and a very bitter pill that the condition of my health withdraws me almost entirely from active participation in this work, to which I have been looking forward with so much pleasure. I hope that instead of my withdrawal, which, as most of you know, is rendered imperative by medical advice, frightening anybody, it will rather, if I may appeal to your affection, make you all feel the more need for you to gather round my dear friend, Gipsy Smith, who is going to conduct these services. I have the fullest confidence in him and in his work, and the warmest anticipations of large spiritual blessings to flow from the services. I appeal especially to the members of my own church and congregation, that they will do what they can by their sympathy, their attendance, and above all by their earnest prayers, to make this coming week a week long to be remembered in the history of this church."

My testing-time came in the afternoon. I had had a sore conflict with the Evil One throughout the whole of the preceding week. The tempter whispered: "Your methods will never do for Union Chapel. Do you know that that is the most brainy and the most cultured congregation in England? These people have listened to the prince of preachers for many years. They have never had a mission such as you propose to conduct in their church. They do not understand it. Don't you try your methods there. They will not have them. If you insist on the methods that you adopt in other places the people will not come and listen to you. You will have the church to yourself." This struggle with Satan was very real. My heart and mind were sore distressed, but God gave me the victory. As I proceeded from the vestry into the church, I paused for a moment on the first step of the pulpit stairs and said to God: "Oh, my Lord, Thou hast given me all I am and all I have. Thou hast set Thine approval on my poor, weak methods. I place myself and my methods in Thy hands. In this church I will be true to what I believe Thou hast been pleased to use." Throughout this mission I adopted my ordinary style of discourse and of dealing with people, and I never heard one sound of disapproval. The whole church was with me.

People from all parts of Lancashire, who had for long been desirous of hearing me, but had suspected something sensational, thronged into Manchester to attend these meetings, for were they not in Dr. McLaren's church, and did not that mean that they must be safe? Many Church of England people, too, waited upon my ministry. In the inquiry-rooms ten or twelve Anglican churches were represented. Altogether six hundred people professed to give themselves to God.

The last Sunday was a crowning triumph. So great were the throngs that the roads were blocked, and even the trams were brought to a standstill. The conductors were shouting: "This way for Dr. McLaren and Gipsy Smith." Alister McLaren went out to pacify the people, who were becoming somewhat tumultuous. He lost his hat, and was himself unable to get into the church.

A remarkable scene took place at the closing service on Monday night. Turning to Mr. Roberts, the co-pastor, who sat beside me, I said: "I am going to close now." "Wait a minute," he said; "there are others who ought to come out." I asked the people to be seated, and then said: "I know some of you are saying something like this to yourselves, 'I owe all I am to Dr. McLaren—all that I possess of mental grasp and spiritual desire. He is my pastor. I have grown up under him. Is it quite fair to him that when I settle the most momentous question of my life I should do it at the invitation of a stranger? Is it loyal to my pastor?' I respect that feeling. I want you to be loyal to Dr. McLaren. But will you remember for one moment at whose invitation I am here? It was Dr. McLaren who brought me here. He was anxious about *you*. That was why he asked me to come and help him to beseech you in Christ's stead to be reconciled unto God. I do not think anything would gladden Dr. McLaren's heart more than to learn that in this mission, which he arranged for you, the desire of his heart had been accomplished. He is ill. You know it. Do you think that anything could be a greater joy and comfort to him than the receipt of a telegram saying that you had at last intelligently and honestly given yourself to Jesus Christ?" In less than five minutes fifty of the brightest and best young people in the congregation walked into the inquiry-room.

So ended, as far as I was concerned, one of the most remarkable missions of my life. I have always felt that this campaign in Dr. McLaren's church set the hall-mark upon me as an evangelist. I have needed no further recommendation to many min-

isters than that I have had a mission at Union Chapel.
As a consequence I have reached hundreds of people
who from ignorance have had no sympathy with
evangelistic methods. The mere fact that I have
worked with Dr. McLaren has induced them in the
first place to come and hear me, and afterwards,
in many cases, to take their place among my closest
friends.

The Rev. J. E. Roberts, B.A., B.D., has kindly
sent me the following notes concerning that memorable mission:

" I think that I may confess now that the mission which
was held by Gipsy Smith in Union Chapel six years ago
was awaited with some apprehension by the members of
the church and with much curiosity by outsiders. It was
the first ' mission ' of any importance ever held in connection
with the church. And the choice of Gipsy Smith as the
missioner gave rise to many questionings. Gipsy Smith
was not known then so widely as he is to-day. And people
did wonder whether it was wise to ask him to conduct a
mission from Dr. McLaren's pulpit.

" Anyhow, the workers determined to do their best.
Gipsy Smith had been asked by the advice of Dr. McLaren,
and they worked earnestly and prayerfully to make the
mission an apt instrument for God's Spirit to use. Never
was a mission prepared for more faithfully or more willingly. The services were advertised thoroughly. Largely
attended prayer-meetings preceded the mission. And
then came the opening night. At once it was seen that
the mission would be a great success. Crowds flocked
to the chapel. The Gipsy preached and sang with persuasive power and pathos. From the first a considerable

number entered the inquiry-rooms. Here was a large staff of specially selected and trained workers. But they were fully occupied, dealing with the numbers who were seeking salvation.

" It is impossible to say how many of the five hundred persons who passed through the inquiry-rooms have stood the test of time.   They came from every church and chapel in the neighborhood.   In our own church we reaped large results.   Many of the converts were gathered into classes, where they were further instructed in the principles of church membership.   None were proposed for membership until three months had passed.   Then great numbers were added to the Church, of whom the large proportion have continued steadfastly in the Church doctrine and breaking of bread, and prayer.   Some of our best workers to-day were converted under Gipsy Smith.

" Our missioner left delightful memories in our midst. He became a dear friend to many.   His subsequent usefulness in an ever-widening sphere has given us great joy, but no surprise.   He is ever a welcome visitor at our services.   And he seldom comes to any service without being gripped by the hands of several whom Christ found during the mission through his agency.   We love him, and we thank God for him, and we pray God to bless him yet more abundantly."

I will not weary my readers by giving them details of the various short missions that I conducted in English provincial towns during 1895.   But I will note one or two incidents that seem to me to be of more than ordinary interest.

During this year I began to receive invitations for mission work from Free Church councils.   At

Bilston, upon the invitation of the local council, I conducted a ten days' campaign at the Wesleyan Church, the church in which Dr. Berry afterwards died. I am told that the doctor whose funeral the great preacher was attending dated his decision for Christ from my mission in Wolverhampton. But this is anticipating. My host at Bilston, Mr. Bussey, was a very excellent man. Of his nine children, seven passed through the inquiry-room. The eldest son is now a local preacher in Bilston, and conducts missions with blessed results. Among the other converts was the organist.

I had an amusing experience at Swansea. At the beginning of my career as an evangelist a young Welshman taught me a verse of a Welsh hymn. At one of my Swansea meetings, making the most of my knowledge of Welsh, I sang this verse. It was the only verse I knew. But, when I had started the people at hymn-singing, I could not stop them. My Welsh accent must have been good, because I was asked by some zealous patriots if I would preach in Welsh. "No," I said, reflectively, "I think I prefer English."

At the close of 1895, I worked for six weeks in Edinburgh in connection with various free churches. The Rev. John Morgan, of Viewforth, in whose church I had labored, contributed to the *British Weekly* an interesting account of this campaign, from which I quote:

" Great crowds have gathered to hear the Gipsy preach and sing. All who have been associated with him bear

grateful testimony to his marvellous success. His remarkable personality contributes not a little to this result.
There is a romance associated with his name and history.
His gift of song also adds greatly to the charm and fascination.

" In private the Gipsy has the mien and bearing of a
Christian gentleman, and those who have had him sojourn-
ing with them can best give their testimony as to his meek-
ness and modesty, as also to the geniality and true man-
liness of his character. He is regarded with the greatest
respect and affection by all who have come to know him
intimately, and has made himself a universal favorite in
the family circle.

" There are multitudes among us to whom Mr. Smith's
visit this winter will be ever memorable as the beginning
of days to them, and many more to whom his bright,
hearty, happy Christian spirit has strikingly commended
his gospel message, and conveyed the marked and unmistakable impression of a true evangelist endued with rare
spiritual power.

" On New Year's Day Mr. Smith is to sail for New York,
and many friends will follow him with genuine sympathy
and earnest prayer during a lengthened evangelistic tour in
America. He may rest assured that a very cordial welcome
awaits him whenever he shall again revisit Edinburgh."

I heard the Rev. Andrew Murray, the well-known
South African, at the Synod Hall, Edinburgh. At
his meetings I made my first acquaintance with a
hymn which I have often since used with great effect—" Moment by Moment."

I stayed during part of my visit with the Rev.
Thomas Crerar, whose wife is the sister of Profes-

sor Henry Drummond, and I became very friendly
with their little baby girl. She was just learning to
speak, and called me "Gippo." She spoke of sugar
as "lulu." She would tap the sideboard door with
her little hands and say, "Lulu, lulu." But neither
her parents nor her nurse would let her have any.
However, she completely overcame me, and when
we two were alone, I used to give my little sweetheart a small piece of "lulu." Some weeks after
my departure from Edinburgh, I sent Mr. Crerar
a photograph of myself. When baby saw it, she
clapped her fat, chubby, little hands, screaming with
delight, "Gippo, lulu, lulu!" "You rascal!" wrote
Mr. Crerar to me. "We have found you out."

When I first visited Edinburgh and stayed with
Rev. George D. Low, M.A., his youngest boy, a
little fellow in kilts, was taught to pray, "God bless
Gipsy Smith." He was still a small boy and in the
same garb when I returned, and in the meanwhile
he had kept up that simple prayer. He had become
fired with ambition as a preacher, and was accustomed to hold forth in his nursery. My little friend
prepared his sermons regularly on Friday. The
maids and his mother formed his usual Sunday-
evening congregation. He stood on a table with
a clothes-horse, covered with a white sheet, in front
of him. Only his little head was to be seen peeping
out above this pulpit. The collection at the door
of the nursery were for my Gipsy Wagon Mission.
On the occasion of my second visit he had a meeting
on the Saturday—a *soirée*. There was a large at-

tendance.   The little minister said, in a stern, solemn tone: "I notice that when I have a *soirée*, I can get my church filled; but you do not come to the preaching on Sunday."   His text on the Sunday evening was, "It is I.   Be not afraid," and a beautiful little sermon he preached.   He said that "when Jesus comes to us it is not to frighten us, it is to take away the frightening, and it is to bring to us a sort of feeling that makes us feel sure, sure."

The closing meeting of this Edinburgh campaign was for ministers, workers, and inquirers, and was held in Free St. George's (Dr. Whyte's).   There was an overflowing congregation, at least two-thirds of which consisted of young converts.   Rev. Dr. Macphail, of Pilreg, Edinburgh, a noble specimen of a Highland Christian gentleman, presided.

CHAPTER XXVII

MY FIFTH VISIT TO AMERICA

I SAILED for New York on New Year's Day, 1896. I had arranged to go straight to Boston and conduct a mission there. This was the only fixed item on my programme. I felt that this would be an important mission, and that I ought not to entangle myself with promises of other work until I saw what God was going to do by our hands in that city.

The mission was held in the People's Temple, at the time the largest Protestant church in the city, seating two thousand five hundred people, and possessing school premises which could be added to the church, bringing up the accommodation to three thousand. Mr. James Boyd Brady was the pastor. As I was driving to the house of my host I passed the People's Temple, and I observed a great placard on the building, announcing me as "Gipsy Smith, the greatest evangelist in the world." My first words to the congregation that greeted me at my first service were to disclaim any responsibility for the announcement in front of the church: "I do not feel that I am the greatest evangelist in the world, and you do not believe it. That being so, we will have it taken down." I believe in advertising, but the placard in question was a ridiculous and undignified extravagance of statement. I felt hurt and annoyed as soon as I saw it. My repudiation of it did not a little to win my way into the esteem and affection of the Bostonians. It soon became manifest that a blessed work of grace was being done. The mission was the talk of the city. Those who had known Boston the longest said they had never seen anything like it. The Boston papers wrote about our work in their best style. I was described as the greatest of my kind on earth, "a spiritual phenomenon, an intellectual prodigy, and a musical and oratorical paragon." It seems that in appearance I at once suggested an Italian *impresario*, that in costume I would have made a good double to Jean de Reské, and that my language might serve as a model for a high churchman!

Several incidents of this mission are, I think, worthy of record. On the morning after the first meeting I was aroused from sleep very early. I was told that there was at the door a man in a very excited state who wished to see me. I requested that he should be brought to my room. He rushed in, waving wildly a copy of the *Protestant Standard*, which had devoted half a page to our meeting. ' What have you come to Boston for?" he demanded, angrily. "Can you not leave me alone?" I perceived that my visitor was an old Pottery man, who years before had heard me preach many times. He had deserted his wife and children, and was now living a very sinful life. In the interval, during moments of acute shame and remorse, he had written to his wife in the hope of finding her, but his efforts had been unsuccessful. Either he received no reply or his letters were returned, and he did not know whether she was dead or alive. His conscience seemed to tell him that I had come to Boston to discover and accuse him. "Why can you not leave me alone?" he asked. "Can you not stay at home?" This man had not been at the meeting. But as he was returning from night duty at a large restaurant, he had come across a copy of the *Protestant Standard*, and had learned that I was in the city. I spoke to him faithfully about the old days, his present condition, his sin and want, and he promised to come to the next meeting. To my joy I observed him among the first who came forward to give themselves to Christ. It was a sincere, absolute surrender, a real conversion. He gave me the name of his wife's parents and the address of the house where he knew her to be living last. I wrote to my brother-in-law, Councillor Ball, of Hanley, giving him all the particulars I could gather. He published an announcement in the local papers and set the police at work, with the result that the wife and family were found. After years of separation she and her children crossed the Atlantic to find the husband and father. She was welcomed with all the old love and the new love that had come to him from the Lord. They are now living happily together, doing a noble work for the Christ who saved them.

One night, going to church, I jumped into a car. Sitting beside me was a lady with a pair of opera-glasses in her hand. She was not going to church. People do not take opera-glasses to church. I suppose they think that they see enough of the parson without them. Presently a lady on her way to my meeting entered the car and said to me, "What are you going to preach about to-night, Mr. Smith?" "Wait and see," I answered. If you tell the people what you are going to talk about, they can fortify themselves. Glorious surprises are what we need in our preaching more and more. Some men will never be saved unless they are taken off their guard. However, I said to my questioner, "We shall have nearly three thousand people to-night, and whether we preach or not we shall certainly pray. And the burden of our prayer will be, 'O Lord, send down upon us the Holy Ghost.'" "Sir, sir," said the lady with the opera-glasses, "are you not afraid something will happen if you pray like that?" "Oh, not at all," I said, "not *afraid ;* we hope something will happen. We are going to church because we expect something will happen."

When the month was finished it was evident that we could not stop the work. It would have been a sin so to do. Fortunately, having a presentiment that this was going to be a great and noble mission, I had kept myself free from other engagements. The four weeks extended into seven. On the fifth Sunday morning I preached to a crowded congregation on "Be filled with the Spirit," and at the close of the sermon a memorable, and indeed indescribable, scene was witnessed. Dr. Brady rose, and, in tones of deep emotion, said, "The sermon this morning has been for my own soul. I feel my need of the experience of which our brother has been speaking, and I am going down to that communion - rail for myself. I am going there to seek my Pentecost. I shall never be able to rear the young souls that have been brought to God during this mission unless I am filled with the Spirit." Presently between two hundred and three hundred people from all parts of the church were kneeling at the communion-rail on both sides of their pastor. When we dispersed we all felt that we had seen strange things that day.

During this week I addressed the divinity students of the Methodist College on "Soul-winning." I had also the distinction of being invited to speak to the students of Harvard University, an invitation which is only given on very rare occasions. The one hour of the day I was free was from 6.30 to 7.30, the dinner hour of the students, but they were willing to set that aside in order to hear me, and we had a happy meeting.

As a result of the mission eight hundred persons were received into the church on probation. I was three times asked to become pastor in succession to Dr. Brady when his term of the pastorate was fulfilled. The people were willing to free me during three or four months every year for evangelistic work, to give me an assistant and a handsome salary. But I did not see my way to accept their offer.

My next mission was held in the Metropolitan Episcopal Church at Washington, of which Dr.

Hugh Johnstone was then pastor. When the President of the United States is a Methodist he attends this church, as do also almost all the Methodist Congressmen. Dr. Milburn, the blind man eloquent, and chaplain to the Senate, is also a member of the Metropolitan congregation. Dr. Milburn and I became good friends. I chanced to mention in the course of an address that I was not ordained. At once the old man rose, and, placing his hands upon my shoulders, said, "I will ordain you—without a question."

Dr. Milburn told me the interesting story of how he became chaplain to the Senate. As a young man he had been preaching in the far West, and was returning to the East on one of the river steamers. Among the passengers were a number of Senators and members of the House of Representatives who spent their time in gambling and in fearful swearing. Dr. Milburn (Mr. Milburn he then was) was invited to conduct a religious service in the saloon on Sunday morning, and the Congressmen were among his congregation. He rebuked them sternly and faithfully for their gambling and swearing, and asked if their conduct was such as became men who were the representatives and the lawmakers of the nation. After the service Dr. Milburn retreated to his cabin. The men whom he had rebuked were wild fellows from the South and West. He expected every moment to receive a visit from some of them, bearing a challenge. He had reckoned on this likelihood before he had preached his sermon. Pres-

ently there was a knock at the door. "Here it
is," said Dr. Milburn to himself; "sure enough,
what I expected. They have come to challenge
me. I expect I shall get a severe handling. May
God help me to be faithful." Several tall, awkward,
fierce-looking men stalked in. But there was no
fight in them. They ranged themselves up before
the doctor, meekly confessed that they had deserved
his rebuke, thanked him for his sermon, and asked
him if he would allow them to nominate him as chaplain to the Senate. Dr. Milburn was as delighted as
he was surprised, and readily consented to be nom-
inated. Thus he was elected to the post which he
has filled with such conspicuous ability and dignity
for nearly sixty years.

Dr. Johnstone entered into the work most heartily.
He sank himself entirely in order that I might have
the best possible chance. The church, which holds
fifteen hundred people, was crowded at the very first
service. An amusing and somewhat awkward incident occurred. I was preaching on "Lifting the lame
man at the gate of the Temple." The church has no
pulpit, only an open rostrum, with not even a rail
in front. "If," I said, "you want to lift anybody,
you must stand on solid ground yourself," and
thereupon I stepped off the platform, falling a distance of three or four feet. I flatter myself that
I have always been rather quick in extricating myself from an awkward situation, so after I had risen
I said to the people, "That was not as solid as I
thought. You are witness to this, that I fall some-

times, but "—marching quietly back to the rostrum—
"I get up again." Next day a Washington paper
stated that Gipsy Smith illustrated his own sermons.
The mission lasted for three weeks. Every night
the communion - rail was crowded. It was a very
pleasant thing to see eminent doctors, business
men, and Congressmen kneeling by the side of the
anxious inquirers, encouraging and directing them.

Dr. Milburn presented me to President Cleveland
at the White House, told him about me and my work,
and invited him to my lecture on my life story. The
President said that if they had known sooner, he
and his wife would gladly have come, but that their
present arrangements made it impossible.

I was taken by my friends, Mr. and Mrs. Washburn,
to Mount Vernon to see the room in which Washington died, and the tomb in which he is laid. At the
sepulchre we came aross an old colored man who
had formerly been a slave. Mr. Washburn asked
him if he had read about Gipsy Smith, the evangelist.

"Oh yes!"

"Well," said Mr. Washburn, pointing to me,
"that is the man."

"Oh, is that the man?" inquired the old negro.
Whereupon he came up to me and said, "My young
brudder, I loves de Lord, too!"

"That is right!"

"I preaches, too."

"Good!"

"I preaches nearly every Sunday to my people."

"I hope you have a good time?"

"Oh yes, I have, and let me tell you this—when next you preaches just you give the people what they need, not what they axes for."

For the second time I took a journey across the continent to Denver and preached to great crowds in the Colosseum, a building seated for between three and four thousand people. Everywhere I found striking and enduring results of my former mission there. Converts were standing well, and many were good workers in the churches. I was the guest of my dear friends, Mr. and Mrs. Thomas.

The feature of the mission was the restoration of a large number of backsliders. Many persons had come out to Denver from the Eastern States with their certificate of church membership in their pockets, but they had never produced them and had gradually drifted away from church connection.

Twelve years ago Denver was growing at the rate of two thousand people a month. The Rocky Mountains, twenty miles off, are rich in minerals—gold, silver, copper, and lead. The climate is most delightful and most healthful. The doctors in the Eastern States send their consumptive patients to Denver, where they are often restored to health. Many fortunes have been made in Denver and many lost. On the occasion of my first visit a rich man in the town offered to pay me a handsome salary, to provide me with a permanent railway car sumptuously fitted up in which I might travel across the country, accompanied by a troupe of singers, conducting evangelistic meetings in the great towns.

When I returned to Denver ill fortune had overtaken him, and he was earning his living by keeping a restaurant in New York. The decline in the value of silver has seriously diminished the prosperity of Denver, but I believe that in years to come it will be one of the great cities of the world.

The physical peculiarity of the place is the remarkable clearness of the air. With the naked eye you can see a two-hundred-mile stretch of the Rocky Mountains. A good story is told to illustrate the trick that this clarity of the atmosphere plays with one's estimates of distance. A tourist living in a hotel at Denver rose early in the morning and told the waiter he would take a walk to the Rockies and back before breakfast.

"You will never do it," said the waiter; "it is twenty miles to the Rockies."

"Nonsense," said the tourist; "don't you try to fool me; they are just across the fields there."

"All right," said the waiter; "you know best. But I tell you it is too far for you."

The tourist set out, crossed the fields, walked on, and on, and on, and still he did not come to the Rockies. A party was sent out in search of him. They discovered him standing on this side of a stream, stripping off his clothes in order that he might swim over it.

"Why," said the leader, "what are you doing? You can step across that stream."

"Oh," said the tourist, with a knowing wink, "you won't take me in again. I know how decep-

tive your distances are in this darned State; I know
I shall have to swim over this."

I can tell one or two good little stories about this
American tour. At Boston I lived with a couple
whose only child was a little boy who slept in a cot
in his parents' bedroom. In the night he fell out of
bed, and at once his two loving parents, hearing his
cry, jumped up to place him in his cot again, and
met over his prostrate form. At breakfast his father
teased him about this accident. He said, "Johnnie,
do you know why you fell out of bed last night?"

"No, father, I don't."

"Well, the reason is this: you slept too near to
where you get out."

The youngster received this explanation in silence.
Pondering deeply for a few minutes, he suddenly
exclaimed, "Father, the reason you gave for my
falling out of bed last night was not the right one.
I know why I fell out."

"Well, my son, why did you?"

"Because I slept too near where I got in."

When addressing young converts I always draw
a moral from this story. If they desire to remain
in their Christian life let them get well in.

Mrs. Margaret Bottome, the founder of the King's
Daughters, during this visit told me a story which
illustrates the same point. She was walking along
the front at a seaside place. A young friend enjoying himself in a small boat beckoned to her and
asked if she would like a sail. Mrs. Bottome said,
"Yes," and the boat was brought in to the side.

Mrs. Bottome, in essaying to step in, touched the boat with her left foot and at once it skidded off some distance into the water. Back again the young fellow rowed. This time Mrs. Bottome touched the boat with her right foot and again it sped off some distance. When the youth brought his boat alongside the third time, he exclaimed to Mrs. Bottome, "Why don't you come in, all of you?"

If young converts wish to maintain their religious life strong, fresh, and secure, they must throw the whole of themselves into it; they must hold nothing back.

I met Miss Fanny Crosby, the well-known hymn-writer, at New York. Many of her compositions appear in the *Free-Church Mission Hymnal*, but her identity is there disguised by her married name, Mrs. F. J. Van Alstyne. Miss Crosby is seventy years of age, a very tiny woman, and quite blind. At one of my meetings, sitting on the platform beside me, she heard me sing a hymn of hers:

"Like a bird on the deep, far away from its nest,
   I wandered, my Saviour, from Thee,
  But Thy dear loving voice called me home to Thy breast,
   And I knew there was welcome for me."

When I had finished Miss Crosby said: "Brother Smith, I did not know there was as much in that song. You have broken me all up." Speaking about her blindness, she said, "I would not see with these natural eyes if I might, because I should miss much that I already see."

CHAPTER XXVIII

SOME FRESH STORIES ABOUT PETER MACKENZIE

I REACHED England again on the 18th of May, 1896. From that date until September, 1897, when I began my work as the first missioner of the National Free Church Council, I was occupied in conducting brief campaigns in different parts of England. Let me note some interesting points in connection with this period.

At Consett the miners were so moved that they started to hold prayer meetings down a coal-pit—in the month of June, too, when it was very hot. I worked at Norwood Grove Congregational Church, Liverpool, with the Rev. E. R. Barrett, B.A., the pastor. We had a most fruitful week. Two years after this date Mr. Barrett told me that he had never had a communion service since the mission at which some persons who dated their awakening from my visit were not admitted to church membership.

One of the most notable missions of my life was conducted at Wolverhampton in October, 1896. Dr. Berry was the life and soul of the enterprise. He gave up all other engagements in order to be present at the meetings. The annual Mayor's dinner fell due during this campaign, and Dr. Berry was invited to attend. His reply was that the most im-

portant thing in creation to him at that moment was
the mission.   What would his people think of him if
he were feasting at the Mayor's banquet while sinners
were being converted?   All the other ministers of
Wolverhampton loyally supported Dr. Berry.   The
mission had been arranged by the local Free Church
Council, and I am sure that it did a great deal towards bringing Dr. Berry to the point of supporting
the engagement of a free-church missioner.   No
man ever stood by me more sympathetically than
Dr. Berry, whether in the meetings or out of the
meetings, in his study or in my lodgings.   I have
for years had a great longing for a peaceful period
of calm study, and I chanced to say to Dr. Berry,
"I wish I could sit down and do nothing but study
for a year."   He retorted, "Yes, and then you would
be spoiled.   Just you go on with your work and do
as much reading as you can."   We had eight hundred
inquirers.   One hundred and forty of the converts
elected to join Dr. Berry's church.   Dr. Berry summoned a church meeting, and, choosing one hundred
and forty of his best members, put a young convert
into the charge of each.   The member was expected
to visit the new convert, and report to Dr. Berry every
week or two for two, three, or four months.   I heartily
commend this plan.   It is good for the young convert and good for the church member.

In accordance with my custom, I told the story
of my life on the closing night.   All the tickets were
sold long before the meeting.   The crowd who had
been unable to get tickets gathered outside the build-

ing in the hope of squeezing their way somehow into the hall. They knew there was a little standing room. The policemen were utterly unable to keep the people in order. They sought to charge the crowd, but the crowd charged them. They pinned them against the walls and knocked their helmets about in all directions.

My mission at Dewsbury was conducted under the shadow of the great name of Peter Mackenzie. I enjoyed the intimate friendship of Peter, who was a sunbeam in the lives of thousands. I met him for the first time, sixteen or seventeen years ago, on the platform of Hull station. Both of us had been preaching in the town. We were leaving in the same train, though not in the same compartment, because our destinations were different. I told him that a great work of grace had been accomplished in Hull. "Glory to God!" he shouted, "I will send you a goose at Christmas." Three months passed away. I had forgotten all about the goose and Peter's promise, but he had not forgotten. He sent me the following letter:

" HONORED AND DEAR SIR,—I have had no time to purchase a goose. But I send you 10s. and a photo of yours truly, which when you receive you will have goose enough.   PETER MACKENZIE."

I met him again at Crewe some time after I had addressed the Congregational Union at Hanley. Said he to me, "What a lot of steam we should waste if we stopped the engine every time a donkey brayed and went to inquire into his bronchial tubes." He bought a rose at the station and put it into my coat. Then he hailed a newspaper boy, and shouted to him, "Penn'orth o' Tory, penn'orth o' Liberal, a penn'orth o' fun." Then, handing the papers to me, he said, "Here is your train; read how my Father is ruling the world."

Peter came to Hanley, while I was there, to preach in the Wesleyan Chapel, and to lecture in the Imperial Circus on "The Devil: his Personality, Character, and Power." The lecture was announced over the town in black letters on a huge green poster. As I was passing along the street a half-tipsy man accosted me, and pointing to the placard said, "What nonsense! There's no such person as the devil." I asked him what he had been doing of late. "Oh," he said, "I have been drinking. I have had a six weeks' spree. I've had a fearful time—the blues terribly." "Oh, indeed," I said; "what do you mean by the blues?" "Don't you know? — little uns." "Little uns?" "Yes, little uns. Don't you know what I mean?—little devils, scores of them." "Well," I said, "don't you think, now, that if there are lots of little uns, there must be an old un too?" When I seconded the vote of thanks to Peter for his lecture, I told this story. Rising from his seat and waving his chair over his head, he shouted, "Glory, glory I'll tell that all over the country."

When Peter was brought home ill to Dewsbury, the Wesleyan minister of the town, Mr. Martin, called to see him. "I am very sorry, sir," he said, "to find you in bed and so ill." "Yes, yes," said Peter, "I am in the dry-dock, undergoing repairs." Mr. Martin heard that Peter had become much worse, and again called on him. "Ah," said Peter, "Father is going to send down the angel and let old Peter out of prison." A few days later he died.

CHAPTER XXIX

AS THE NATIONAL COUNCIL'S MISSIONER

On my return from my last trip to America, my pastor, the Rev. S. F. Collier, remarked to me that the position I ought to fill was that of recognized free-church evangelist. He said that he intended to suggest this to some leaders of the National Free Church Council. Dr. Pope met me one day in Manchester and made the same remark. Not long after these conversations, I received a letter from the Rev. Thomas Law, the General Secretary of the National Council, asking me to meet him at the Central Hall, Manchester. I believe that Mr. Law had developed in his own mind, and had suggested to the committee, a great scheme of evangelism to be undertaken by the National Council, and that, in this connection, his thoughts had been turned towards me. I did not gather from this first interview that Mr. Law at that time was empowered to invite me to become the free-church missioner. I understood that he merely desired to ascertain my views on the matter. I agreed with him that official connection with the National Free Church Council would certainly be a great strength to me and would open up to me a wider field. I talked the matter over with my wife, and she advised me to accept the position if it was offered me. I had not sought it. It had come to me, At a second interview with Mr. Law I consented to become the National Council's missioner. It was arranged that I should begin work on the 1st of September, 1897.

I have now been in the service of the National Council for over four years, and, all being well, I hope to end my days as their missioner. I consider my present sphere of operations the biggest and most important field I have ever touched. When it is properly worked it will do more to break down local prejudices and to bring Christians and churches together than anything has done for ages. I owe a debt of gratitude to Mr. Law for the wisdom and discretion he has displayed in arranging my missions at centres which give me the best opportunity, and also for his kind thought and care for my health and comfort.

Between my engagement and the commencement of my work for the National Council, there was an incident in my life of which I am particularly proud. In 1897, the Wesleyan Methodist Conference was held in Leeds, and I took two conference appointments—preaching in the Coliseum twice on Sunday to over six thousand people. I believe that I have the distinction of being the only layman who has ever taken a conference appointment. When the official plan was first published, my name was omitted. As I had hesitated to accept the invitation of the Rev. S. Chadwick to preach these discourses, I concluded, when the plan came out without my name,

that he had managed to do without me. I wrote to
Mr. Chadwick to that effect. He wired back that I
was advertised all over Leeds. The explanation of
the omission was that, a layman never having taken
a conference appointment before, the Plan Committee
did not know whether they ought to announce the
fact, and thought the safest thing was to take no
notice of the lay evangelist. There was a short
debate at the conference on this matter, in which
Mr. Chadwick, Mr. Price Hughes, and Mr. Watkinson, pointing out the absurdity of the omission, took
part. Their conclusive argument was that if a man
was fit to preach, he was fit to be announced.

I could write a volume about my work for the
National Free Church Council. It has been greatly
blessed, and it is full of interesting and encouraging
incidents. Let me tell a few anecdotes. When I
was conducting a mission at Lancaster I overheard
two men discussing my career. One of them was
somewhat deaf, and like most deaf people, spoke
very loud. My life story, according to this deaf
man, was this: "When Gipsy Smith was a little
chap—quite a kid, you know—they sold him to
a rich old bloke with plenty of brass. This old chap
was religious-like, taught the Gipsy to read the
Bible and be good, you know; and then the old chap
died and left the Gipsy all his money—plenty of
brass! Oh, lots of brass! Then Gipsy took to
preaching, and they called him 'Gipsy Smith,' because he was a gipsy when he was a kid. He is a
splendid preacher. He preaches just for the love

of it. He need not do it. He has plenty of brass;
the old chap left him such a lot. Now, that's the
man. I am going to hear him." When I appeared
before my congregation in the evening I saw this
man and his wife sitting immediately in front of me.
I told the people the story of my career that I had
overheard. The author of this strange romance
listened with his mouth wide open. I said, "That
story is not true, and if you will come to this church
on Monday night, you shall hear the true story."
The man and his wife were converted during this
mission.

My wife and I, with some friends, were spending
a week at the seaside. I had wandered a little bit
away from them. An Italian girl, who made her
living by singing and playing to the people, evidently
mistook me for a countryman of hers. I was dressed
in a velvet jacket, and beaver hat. She began to
talk to me in what I took to be Italian. I told her
that I was not an Italian, but a gipsy, and that she
must speak in English.

"Gipsy!" she said. "Tent?"

"Yes."

"Woods?"

"Yes."

"Wild?"

"Yes."

"You lie."

Presently my wife came up to me, and the Italian
girl said to her: "You go away; this is my young
man." I explained to my new sweetheart that the

lady she was sending away was my wife. In broken English, she asked Mrs. Smith the same questions she had put to me, whether I had been brought up in a tent, lived in the woods, and run wild? She replied, "Yes." Then said the Italian girl, "Where did you catch him?"

I asked a number of Sunday-school children one day what a gipsy was. A little boy replied: "A man who goes round and round and round to see what he can find." Not at all a bad definition of many gipsies.

A pretty incident occurred during my mission in Cheltenham. A sweet, beautiful young lady, who was converted one night, brought with her, two or three nights later, her dearest friend, a deaf and dumb girl. As my sermon proceeded I saw the new convert interpreting to her friend what I was saying. This deaf and dumb girl was the first person to rise for prayer. Presently the two went into the inquiry-room. "Will you please help my friend? She is seeking the Saviour," said the new convert. The inquirer being deaf and dumb, none of the workers was of any use, and so we told the young lady that she was the proper person to bring her friend to Christ. The two went away happy in their Saviour.

It was during a mission at Taunton that I learned the hymn "Count Your Blessings," which through its use at my services has become exceedingly popular in many parts of England. At the request of Mr. Tom Penny, my host, I visited the infirmary. Most of the patients had been carried out onto a lawn for a sun-bath. I spoke a few words to them, and then Mr. Penny said: "Before Mr. Smith goes, won't you sing something for him?" "Yes, sir," said a little girl. "What will you sing?" said he. "Count Your Blessings," was the reply. Immediately I was deeply touched and impressed. Here was I in full enjoyment of health and of many priceless benefits of God, yet I had never counted my blessings— it had never occurred to me so to do. I felt sure that thousands of others had been guilty of the same omission. I reflected that the Psalmist must have been thinking of this disposition of our hearts when he sang, "Forget not all His benefits." Many of us, alas! are never so happy as when we are talking about our miseries. The sweet song fastened itself upon my heart and soul. I sing it at my meetings very frequently. The hymn attained extraordinary vogue during my mission campaign at the Metropolitan Tabernacle. Wherever one might go —in the streets, in the trams, in the trains—some one was humming or whistling or singing, "Count Your Blessings." The boys pushing their barrows along, the men driving their horses, and the women rocking their cradles—all these had been caught by the truth and melody of the hymn.

My last mission for the nineteenth century was conducted at Luton. The inquirers numbered 1,080, rather more than one in every forty of the population. Rev. W. Henry Thompson, the Wesleyan minister of the town and the chairman of the dis-

trict, said to me that the people in Luton never ask
"Where are the new converts?" They have no
need to put the question. The new converts are
everywhere—in the Sunday services, the week-night
services, and Christian Endeavor meetings. Said
Mr. Thompson to me, "I have never been connected
with a revival which left such a genuine crop of new
converts as yours." As I have said elsewhere, to me
the most memorable incident of this mission was the
restoration of my sister, Lovinia (Mrs. Oakley), who
had been a backslider for years. Her health has not
been good, and a week or two ago I visited her. I told
her I was going to put her into my book. She said
"Yes, all right; tell your readers I am holding out,
and that I may soon be in the presence of my Lord.
I do not fear the great day. I have placed my trust
in Jesus Christ."

During the mission at Luton, my brother-in-law,
Mr. Evens, was sent for to conduct the overflow
meetings. On the Saturday I took him to the place
of my mother's death and burial—at Baldock, about
twenty miles off. I pointed out to him almost the
exact spot in Norton Lane where she lay sick unto
death, and together we trod the path along which her
coffin must have been carried to the grave, with my
father following as the sole mourner. When we
stood by the grave, I said to my brother-in-law : "I
have been feeling for some time that I should erect a
stone here." "I am rather surprised," he answered,
"that you have not done so before." "Yes, indeed,
but I have made up my mind to do it now." Alder-

man Giddings, the Mayor of Luton, presided at my lecture on the Monday evening. When I reached the part where I tell of the death and burial of my mother, he turned to Mr. Evens, who was sitting beside him on the platform, and asked, "Is there a stone over that grave?" "No," he replied. "Well, I will put one up; that is my business." At the close of the meeting he told me of his decision. The incident seemed to me a remarkable comment on the text: "Before ye call I will answer. While ye are yet speaking I will hear."

The opening weeks of the twentieth century were made forever memorable in the history of the evangelical free churches of England by the simultaneous mission. From the beginning of the Federation movement—a movement which commands the support of all the leaders in the free evangelical churches of England and Wales, and has succeeded in welding these churches together into one mighty army—evangelistic work has had a prominent, and indeed a foremost place. Most of the local councils, which now number nearly eight hundred, have at one time or another held united missions with conspicuous success. It occurred to the Rev. Thomas Law, the general secretary of the National Council, that no better way of inaugurating the new century could be devised than that these councils should at the same time be engaged in an earnest endeavor to reach the masses outside the churches. It was impossible to conduct the campaign with literal simultaneity. The work in London extended from January 26th to February 6th; in the provinces, from February 16th to February 26th; and in the villages from March 2nd to 6th. This great enterprise was crowned with the richest spiritual blessing.

I worked at the Metropolitan Tabernacle during the London campaign. The vast building was crowded at every service, and more than twelve hundred persons passed through the inquiry-rooms. I had the great joy of my father's presence with me every night. Mr. William Chivers, whose mother bought clothes-pegs from me when I was a boy, brought my father from Cambridge to London with him as his guest, and entertained him during the week. Several other relatives came up to that mission—some aunts and cousins that I had not seen for twenty years or more. My father was in his element. It was the crowning experience of his life. Mr. Meyer afterwards said that it was beautiful to witness on the old man's face the exact correspondence of sympathy with the emotions that filled the heart of the younger man as he proceeded with his discourse. It was hard to tell which the sermon cost more, the father or the son. One night as we two got into a cab, my father was full of uncontrollable joy. Jumping up, he said, "I tell you, my dear, I seemed to creep right into your waistcoat to-night." That was his vivid and characteristic way of expressing the perfection of his sympathy with me. My father, uninvited, assumed control of the inquiry-room workers at the Tabernacle, but so gracefully and so sweetly did he do it that the workers quite willingly submitted to his direction, feeling that it was only what should be.

The Rev. Thomas Spurgeon, the pastor of the Tabernacle, was present at nearly every service, and a few days after the mission he wrote the following notes about it: "From the outset Gipsy Smith secured the ear of the people, and soon he had the joy of winning their hearts for Christ. He emphasized the need of repentance, and the necessity for the new birth. He denounced every form of evil, and warned men to flee from the wrath to come. He preached a full and free salvation, and illustrated all with thrilling incidents culled largely from his own wonderful experience. It was evident at each service that he had spoken to good purpose. The demonstration of the Spirit was never lacking. No sooner was the address over than scores were ready to testify as to their desire to be saved, and to respond to a singularly persuasive appeal to 'come along' into the inquiry-rooms. One friend, who has been in the thick of many such movements, assures me that better work was never done before, so evident was the breaking down, and so manifest the breaking in of the marvellous light. We were all constrained to say, 'This is the finger of God.'" Writing in October, 1901, Mr. Spurgeon said: "Converts resulting from Gipsy Smith's mission are still appearing and asking to be united with God's people. Those who have already joined us seem to be of the right sort, and these later applicants are bright examples of Christ's power to keep and save. Writing eight months after the mission, I can only confirm my original verdict of it—full of real power and blessing."

Rev. F. B. Meyer, B.A., has also kindly sent me the following note about my work at the Tabernacle:

"I shall never forget one evening when the father of the evangelist was present on the platform, and seemed to be adding the force of his own devout, fervent spirit with every word uttered by his son. Our beloved friend enjoyed unusual liberty that night. It seemed as though the fragrance and music of his own early life were being wafted like a fresh breeze to the audience, which alternately was melted in tears or stirred to enthusiasm.

"We are still continually hearing of blessing which was not recorded at the time, and the secretary tells me that he has received many satisfactory reports from clergymen and ministers of the neighborhood of the cases handed over to their care. It is believed that nearly every church in the locality received some new converts, while the quickened life of many Christians testifies to the benefit they received.

"It is interesting to see the evangelical nature of our friend's spirit and work. He attracts around him ministers of all denominations, and even Christians of the Established Church are drawn to him. God has greatly gifted him, and we can only believe and pray that he may be spared for many years, like a stalwart reaper, to go through the harvest field of the churches, gathering in myriads of souls."

This seems a fitting place to say that my missions

in London in connection with the National Council have all been blessed with gratifying success. Perhaps the two most notable were those at Marylebone and Paddington. Dr. Monro Gibson contributed an account of the former to the *British Weekly*, from which I may make the following extract:

"There is a charm about Gipsy Smith's personality which wins from the outset, and prepares for that response to his earnest appeals which has been marked in every service. He is more expository than any other evangelist whom I have heard, and neither his exegesis nor his theology would do discredit to a graduate of our theological schools. There is an air of culture even in style which is nothing less than marvellous to those who know the story of his life, and of which I cannot give any other explanation than that he is a graduate of the same school which prepared John, the fisherman, for his literary work. But the great factor is the power from on high with which he speaks, and which, manifest the first evening, was increasingly so as the days passed on. There has been much quickening among Christians, and a goodly number giving evidence of having been turned from darkness to light."

Dr. Clifford gave his impressions of the Paddington mission in a long article published in the *Christian World*. He said:

"It has been a most helpful time; there is not a church in the council that has not been represented among the visitors in the inquiry-room. Members and ministers thankfully testify to the quickening they have received.

The message of the evangelist goes straight to the heart of the gospel, and his methods are as sane as his gospel is clear. He has no fads. He is not the victim of vagaries. He does not air any visionary theories. He knows his work and does it. He does not quarrel with pastors and call it preaching the gospel. He is their helper. Exhaustless resources of pathos are his. There is a tear in his voice. He moves the heart of his audience to its utmost depths. But he never forgets that man has an intellect, and thinks and reasons; and when the hearer is most roused to cross the Rubicon he holds him in thought as to the meaning of the step he is taking, tells him that going into the inquiry-room — important as that is as a definite and distinct choice of discipleship to Christ—is only a beginning, and must be followed by a resolute, patient, and thoroughgoing obedience to Christ, the newly accepted Master. His humor is irresistible. It is one of his sources of power, for humor is human. It is one of the elemental forces of life, and it never fails to attract. He suffers no conventions to stand between him and it. He despises conventionality, and is as incapable of dulness as he is of obscurity. Every hearer sees what he is aiming at, and knows and feels that he is seeking the highest good. Hardly for a moment does he seem to lose touch of God or of his audience, and after a broad flash of humor instantly swings back into a direct and searching appeal, or else ascends in prayer not less direct and still more earnest.

" The ethical rings out in his teaching with terrible resonance. Most of his strength is derived from the directness of his appeals to the conscience. He searches the heart, exposes the subtle devices with which we shirk our responsibilities as Christians, and compels us secretly to admit, if not to confess, our sins. The value of the mission

to the avowed disciples of Christ is not less than to those
who are constrained to make the great decision."

I worked at Birmingham during the provincial
campaign of the simultaneous mission. Alderman
Edwards, the Mayor, who is a prominent Congregationalist, postponed the mayoral banquet in order
that it should not interfere with the mission and
appeared by my side as often as possible. I was
greatly helped by the best choir (conducted by Mr.
Thomas Facer) and by the strongest band of workers and stewards that I have ever had anywhere.
The town-hall was crowded every evening; indeed,
sometimes we could have filled it thrice over. Dr.
Clifford, my colleague in this campaign — and no
better colleague could a man have—delivered a
series of noon-day addresses on "Be ye reconciled
unto God," which made a profound impression. His
meetings were attended by from one thousand to one
thousand five hundred people. When the last lecture was delivered, I was moved to propose a vote
of thanks to Dr. Clifford, and to urge that the discourses should be published. At the evening service
Dr. Clifford sat by my side, except when he was conducting overflow meetings in Carrs Lane Chapel. I
felt in every service that he was praying for me
and supporting me by his deepest sympathy. One
night the first three rows in the town-hall were
filled entirely by men, and not one of them had a
collar on. At the close they all went into the inquiry-room. As the mission proceeded the crowds

grew. People came and stood two hours or more in the hope of getting in. The local papers stated that even Joseph Chamberlain could not draw such crowds as were attracted by Dr. Clifford and Gipsy Smith.

On the second Sunday of the mission the people began to gather in the morning for the afternoon service. Five minutes after the doors were opened the place was crowded. There were more persons outside seeking admission than there were inside the hall. Those who could not get in did not go away. They simply waited for the evening meeting, which was announced to start at seven. So large were the crowds that we began the service at five o'clock. Four policemen carried me into the hall over the heads of the people. An unaided attempt to force my way through the crowd was hopeless. Dr. Clifford was preaching that night at Carrs Lane. He had a rather curious experience. The policeman at the door refused him admission.

"I want to go in," said Dr. Clifford.

"Are you a seat-holder?"

"No, I am not."

"Well, you cannot get in."

"I think there will be room for me in the pulpit."

"I am not so sure of it."

"But I am Dr. Clifford; I am going to preach."

"Oh, are you? I have let in two or three Dr. Cliffords already."

In the end Dr. Clifford succeeded in establishing his identity to the satisfaction of the officers of the law, and was permitted to enter.

One thousand five hundred persons passed through the inquiry-rooms during the mission.

Rev. J. H. Jowett, M.A., has kindly supplied me with the following note concerning the Birmingham campaign:

" Perhaps the most marked impression that remains in my mind, when I recall the great mission of last February, is the marvellous power of the missioner's self-restraint. There was nothing of the ' scream ' in the meetings! The sensational was entirely absent. I always felt that the leader was perfectly self-possessed, and that in his heart there dwelt the quietness which is the fruit of a steady faith in the Lord. In the final appeals the missioner himself was overlooked in the mighty sense of the presence of God. The moving power was not so much a voice as an atmosphere. Hard hearts were melted in the constraint of an all-pervading spiritual power. It was not only the ignorant and uncultured who were won; those whose minds had received mental illumination were also wooed into the light of life. I have in my congregation young fellows of no mean ability who were led into definite decision for the Christ."

POSTSCRIPT

I TRUST that what I have written will interest my readers. I have had a life very different, I think, from that of most of my fellows, but a life which God has greatly blessed, and I think I may add, with all reverence, greatly used. It has been full of trials and difficulties. I have been often troubled, but never distressed; often perplexed, but never in despair; often cast down, but never destroyed. Any afflictions that have visited me have been but for a moment, and have worked a far more exceeding weight of glory. I have sought to keep the eyes of my heart open to the things which are not seen, for the things which are seen are temporal, but the things which are not seen are eternal.

I have had rich and strange experiences. I have lived in many houses, the guest of many sorts and conditions of people. I have been presented to two Presidents of the United States, dined with bishops and archbishops, and slept with two Roman Catholic priests. In my study hangs a letter from her late Majesty the Queen, and one from a royal duchess, but the dearest things in my house are two pictures which adorn the walls of my bedroom. One is the picture of the wagon in which my mother died, and the other a picture of a group of gipsies. I never sleep in that room without looking at these pictures and saying to myself: "Rodney, you would have been there to-day but for the grace of God. Glory be to His name for ever."

THE END